ON WHOM I HAVE MERCY

A NOVEL BY
VERONICA FOLDES FRAME

Christian by faith and Jewish under the law, Katalin struggles with her dual identity in a Hungary caught up in World War II and its aftermath. She and Istvan, a Jew, fall in love. They struggle with their desire for marriage and to have a child in the midst of the increasing threat from Nazi violence. Istvan is deported to a concentration camp; Kata and family seek refuge with Christian friends. Some are paralyzed by fear; others, acting on their faith, risk their lives to protect them. Even the welcomed "liberation" by the Russian Army poses its dangers.

With the war over, the arduous attempts to survive in a devastated country and to assemble the family merge into a new struggle: power is shifting toward Communism and society is more polarized than ever. Katalin needs to come to terms with her faith and identity, to make sense of her survival out of the Holocaust and to find a direction for her life. In her soul-searching, she recalls Parsifal's quest for the Grail—a recurring motif in the novel—and knows that her own quest will continue.

ON WHOM
IHAVE MERCY

To the wonderful church
community in Essex — a past.

[signature]

ON WHOM
I HAVE MERCY

A NOVEL

VERONICA FOLDES FRAME

RIVERVIEW PUBLISHING
NEW YORK

First Printing

Library of Congress Catalog Card Number: 92-63008

ISBN 0-9635160-0-0 (Hardcover edition)
ISBN 0-9635160-1-9 (Paperback edition)

To Matt—My Son, My Friend

ON WHOM I HAVE MERCY is a work of fiction. While the major thrust of the story is based on personal experience against the background of historical events, the characters and their actions were crafted to serve the purposes of the novel.

Veronica Foldes Frame

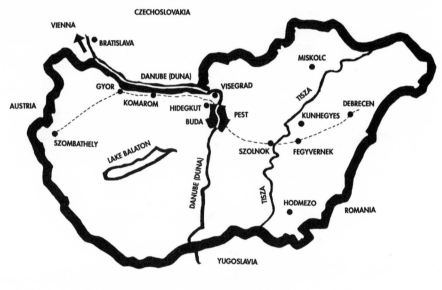

CZECHOSLOVAKIA

VIENNA

BRATISLAVA

MISKOLC

DANUBE (DUNA)

GYOR

VISEGRAD

TISZA

AUSTRIA

KOMAROM

HIDEGKUT

DEBRECEN

KUNHEGYES

BUDA

PEST

SZOMBATHELY

LAKE BALATON

SZOLNOK

FEGYVERNEK

DANUBE (DUNA)

TISZA

HODMEZO

ROMANIA

YUGOSLAVIA

HUNGARY

"I will have mercy on whom I will have mercy, and I will have compassion on whom I will have compassion."

Exodus 33:19 and *Romans 9:15*

ON THE RUN

OCTOBER 1944

atalin Fogaras approached the fence around the church. Her hand on the latch of the iron gate, she drew a deep breath, pushed it open and slowly walked up toward the side entrance. It was four-thirty. She desperately hoped the minister would be alone.

She passed in front of the sign—REV. IMRE SAROSSY—then tapped on the lacquered oak door. There came an impatient "Yes?" and she entered.

Dr. Sarossy, rotund features accented by horn-rimmed glasses, recognized his visitor with a start.

"Mrs. Fogaras! Here? At this time?" He limply responded to her outstretched hand and motioned towards the armchair on the opposite side of the big desk. "What can I do for you?"

The question was preposterous.

It was October 16, 1944, the day after the Hungarian Nazis had taken over the government. The situation was chaotic. The radio announced new orders every minute. But there was one constant theme: The need to deal with the Jewish population of the city.

"Well?" Sarossy repeated. He had known the young Fogaras couple since they had moved into the neighborhood four years ago. Their legal situation was ambiguous. And now—

"It's been a very difficult day," the minister muttered.

"I—I was on my way home," she burst out, "and thought I'd take a chance, perhaps find you here."

He nodded, waiting.

"I needn't tell you, I'm desperate. If only I could get to the Swedish Embassy! I thought maybe—" she added pleadingly. "Could you?"

It seemed daring to request his help. What could she expect of Sarossy? Of course, he was her pastor. Still, he had always struck her as a cautious man, undecided about his own position in the progressively worsening political situation.

"This can't last. A couple of days, perhaps," she started again.

"It's a tragic situation," the minister said.

"If it weren't for the child, I wouldn't ask. He's all right in the country now, but he'll need at least one of us. I haven't heard from my husband for months."

"I know; believe me, I understand."

"I thought if I could reach one of the houses under Swedish jurisdiction—I got a certificate of protection some time ago, but then things seemed to calm down a little and I didn't follow up. And now—" She threw up her hands.

The man opposite her listened carefully. He nervously rubbed his chin. Then he sat back, took off his glasses, chewed on the bow, then spoke.

"Where are those houses? Do you know how to get there?" Sarossy's lenses were back in place now. He looked at her squarely.

"Perhaps tomorrow, perhaps I could get to the Embassy tomorrow and be guided by them. It's too late today. And if I go home, I'll never be able to leave again."

Kata felt better having formulated a tentative strategy. It must have made an impact on Sarossy, too, for he seemed to be pondering further.

Was he thinking of the neutral powers—Sweden, Portugal, Switzerland—the only ones who might provide some escape? There was the Catholic Church, too, those buildings under the protection of the Papal Nunciature. But, of course, the Catholic Church had more power. Still, Sarossy was a minister of the Faith, a proclaimer of Christian love in the best Reformed tradition, as he would say.

He looked at Katalin sharply.

"You say you can find your way to the Swedish Embassy tomorrow?" he repeated.

"I think I can."

Sarossy deliberated another few seconds.

"This is an impossible situation, I agree," he finally said. "It must be over soon—two or three days, perhaps. The Regent would not have issued his proclamation if he hadn't expected the Allies to respond." He looked at his watch.

It was after five.

"All right. Stay here tonight! Of course, I'm risking bullets. But, the church doors are open until eight. Anybody can enter. Understand, I haven't seen you, I haven't talked to you!"

Her "thank you" was barely audible.

"God bless you," Sarossy reached out his hand quickly for the goodbye, almost as if afraid of a change of heart. She didn't tarry.

She slid out into the hallway and took a step in the direction of the side door opening into the sanctuary. Then she stopped, turned and quickly found her way to the choir loft. Once up there she crouched behind the organ. It hid her from the eyes of visitors in the sanctuary, but she could see the ground floor and its now empty pews through the slots of the balustrade.

She was glad this wasn't her home church. With her father's prominence everybody would have known her there. But here, except for the minister, only a few were really familiar with the background of the young Fogaras family.

She took off her sweater, rolled it into a pillow and stretched out on the floor, with the raincoat pulled over her; she lay snugly in the small space. Thank God, the gates would close soon! She felt almost comfortable.

The church bell chimed six over her head—the deadline for all Jews to be in their homes.

She would never have thought yesterday that their already precarious lives would come under even more stringent danger. For the last month or so—in fact, as recently as last week—hopeful signs had emerged on the political horizon. To be sure, life had had its increasing perils since the Germans had invaded Hungary in March. Deportations had been stepped up throughout the country and were accomplished by the end of June, except in Budapest. There, it was said, the Regent had at last taken a firm stand with the Germans. Everybody knew it might be only a respite, but the war was clearly proceeding towards its end. Even during the months of German rule one could perceive some increasingly hopeful signs—Lakatos as Prime Minister; rumors of peace overtures towards the Allies. And finally, yesterday, October fifteenth, the radio had broadcast the Regent's plea for armistice.

Irene, her sister-in-law, heard it first.

"Come, come, Kata, quick!" she cried out to her in the kitchen where Kata had gone for the teakettle.

She recalled now vividly the excited and incredulous call. The two of them had listened to the radio afterwards—exhilarated, yet with premonitions. In an hour the proclamation had been altered. Confusing "interpretations" started; by four the radio blasted those German marches again; in a while the call was for continued fighting. And by ten, they knew for certain. Szalasi had taken over!

Szalasi! Most everyone, even those on the far right, said he was a lunatic. He would be totally at the service of the Germans.

The news paralyzed her at first. What was there to do? Irene prodded her to leave.

"You must try," she said. "The child needs you. You must stay alive!"

It seemed such an impossible task.

"Try your Christian friends," Irene insisted.

And the minister had come through! Still, she might never make it. Not unless the coup were over in a day or two. Then! Only then. Perhaps!

It was impossible to contemplate tomorrow. She ought to get to the Swedish Embassy. But how? It was in Buda, across the Danube. And would they still honor the certificate?

The more she thought of this, the less hopeful she was. She was so tired. All those years under the shadow of annihilation!

She had experienced the first foreboding of personal danger in September 1938 upon her return from Scotland. And by the spring of 1939 everything had begun.

BOOK ONE
IDYLL IN SHADOW

CHAPTER 1
BEGINNINGS

MARCH 1939

THE GERMANS HAVE ENTERED PRAGUE!

It was March 15, 1939. The cry of newsboys hit Katalin Vaghelyi as she was riding the tram in Budapest. She took a deep breath. So it had happened.

Her joy in having just obtained two new pupils was dampened. With all those uncertainties, they might not be interested any more.

Their father was intent, though, on having his daughters continue with languages. They had had their Viennese baby nurse, then came Mademoiselle who was still with them, and now, English was to have its turn. They had started some months ago but their tutor was leaving.

The tram was moving slowly under the shadow of the Buda Hills. Budapest seemed peaceful enough. Above her, at times visible, other times hidden by streets and tall buildings, were the landmarks of the ancient part of the capital, Buda, with its majestic Royal Castle, the sparkling Fisher Bastion a little further away, and the unmistakable contour of the Coronation Church at its side. History and tradition! Little palaces tucked away in tended gardens. They looked down upon the flatter shores across the Danube where busy Pest spread toward the industrial suburbs.

But her native Pest was beautiful, too, even though with less patina. And she looked with pride at the huge neo-Gothic Parliament spreading along the shore on the other side of the river. The tram swerved towards Margit Bridge.

Germans were in Prague, but it seemed distant. Yet, she could not quite dismiss the thought that the German push had been unequivocally increasing ever since 1934, coming closer.

Only five years but packed with events: Anschluss, Sudetenland and now Prague. With each of Hitler's moves, her prospects had narrowed. So, she had given up university to concentrate on practicalities. Still, her year in Scotland had been a real privilege. Few Hungarians could afford such luxury. The invitation had come through her father's connections and she had made sure to use the time well. She'd perfected her English, learned shorthand and tried to understand the ways of the West. She had become more independent, too. That was the most important thing, although she had not been alone. In Scotland there were the Reverend Stewart and his proper but kindly wife. They guided her; yet, it was different from running with everything to Mother and Father. At home, her attire had been modest and makeup minimal. Money was scarce and there were the restrictions of her father's church. And Mother, still quite good looking—taller than Kata, erect, her once blond hair darker now but still reflecting a golden hue. Well, Mother was not a model of fashion. But in Scotland, Mrs. Stewart took her on shopping trips and Kata acquired new tastes. It helped her confidence to grow. If only the minister's wife had not been so worried about eligible young men, and even more about the ineligibles!

Kata liked her, though. She had learned a great deal from her, about Britain, history, customs—and proper manners. Not what she needed in Hungary now!

They had crossed to the Pest side; the news was back on her mind. There were worried faces entering the tram; the people on the street seemed to carry a burden.

She could hardly wait to get home.

The streetcar reached Kiraly Street, time to transfer. But she decided to walk the eight blocks to her home.

Running up the one flight, Kata opened the door of their apartment. It was good to be greeted by her mother, even with the familiar words: "Kata, so late! I was so worried."

"You're always worried, Anyuka." She kissed her mother.

"Is Father home?"

"He went down to get the evening paper. We can eat as soon as he's back."

Kata went into her room.

"Her" room? She grimaced at the thought. It was the family dining room with a daybed. They seldom used this room for meals, however, generally eating in Father's reception room. Kata could usually enjoy her privacy here. In her high school days she could spread her homework out on the big dining table or sit at it with the French instructor who came to practice with her twice a week. But in the spring she preferred the desk near the window where she would push the glass panes open to savor the scent of acacia wandering into the room.

She pulled the shades down now, and had just changed to comfortable clothes, when she heard her father's voice in the hallway. "So, Dr. Vaghelyi is at home," Kata exclaimed, opening the door and giving him a warm hug. She and her father had always had a special rapport.

Minutes later the three were at the table. Father and daughter began a conversation, and Mother, quietly remembering that she had forgotten to bring in the teakettle, rose without a word and returned with it.

"You should have asked me, I could have done that!" Kata protested.

"It's all right. You've had no chance to talk to your father since yesterday evening."

This was always the way. Sarolta Vaghelyi would serve her little family willingly and with apparent enjoyment, though at times she would complain about prices and demanding washerwomen. In earlier days the full-time household help would perform the cruder tasks of housekeeping, but Mother was the undisputed mistress of the kitchen and she did not particularly want her daughter in it, either.

"You study, learn to be on your own," she would tell Kata, and Mother indeed did everything so that Kata could have uninterrupted time for her work.

Thus, a separation of domains had developed, at least at home: Mother in the kitchen, Kata at her desk. Then together, off to the weekly swimming classes, window-shopping on nearby Erzsebet Boulevard, a visit to some relative, and in later years chats around the built-in tile stove in the winter when Kata needed a break. Mother was there to listen while the needles in her hand busied themselves with the sweater or skirt she was making for her daughter.

The real talks—they were with father.

"What do you think, Apu?" Kata nodded towards the evening paper lying on the armchair.

Her father took time with the answer. "In a way, it should not surprise us after yesterday's news. And Hungary has gotten back the rest of Ruthenia!"

Kata smiled. No matter how bad the news was, Father would always find something hopeful to report. She wondered whether he was always right. But Hitler was returning parts of Hungary taken away after World War I. How could she remain indifferent when the country was receiving its share of long-due claims?

"What happened?" Mrs. Vaghelyi seemed to sense she might have missed something important.

"Don't you listen to the radio, Mother? It's in the paper, too, of course." Kata picked up the *Esti Kurir* and she reached over the table with it.

"I need my glasses." Her mother looked around for a second, then abandoned her search. "I'll read it after supper. This isn't the time."

Wasn't this typical, Kata thought with a sense of condescension that immediately made her ashamed. "Look, Anyu," she explained, wanting to be helpful, "the news isn't good at all. You know the Germans had designs on all Czechoslovakia, and now they've entered Prague."

"That really isn't good, is it?" her mother said. "Where will this lead?

"Let's see what Britain will do; it makes a big difference. I can't imagine they would let the Germans go much further. They can't!" Dr. Vaghelyi said.

"But what if they do?" Kata asked.

"I look at historical perspectives. Subjugation never lasts forever. Look at Babylonia, the Roman Empire."

The telephone rang in the other room. Kata went to pick it up.

"On Saturday? Yes, I'm free Saturday. Let me call you back after supper." Her reply was heard clearly at the table.

"Who was it?" her mother asked as she returned to the meal.

"Eva is having another party; she wants me to come, Saturday."

"You're going out again?"

"Again? Oh, Apu!"

"Who will be there?" Mrs. Vaghelyi asked.

"The usual crowd."

"You ought to wear the blue dress you bought in London. It's very becoming."

Her father was not so easily mollified. "Another party," he mumbled.

"Apuka, really, please understand. What do you want me to do at nineteen? Sit home on weekends?"

He was quiet for a second but then said, "I understand you need company. I'm just not sure you need to go to these dancing parties for that."

Kata shrugged her shoulders.

"How about the young minister from Scotland, or the Ordassy boy?" her father suggested.

"You don't want to send her back to Britain, Erno, do you?" her mother asked.

"No," Kata replied. "Father just wants to fit me into a saintly mold. Of course, Jack Browning dances, too. It was not a sin in Scotland as it is with some of your friends."

Her father frowned. "You're being unfair, you know that. I don't really care one way or the other as long as you put the emphasis on essentials."

Kata did not respond at first, then reached out to him touching his arm. "I know, Apu. Just as in school you wanted me to learn. Grades weren't important. And you taught me a lot. But there are so many other things, too."

She drew a deep breath. "Browning is going home next week. I'm getting two of his pupils."

Her parents seemed to be pleased about the students. "And Ordassy? Well, that would never work either," Kata said, "he could never marry me. A Gentile? And with the new laws?"

"It may not be so simple, it's true," her father admitted. "We must learn to make social adjustments. But who knows? Things may not get so bad, not here, in Hungary."

* * *

Kata's work as secretary in three languages in the international law firm that had hired her after her return from Scotland had proved to be

easier than she had anticipated. The prolonged absence of her immediate boss on a family visit to Sweden had lightened her daily schedule
for the time being. The other two partners of the firm were also abroad
on extended business trips, and in their absence, the office closed at
three. Would they ever return, she wondered.

After a late lunch at home, she would proceed to her students. She
had had two up to now, and with the newly acquired sisters another two
afternoons were taken. It kept her occupied. She had to read and study,
to sustain her skill. But she enjoyed it. And the lessons brought in extra
money.

This was the first week she had been tied up every day until the
evening and she looked forward to a change of pace tonight. It was true
the parties were not always as successful as she intimated to her parents.
Eva was not a very profound girl and her friends, too, were often on
the frivolous side. But Kata had known Eva for thirteen years, ever since
they had started to walk home from school in the first grade. She had
most hospitable parents, too, important in a world where she could not
move freely without chaperons.

And now, Saturday night, Kata was ready at eight to leave for Eva's
home. On her way out she threw a last glance into the mirror. Not so
bad, she grinned. She remembered what an ugly duckling she had
thought herself in her early teens. How come, with handsome parents
as hers? Of course, her mother always complimented her on her pretty
mouth and greenish-grey eyes. "And you look people straight in the
eyes, Kata. People like that," she said. "Don't worry about your freckles:
they go well with your brown hair, with its highlights."

Well, she was truly not as worried any more. Scotland had done
wonders! And she walked out of the house with anticipation.

The tram took her to the short bridge spanning the railroad tracks,
just a few blocks from Nyugati Station, the bridge leading into the
relatively new district where Eva lived. The streets were well lit and
clean.

"My parents have gone to the movies," announced Eva happily.

This was a pleasant feature of the Vidors—they were quite willing
to disappear when their daughter's friends gathered. They would be
home before the party was over, of course.

The apartment reflected the festive mood of the visitors. There was music, the bar had drinks and the lights were soft.

Soft? Kata noticed no light at all in the study, though it was obvious the room was not empty.

She accepted a small glass of cherry liqueur and exchanged some superficial news with people around her. Then, she agreed to a waltz with Marton, a young man she had known for years. As he was taking her back to the chair after the lively whirl, someone called him from the bedroom where the phonograph was giving trouble.

"Where is our electrical engineer?"

Marton excused himself.

Kata looked for her purse and the seat that was hers before. A tall young man rose.

"Did I take your place? Won't you sit down here?" He pulled another chair alongside. "But let me introduce myself first. Istvan Fogaras." He bowed slightly.

"Katalin Vaghelyi." She was trying to place the young man. "Have I seen you before? Maybe I shouldn't need to ask."

"No, I don't think so. Kata?—this is my first time with this group except for Antal," and he pointed to a young man whom Kata knew quite well through Eva.

The music was restored.

"Do you want to dance?" he asked.

"I feel a little breathless from the waltz, but I don't want to hold you back!"

"Not at all. Look, would you like to move over to the foyer? Those two armchairs in the corner—we can talk better there."

For a short time they exchanged casual remarks—the weather, the music, the crowd in the other room.

"A cigarette?" Istvan offered.

Kata took one from the silver case.

"I'm only an occasional smoker," she blurted out self-consciously.

"Good for you. It's a useless habit, to say the least."

He rose halfway to help her with the light.

"I've heard about you before, Kata, I must confess," Istvan said as he resettled in the armchair.

"You have? Really? Shall I ask what, or is that awkward?"

The young man laughed. "I have the suspicion you don't care for gossip. In any case, I'm eager to find out things for myself."

"All right. Where do you want to start?"

"I'll tell you what I know, shall I?"

"Please."

"I know you are studious, like books and know English. That's all."

"Well, I hope that's not all I am!"

"What else?"

"Well—but look here, why should I make this so easy? You already know more about me than I do about you. It's not fair, is it?"

"No, you're right. I shall start then. Let me think: To impress you and still be truthful," he pondered. "I probably can't call myself studious—not much while in school anyhow—I can't speak English but I love to read."

"Favorite author?"

"Thomas Mann."

"Hm. You make up for the lack of studiousness."

"I like him. A bourgeois bohemian. Sort of a contradiction in terms."

Antal suddenly entered. "So you found Kata," he said to Istvan. And to her: "My good friend here is a little too much for me at times, but we have known each other for years—used to live in the same building as kids. I was glad he was free to join us tonight and I promised him he wouldn't be bored. See you later," and he was off, his arm around Eva's waist, to the rhythm of "Mon Amour."

While waiting to see in which direction her newfound companion would lead the conversation, Kata tried to take a better look at him. Although he could not be described as handsome, there was some unusual appeal in his features—his lean face, alert eyes looking at her intently through gold-rimmed glasses, cheeks sunken below the prominent cheekbones, high forehead. The face was alive. And the words came easily out of the longish lips under a narrow moustache.

So she kept listening to his stories and the beginning of his self-disclosures.

Istvan had spent some time abroad, too. In Vienna—attending university.

"Did you like it?" Kata inquired.

"Oh, I had a good time, but as to studies, I'm afraid I didn't do so well. But then, my choice of subjects— I should have taken up liberal arts, not economics."

"Well, why didn't you?"

"My parents—had different ideas."

"And you had to go along?"

"In a way. It seemed sensible—then."

"And now? What do you do?"

"Very prosaic, I'm afraid, at least my everyday occupation. I help out in my parents' business—men's and women's wear. They want me to be equipped to take over."

"Are you?"

He laughed. "I think you've guessed."

She liked the sound of his laugh.

"A cup of espresso?" Eva called from the other room.

They moved toward the tray of demitasses. Istvan handed her a cup. They sipped the coffee in silence.

"Everyday occupation, you said. Is there anything else?" She returned to his comment.

There was some wavering, a slight hesitation, but his reply was matter of fact.

"Not really. Nothing to speak about."

She did not press further.

"How about a tango?" Istvan asked. "This is a party after all!"

She slid into his arm and enjoyed the languid steps. It was nice to leave the words, nice to be in the arms of Istvan Fogaras. He seemed tall to her, compared to her, but she liked that.

The evening passed quickly—a dance now and then with others, too, some chatting with friends, joking, one more drink, another dance.

Kata looked at her watch. She realized it was past one o'clock. It was time to go home. The Vidors arrived and there was a short period of polite intermingling between the generations.

As the various couples and groups were discussing how to get home, Istvan came up to her.

"Where do you live?" he asked.

Kata gave him her address.

"May I see you home, or do you have other arrangements?" "No, it will be fine. Nobody else lives in that direction."

They went downstairs with the rest. Indeed, most of the people were heading away from Kata's neighborhood. They said good night.

"Shall we take a cab?" Istvan offered.

"I like to walk; do you?"

"I do. It's a bit chilly, though. You seem to be shivering."

"It will pass."

They moved on briskly.

"So you like to walk," Istvan picked up her statement. "Hiking?"

"Yes! I love to spend Sundays in the Buda Hills. It interferes with church, but I do it anyhow. I just need to get out."

"Church?" There was a moment's pause. "Are you—you're not Gentile, are you?"

Kata shook her head. "No. I'm Christian, though."

"This is something I didn't know. Something recent?"

"No, not so recent." She thought for a moment, then added: "It's a complicated story."

"I'm sorry. I shouldn't have intruded, not the first time I met you. What a clear night!" Istvan turned to a safer topic.

It was a joy to walk under the bright stars, their legs stretching, their faces tingling in the chill air, exchanging only a word here and there as they stepped along.

As they reached her house and she was ready to shake his hand goodnight, she realized with some embarrassment that all this time her hand had been in Istvan's warm coat pocket, held gently by his long, bony fingers. She blushed slightly and gave him her hand—now officially.

"Good night, Kata, I enjoyed the evening."

CHAPTER 2

VISEGRAD

MARCH 1939

It was Easter morning. A crowd was gathering on the pier. The excursion boat to Visegrad was quietly resting in the cool water of the Danube awaiting the passengers.

Kata arrived a little breathless, looking for her friends. It was Eva who had made the suggestion ten days before that they go away for the weekend. Her parents were free to chaperon and—"Istvan Fogaras may come, too!"—she added with a teasing challenge in her voice.

"It will be a wonderful change from the gloom of the city," Kata quickly responded.

"I bet it's the only reason you are coming!"

Now, as Kata arrived, the person she first spotted was Istvan. He was leaning against the wharf's railing, immersed in the morning paper. But he looked up, waved and was on his way to greet her.

"Imagine, it's been three weeks! The elements favor us," he said, pointing to the bright climbing sun breathing life into the crisp morning.

Kata's reply was interrupted by the arrival of the Vidors. The rest of the group came and there was a happy flurry of anticipation about a weekend away.

The pier buzzed with noise and laughter. Here and there, solicitous mothers anxiously called out to their disoriented offspring; firm male voices cut into the melee. There was a long-drawn call to a lost partner—happy confusion. Finally, the crowd was allowed to move across the gangplank.

The boat's horn sounded. They were leaving. It puffed upstream under the heavy load.

Men and women stared into the resisting current as the boat carved its way toward the arching span of Chain Bridge, then gracefully slid through the pillared tunnel of Margit Bridge on its slow progress out of the city. The passengers held their jackets close against the breeze as they leaned on the railing. At times the six young people were all together, at other times they distributed themselves into couples; occasionally the girls and men formed into separate groups.

Only a few small craft were visible in the water now, though the beginning activities of shoreside boat colonies could be detected from the slowly moving steamer.

"Do you ever get out on row boats, Kata?" Istvan inquired.

"No. I'm embarrassed to say it, but my mother is awfully fearful of the water."

"Can't you swim?"

"Very well, in fact. But you know those whirlpools, the strong current and who knows what—that's what I'm told. It must be fun, though."

"Mothers!" Zsuzsa caught the word as she passed by. "If they're not worried about accidents they want to know every move you make. A rowing trip for us? Forget it, Istvan."

She waved a mocking good-bye as she proceeded with Gyuri to examine the upper deck.

"Did I touch a sensitive chord?" Istvan guessed. "Boating is fun, though, it really is, particularly when one can stay for more than just one day. Antal and I had some experiences, didn't we?" Istvan asked as his friend returned with Eva from an inspection of the other shore.

The boat colony of Romaifurdo gradually gave way to the steeples of picturesque Szentendre. After a while the summer youth camp of Tahitotfalu could be seen. On the right, they passed endless rows of summer cottages nestled in the elongated island separating the two shores of the Danube for a stretch of sixty miles, up to where the river took a sharp turn to the west, and the hills rose once more and the great pyramid of a moderately tall mountain could be seen. It signaled their destination. The five-hour ride would soon be over.

The crowd began to throng the narrow corridors, impatient to set foot on the Visegrad shore.

"Eva, Zsuzsa, Kata—and you young fellows," Mr. Vidor turned toward Antal, Gyuri and Istvan. "Follow my wife and me!" And the Vidors, with remarkable agility for middle-aged parents, marched toward the cottage, the rental of which they had arranged for their party. They had long known the elderly couple who owned the house and who usually retired into a back room as spring arrived to supplement their income from rentals by weekenders and summer vacationers. Visegrad was a popular excursion spot.

Upon arrival, Mr. Vidor continued the role of manager: "This room is for the girls, that for you fellows, and this for us old folks," he exclaimed. The young people accepted the arrangement and proceeded to freshen up before they went to look for food.

The raw wooden tables of a restaurant under the incipient foliage of mulberry trees invited them and they decided to settle outdoors in spite of the breeze; soon they were sated with fried chicken, mugs of beer and luscious *palacsinta*.

A leisurely walk along the shore followed the repast. They stopped from time to time, picked up pebbles and challenged the water with them, ran a few minutes then stopped again to marvel at the beauty of the river. They walked and talked and enjoyed being alive.

Time passed quickly—they were tired.

Back in the village, they stopped for a snack and soon were meandering back to the cottage.

They decided to turn in early, to be ready for the next day's trip—a walk to the top of Visegrad Hill.

As they said good night, Istvan gently touched Kata's arm before heading to his room.

* * *

Easter Monday arrived in brightness. The balmy morning air heralded a wonderful transition from the bright but still somewhat cool previous day. Now they felt that several hours spent outdoors would not be excessive and the thought of a slow-paced walk up the hill filled them with joy.

At first, they threaded their way on the clean, upward-winding main street. A neat little church on its higher slope dominated the small village. It served as a turning point on the path leading to the castle. The path itself—a walk of one or two hours—was crowded with visiting city folk. Lovers marched hand in hand swinging their arms back and forth, in rhythm with the movement of their legs. Children dashed ahead, screaming with pleasure, then quickly returned to be within the protective sight of their parents. Some middle-aged folk setting out with the others had no intention of reaching the top. They would stroll as long as they felt up to it, then stop, munch on sandwiches, absorb the spring foliage, breathe in the sweet air of renewal, get a view of the river and then turn back for a relaxing afternoon nap.

As the older generation and those couples with younger children were left behind, the path became less populated. Several tree-marked trails led to the top and Kata and Istvan, already separated from their faster moving friends, decided to follow one of the trails, rather than the regular winding road preferred by the average city tourist.

They were in no hurry.

As they walked, from time to time the river's view could be seen. At times its bluish greyness appeared as if through a window—an opening in the young foliage. Then the river disappeared and the woods offered its delight to the explorers.

"I'm happy you could come," Istvan said.

"It's good to be away from the city! I've had a hard time there in the last few weeks. Everything seemed hopeless. But it didn't last, thank God," she said with a big sigh.

"One's mood changes, doesn't it? I feel quite depressed at times. Of course, now it's the world situation."

The recollection of it quieted them both, absorbed in their thoughts.

Then Kata asked: "What do you think of it?"

"Extremely discouraging. We may have a war soon. Besides, for us Jews the outlook is miserable. I am one of those who at times dwells on the events and becomes paralyzed. Or else, I chuck the whole thing and escape into esoteric activities."

"Esoteric?"

"I was speaking ironically." There was a noticeable pause before Istvan came out with it. "I write, you know."

"Really? I had no idea. Fiction?"

"Yes. Only short stories so far."

"That's exciting! Has anything been published?" She immediately wondered whether that was wise to ask.

"One short story—in the *Ujsag* two years ago. I was lucky. They took it immediately upon submission."

"Oh? But then they must have considered it good. Imagine, no rejection!" She turned toward him in amazement. "And since?"

Istvan quietly walked on before answering. "Nothing since then. I really must perfect myself first. It's nice to know, though, it may not be hopeless!"

"It takes patience, doesn't it?" Kata tried to understand a writer's point of view. "I would have been on their necks, I'm sure. But then, I'm not an artist," she said with some humility. "It must be a wonderful feeling."

There was awe and pride in her statement. Istvan was the first live writer she had known. There was Father, of course, but that was different. His forte was philosophy, religion—and law!

"I always thought it was a marvelous thing to be creative. I wish I could—"

"Marvelous? I don't know. It's quite painful at times." He stopped, then continued the explanation: "Surely, when a baby is born and he looks healthy and is full of life and vigor, it is a joy to watch. But the time preceeding its struggle from the womb! The thrilling moment of conception is followed by months of agonizing expectation, and delivery is at times excruciatingly painful, I understand," Istvan continued. "Besides, you must know artists are not the most happy people. Not as a rule, anyhow. But they do have exceptionally satisfying moments."

Kata listened to every word. She smiled and said, "But you seem happy."

He returned his smile and reached for her hand. "With you now, yes. But I ought to warn you, I'm quite moody at times."

"Warn me?" She looked up at him.

There was a pause.

"Well, I didn't call you, did I?"

"No."

"I don't really know why I am trying to justify myself!" He looked at her thoughtfully. "But I've been thinking of you quite a bit. An old wolf like me and an innocent young girl!"

"Come on! Your thirty years must be weighing heavily on you! Do you mean to frighten me?" she asked now as he turned toward her.

"It sounds like that, doesn't it? No, I don't think I do."

He steered her by the elbow through an arch of branches lying low across the trail.

"Seriously, I'd like to know you better. I felt amazingly light and carefree after taking you home the other day. I was surprised. You surely aren't the first girl!"

Kata laughed. "I believe that."

They walked on. As the path broadened at one point Istvan squeezed her hand. For a while they proceeded in silence. They came to a bench in a small clearing and Istvan suggested they sit and rest for a while. They absorbed the peaceful beauty below—the slow-moving, undulating river containing the blue of the horizon and the darkness of the shoreline. The red brick roofs of Nagymaros spotted the greening landscape across the river, and the hills further to the north and west bordering Czechoslovakia framed the still life.

"The world is at peace, at least from here," Istvan said. "Let's see if we can't transplant some of the magic to the city!" He seemed to have his plan. "Kata, do you like classical music? I have two tickets to *Parsifal* for next Friday. Would you care to come?"

"*Parsifal*? Yes, I'd love to! I'm not an expert on Wagner, though. I must confess, I haven't seen any Wagner opera yet."

"I'm glad I'll be able to tell you about it then. Do you know the story at all?"

"Yes, I took a literature course in Edinburgh. I learned of King Arthur, Sir Galahad, the search for the Holy Grail. I think the Wagnerian story is not the same but I do have an idea about the theme."

"You know more than you need to know. The rest will be there on the program. As to music, it may be best if you experience it on your own, without my giving you advance coaching. I love Wagner—the *Ring, Tristan, Tannhauser. Parsifal* is a little too long. It's good I'll not have to feel lonely!"

He looked at her laughingly. "But, what a silly thing to spend our time here with Wagner!" And as if wishing to rectify the mistake, he drew her to himself. It was but a touch of a kiss—a tender, enchanting prelude. She responded for a second. Then she rose. After all, she thought, this was only their second meeting.

"Don't you think our friends will be waiting for us?"

Istvan smiled. "I need a girl who knows when it's time to get off the clouds. Let's go."

In a few minutes they reached the plateau on the top. The others were there already. "It took you a long time to arrive!" they teased.

They looked for a quiet spot to settle down to eat their sandwiches. Then the six of them stretched out on two blankets spread on the young grass. Istvan and Kata turned their heads slightly towards each other. There was desire and laughter in their eyes.

After a while, the six descended together on one of the broader pathways. Some of them were singing in unison. Istvan and Kata joined in here and there. Then they continued in silence, stealing glances at each other. They hardly heard the familiar tunes carried by their friends.

* * *

As they returned to the city in the evening, Kata and Istvan stood at the rail and looked across the dark water. Except for a sliver of light around the vessel emanating from the boat, the blackness seemed as impenetrable as the future. But the little light provided comfort against the unknown beyond. And there was comfort in the people around them, too, some of whom they knew and had greeted earlier with casual recognition. Threads of sweet music came from below; relaxed chatter brushed them by, and the two, side by side, gazing at the upheaving water, stood there with welling joy.

"So you agreed to see me in the city, Kata?" Istvan turned to her after a while.

"I did. You asked me, didn't you?"

"I told you I'd like to know you better." Istvan's voice was warm and positive. Then a slight halt: "I also wonder about the wisdom of it."

"Wisdom? Is there any cause for doubting?"

His gentle laughter was reassuring. "No, no real reason, Kata. It's just that I don't know whether I am the properly eligible type."

He said this with mock formality but then continued in a serious and more self-revealing manner.

"I told you about writing. That's my dream and ambition. But in reality, probably nothing will come of it. Certainly, not while the political situation is as it is now in Hungary—and in the world, for that matter. It looks as if I will be aiming for impossible goals. It can be quite difficult at times. It's true, I have a modest income from the family business—just enough for the bare basics."

Kata smiled in the dark. "I wasn't quite brought up in excessive comfort myself," she stated. "I'll tell you about that sometime. My father is a hopeless idealist. In any case, why think about this now? You invited me to *Parsifal* and I accepted. Unless—you're not retracting the invitation?"

"I can see you're not easily dissuaded. We'll go. But you can't say I didn't warn you!"

They found two deck chairs and sat for a while in the dark. Now they could see the sparkling lights of the city in the distance. Kata's hand rested comfortably in Istvan's grasp. The weekend would soon be over. But the appearance of those lights welcoming them into the city made her think happily of the week to come.

CHAPTER 3
PARSIFAL

APRIL 1939

They met in front of the baroque opera house at half past five.

A light rain sprinkled the avenue as Kata emerged from the underground. It made the same slight impact on the pavement as the street cleaning truck's sweep every morning, but it filled the air with the fresh smell of spring.

She was fumbling to open her umbrella as she moved toward the big clock on the corner.

Istvan came to her rescue. "How about sharing mine?"

"I'll accept. Hi!" She reached out her hand and slid under the protective canopy offered by Istvan.

"So we made it! Our first real date! And how did you spend the last five days?" Istvan asked.

"Looking forward to this evening—to *Parsifal*."

"I'm glad I aroused your interest—for Wagner."

They both laughed.

"I'm really glad you came." He gently steered her toward the side entrance.

"I think I told you, the tickets are for the balcony."

They walked through the gathering crowd of the ground-floor vesti-
bule. Some were waiting for the one elevator in the right corner. Others
stood around looking for friends.

They decided to climb the three flights.

"Oh, I like these seats!" Kata exclaimed. "During the last two years
of school I had season tickets a little higher up. It was all right. But the
first row gives one a chance to see everything—the stage, the audience." And she looked around with rapture at the festive crowd and the
glittering women in the orchestra seats.

She glanced at the stagebill. "The story of Parsifal, a simple youth
become a knight in search of the Holy Grail," the synopsis said. She
could not finish the complicated story in which intriguer and innocent
vie for redemption but she caught the words "salvation through compassion." The lights dimmed. The performance started and the magic of
the music took over.

And while she listened with her hand in Istvan's, the sound, the touch
and the mystical atmosphere of the dark balcony—all these converging
sensations—transformed the story from its message of universal quest
to one of personal significance for Kata herself. *Parsifal* spoke to her in
some specific, as yet inexplicable, way.

A quest for the Grail, search for perfection, salvation through compassion.

She was moved by the hero's determination in the midst of diabolic
schemes and his own stumblings. Parsifal's final victory exalted her. A
destiny fulfilled.

* * *

There was little time to discuss the performance that evening.

She was happy—listening to the music, hearing Istvan's short comments about the singers during the two intermissions, reciprocating the
casual greetings of familiar faces heading from the balcony's door
toward the refreshment counter, and proudly walking the short length
of the foyer with her companion. But she was cautious in trying to offer
a quick commentary on music which she felt she was too unsophisticated to assess.

As the curtain fell at the end, the ovations continued and they finally
moved to gather their belongings at the cloak counter. They could only
share with a word and a smile, a touch or a contented sigh the emotions

of the evening. Then, they were absorbed in the noise and collective movement of the crowd descending the winding stairs.

* * *

The Sunday afternoon after the performance, as they were sitting at Lukacs, there was a glow of anticipation in reliving the experience.

The waitress took their orders and they settled comfortably in the famous confectionary. The place was filled—widows sharing the emptiness of their solitary lives with each other, families feeding delicacies to their youngsters between the movies and early bedtime, lovers in wall-side cubicles enjoying some privacy and quiet. And the crystal chandeliers spread an aura of festivity over all.

"Well, once more, how did you like it?" Istvan seemed eager to get back to *Parsifal*.

"I told you, I was very impressed. It was a great experience."

"Yes?"

"You understand, I don't really know much about music. I love Verdi and Tschaikovsky—entirely different, of course. I must say, though, Wagner didn't frighten me. It captivates by its majesty. It's a bit like the idea of God."

"What do you mean?" Istvan questioned.

"Well, I don't want to be profane, but I feel there are things one cannot quite understand but perhaps it's their being beyond reach that really makes the impression."

"Continue."

Istvan lit a cigarette. Kata waved "no" to his offer of one. Contrary to many people, fumbling with a cigarette distracted her.

"I feel awkward explaining it. In a way this music of *Parsifal* is beyond my depth, but in an appealing, inspiring way."

"Is this how you think of God, too? Out of your reach?" Istvan asked.

She nodded. "This is one way I think of God."

"I see. Other ways, too?"

Kata was quiet for a while. How could she explain? She hardly knew what she believed. Her feelings were still inchoate. The waitress brought the Napoleons. She dipped her fork into hers.

"Well, some other thoughts follow. Are you sure you want to hear them? They are rather rudimentary at this point." She turned to him with some hesitation.

"Kata, I want to know you."

"All right. Where did I leave it? Oh, yes, the idea of God. Well, I said God means incomprehensible, inspiring, majesty. But then how can one really grasp that beyond the feeling? I thought about this during the opera."

"Yes?"

Kata was feeling her way.

"Well, I was touched by *Parsifal*—not only by the music. I suppose I couldn't help thinking of the legend of King Arthur and his knights, which I knew before, but here the emphasis was on the search, wasn't it? Yes, the search is terribly important and compassion, but the whole theme of *Parsifal*, the quest, the seemingly insurmountable difficulties and final victory—they helped me to take in the music. I did not follow every detail of the story and yet, knowing there was a communicable message, brought out the beauty of the music in a more tangible way. Like—I thought of Jesus, the theme to the orchestration that is called God."

Istvan looked at her. "A poetic approach, I must say. So you believe in God?"

"I do." She said quietly. "And you?"

Istvan frowned. "Perhaps, in some ways—in overall, general splashes—some Higher Intelligence or the like. I cannot really say I have faith."

"It's not easy, I know," she agreed, nodding.

"By the way, coming back to *Parsifal*, there was one other important theme beyond the search, the idea of the 'guileless fool.' "

"Do you mean an unsophisticated seeker?"

"Perhaps a little more than that," Istvan said.

"Blessed are the poor in spirit!" Kata continued her own trend of thought and became pensive. "You know I have difficulty with this at times. My father likes to quote it." She shrugged her shoulders.

Istvan chuckled "And you don't like it, I can see that."

"Well, it's hard to take. The trouble is, at times the poor in spirit spills over to poor in purse. I shouldn't say this, but it's 'walking on clouds.' "

"And you prefer being down to earth?"

She blushed. "Not quite. You know, I had a rather different life from my well-to-do and mostly Jewish classmates. Perhaps I am reacting to that. Of course, the wealthy and titled Gentiles attended expensive sectarian boarding schools—convents or the Protestant Baar Madas."

"And the religious and self-conscious Jews go to the Jewish Gimnazium," Istvan quickly picked it up. "It's true, the public college-preparatory high schools are attended heavily by Jewish youngsters. But you said you were Christian, yet you are comparing yourself with the Jewish students—and you're still seeking out Jewish company."

"I know. It always seemed I was both," she said in a somewhat subdued tone. "I'll take a cigarette now."

"Well, perhaps you are," Istvan acknowledged. "But not everyone carries both badges."

"I think you're beginning to see the dilemma."

She was an inept smoker, puffing without inhaling. But the bitter, warm taste felt oddly comforting. "You see, my mother joined the church when I was ten."

"Oh! Then by law, you as a girl had to follow your mother's religion at birth. I suppose you were registered Jewish."

Kata nodded.

"And now?"

"Again, according to the laws, it wasn't possible to change my religion while in school. I had to wait until I became eighteen. That's when I officially joined the church—Calvinist, not my parents' group.

"It must have been confusing!"

She shrugged. "In a way, yes. But with Hitler, things are getting simplified," she added.

"Simplified!" For a moment he seemed to explode. "I feel inexpressible rage. One is so helpless! But we shouldn't ruin the evening. Another espresso?" Without waiting for the answer he beckoned the waitress to fill their cup. He appeared to calm.

They enjoyed the stimulating liquid in silence.

"You know what?" Kata suggested as the waitress cleared the table. "Let's go for a walk. The weather was beautiful earlier."

"A wonderful idea."

He paid, helped her into her coat and they were out on the avenue.

The evening was still mild, though the dusk had swept away the earlier warmth of the sun. There was a faint smell of young leaves and a hint of budding acacia. The gardens of the substantial homes along this part of Andrassy Avenue were swelling with new life. They walked in the direction of Varosliget, the big city park, about a mile from the confectionary.

At the end of the avenue was the Hosok Tere—Heroes' Square. It was brightly illuminated and the obelisk in its center beckoned them from afar. As they moved nearer, the statues of the seven land-prizing Magyars forming two arcs about Arpad, the Chieftain, loomed larger and clearer. The museums on both sides of the square with their classic lines and Corinthian pillars provided a dramatic contrast between the world of civilization and the ideals of the first conquerors who came from the slopes of the Ural Mountain to form a nation. And the enduring immobility of the white marble was accentuated by the green foliage of the park, shivering in the floodlights.

"A beautiful sight!" Kata exclaimed as they stopped on the corner.

"A thousand years of history in the Carpathian basin!" Istvan mused. "A thousand years of pull and tug: wars, attempts at peace, incursive Tartars, Turkish occupants, seductively cultured Hapsburg monarchs. A nation always at odds with itself: The Turks—heathen and alien, a clear foe. The Hapsburgs, a more subtle enemy. And so goes the ever present dilemma, Kata. Belong and identify, fight against or assimilate with, the East or the West."

"You know," she said pensively, "you might think this is romantic foolishness, but, last summer, crossing the Scottish moors by bus and reading a Hungarian newspaper sent by my father, I felt real pain, such desperate longing and a sense of profound loss: 'Can I still be Hungarian?' Remember, the First Jewish Law had just been passed. And even when I came back, I marched along the avenue—was it November?—shouting with the others: 'No, No, Never! Hungary will never give up her former boundaries!' "

"So Hitler helped 'us!' " Istvan shook his head. "The situation is disgustingly ambiguous."

"Yes, the story of our country—ambiguity, I mean," Kata added.

"Let's cross." Istvan steered her toward the Memorial. "I agree," he said as they stood before it, "it does evoke sentiments. Remembering the history—you know, we Jews have been through it all. In a limited way at first, and for a long time not allowed to purchase land, but still, we have been a part of the national ferment. A hundred years ago we joined the Magyars in championing the cause of the Hungarian language as the core of our national culture. And for the fifty years after the Hapsburg Emperor became the Hungarian King, we shared in the opportunities opening to the nation. And in the Great War, we bled and died with other Hungarians. Then came Bela Kun!."

"I was born during the days of the Commune," Kata interjected. "My father told me of the terrible atrocities."

"And I remember the White Terror that followed—I was about ten then," Istvan said. "And just because Bela Kun was a Jew, we were no longer true Hungarians!"

She sighed. "For twenty years it wasn't so clear, was it?"

"Well, we got so used to restrictions—admission quotas at the University, no admittance to civil service positions, a pervasive prejudice, chips on shoulders, arrogance, beatings, Horthy's self-righteous purges. And still lots and lots of intermarriages!"

"So the change is not sudden, though drastic it is!" she concluded. "Istvan," she turned to him, "you should hear my father! A true patriot. Of course, he grew up in the era when things began to move. He went to the university, of course, he was an Army officer, he loved the land, and he himself was disturbed by Bela Kun."

"So your father is a patriot, and a Christian?"

"He certainly is." There was a long silence. "He is a very interesting man, Istvan; I like to talk to him. But to be truthful, he has added to my confusion."

"I don't suppose you find him too patriotic, after what you've said earlier?"

"No, not that. But my father takes his Christianity so seriously, and then goes around declaring his Jewish background to everyone! It's always been like that. That was the price of his becoming Christian, I guess."

"That's a story I would like to hear. What made him become Christian?" Istvan asked.

"It was a long process. But in a nutshell: He was a seeker, Istvan, from a religious home—Orthodox, in fact. The core of life was God, the hope of the future, the coming of the Messiah and the routines of life were garnished with the Law."

"And then he left the village, I suppose."

Kata nodded. "There was a Catholic classmate in the *gimnazium*, a peasant boy, who invited him to a musical Mass. That was only the beginning. Then he was presented with the Gospels in his university days. It was literally a revelation. The Law had been fulfilled! The Messiah had arrived! He preached universal love to all, not just the chosen few. The message gripped him. And ever since, he has been an ardent follower of Jesus Christ—and a loyal son of the race that bred him."

"And your mother? Does she share your father's convictions?" Istvan asked.

"Not entirely, no. At times she is still drawn to the old ways but she is a good wife, and participates with father in the church. Not that she's forced."

"And you?"

Kata shrugged her shoulders. "I am Christian. Scotland helped to make the choice definite. But the State?" There was a long silence. Then a sigh. "My status is being defined."

And indeed, with the so-called Second Jewish Law passed by the Hungarian Parliament in May 1939, anyone not registered as Christian at birth was to be considered a Jew.

There were nuances to be sure. But this one stipulation was enough for the Vaghelyi family. Knowing their place was now beyond their choice.

CHAPTER 4
COURTSHIP

MAY 1939-
JANUARY 1940

Dr. Vaghelyi shook his head. "Kata, aren't you getting involved too soon?" She smiled and brushed off the remark. She had never been so happy.

Kata and Istvan met regularly now—walking, talking, attending some events, seeing friends.

Istvan introduced her to a new circle, some of whom were settled, with businesses of their own, while others pursued professional careers in a world where stability was fading. Their worries and concerns simmered beneath the surface of a deceptive well-being.

They read the papers anxiously every morning, then Kata tried to push the thought of the news away. In this period of her life she could not tolerate any intrusion, any interference with her dreams.

Her friends teased her, of course, though Eva was generally pleased. She took credit for the romance. Zsuzsa was a sharper critic.

"So you're dating Istvan Fogaras! You know, he's not a big match. Smart, yes, but money?"

Zsuzsa had a knack for worldly wisdom, and an entourage of young men. At times she would relinquish the surplus. With her dark eyes, smooth jet-black hair and a slim figure, she was the model of an accomplished female to her less worldly friends. She knew this and was not ready to cater to their sensitivities. Nevertheless, there was genuine warmth and interest in Zsuzsa's hovering over the less sophisticated Kata.

"Watch out!" she persisted. "You, too, like the better things of life!" But in spite of her friend's warning it seemed to Kata that Istvan provided all she needed.

Kata enjoyed the small luxuries her dates with him offered. A supper here and there in small restaurants, a concert in the pavillion of Margaret Island on a hot summer night, an invitation by Istvan's sister to a gala performance of *Rigoletto*. These all afforded Kata what a part of her had longed for: a taste of material well-being and culture over and beyond the comforting realm of the spirit that her own home provided. And, Istvan had a wonderfully creative mind.

"A writer is an observer," he said, "looking from the outside." Indeed, the universe he saw gained life through his own insights and feelings.

"But you don't have any writers among your friends. How's that?"

Istvan shrugged. "I'm not a real writer yet."

"Don't you miss the ambience, though?"

"Maybe. Acually, I was more involved during my Vienna days and the years thereafter."

"You were?"

"Well, I'll tell you. I had a girl friend, wrote poetry,—very talented. Through her I met quite a few Bohemians."

"Oh?"

"Gabriella and I broke up, as you may guess. It was a rather unpleasant thing in fact, so, somehow I turned away from that circle. But the group dissolved in any case."

"I see, No other writers besides the poetess?"

Istvan smiled. "No need to be so formal. Yes, the man she met. We were friends at first, but I was pretty hurt."

"So you turned to bourgeoisie."

"I guess I did. Bourgeoisie has its virtues. Anyhow, the way the political situation is, you know it is impossible to get into the field of the arts now—formally I mean. Journalism has been out of the question for years. My friend, Thomas—you've not met him yet, he's struggling with marital problems—he's stilll a reader for Pegazus Publishing. Who knows how long."

"But you can still write!"

"Probably for the drawer. As a matter of fact, I do."

He began to show her some sketches, discuss a plot or a character and make her feel a part of an artist's world. Kata was totally absorbed in being a writer's confidante.

But her father was troubled.

"Come to church with me today," he asked one early summer Sunday.

Since her return from Scotland she had liked to attend the English service at the local Scottish Mission chapel. But now she agreed to accompany her father. After all, she reasoned, he could claim her presence once in a while.

The congregation was small; the Bible reading copious; the hymns gushed with emotions. For a short while she was back in her childhood and early teens when attendance Sunday morning was an unchangeable routine, the singing a truly "joyful noise unto the Lord" and the people, not many in numbers most of the time—serious and dourly dressed, no makeup, no fancy hairdo, no fashionable clothes—were nevertheless warm and unceasingly interested.

"Brethren and sisters, are you saved?"

The familiar question stirred her reverie. It was the thunder which for her always turned the caressing comfort of the prayer hall into a threatening challenge. Why did they stress that theme? It pushed her into a defensive spiritual stance. If only it were so simple to answer!

"Work out your salvation in fear and trembling!"

Because the wages of sin is death, Kata concluded in her mind.

At the end of the service, the little group of faithful gathered in the yard greeting each other enthusiastically and welcoming the long-absent prodigal daughter.

"It's good to see you, Kata," a black-clad woman, Mrs. Gondos, came up to them. "I wish my son Lali would have come before it was too late."

"Yes, I heard. I'm sorry."

The woman sighed. "Dr. Vaghelyi tried to help but it was in vain. Lali got into bad company—drinking, carousing around. Then came the accident." Her eyes filled with tears. "I told him, 'Repent, repent,' but he only laughed."

They shook a few more hands, then slipped into the street.

"Let's walk toward the park," her father suggested.

When they were on the tree-studded lane of Fasor, Dr. Vaghelyi started: "I've wanted to talk to you for some time, Kata. I am quite worried."

"What about? Istvan?"

"Yes. What's happening, Kata? You're out all the time and are seeing no one else anymore, are you?"

She shook her head. "No, I'm not. But why are you so worried? Don't you like him? It seems the two of you get along well. You with your quotations—Aristotle in Greek, Cicero in Latin. He discussing the mastery of Flaubert in Madame Bovary, the late blooming of Pirandello." She laughed. "Even to mention it seems such an anticlimax after this morning, don't you think so?"

"I do," her father said firmly. "And now that you've brought it up, I did want to ask, what about spiritual matters?"

She tilted her head. "We are not avoiding them! We talk about faith, Jesus. I think Istvan is quite intrigued by the topic."

Her father shook his head. "He's not a Christian!"

"Papa, you're saying that? Haven't you been always on both sides?"

"Not in beliefs and commitments! I am talking about that."

She shrugged her shoulder. "Every time I go to church with you I wonder about you—the constant pounding on the 'Are you saved?' theme! Sure, Istvan is different. But so am I, Apu." She stopped for a moment, looked straight into his eyes and challenged: "What really puzzles me, how can you be one of them? My bright, philosopher father who is versed in the classics, who knows the Bible inside out!"

"You just gave the answer," her father calmly said. "Even the Psalmist says: 'The fear of the Lord is the beginning of wisdom.' "

"This isn't what I mean, Dad, you know that. It's the approach, like this morning. Don't you find it simplistic and frightening, too? Suppose I'm still groping?"

"But we are all sinners! This is the kernel of Christianity—the promise of forgiveness!"

They walked on quietly for a minute, before he continued: "I know their phraseology disturbs you, Kata. But after all, Christianity is about salvation whatever way you put it, isn't it? As for me, many years ago in this group, through some truly wise men who are by now dead, I found a treasure. They gave the Gospels into my hand. The gift received is too great to be diminished by human verbiage. And in this church I know everyone in person, they know me. It's not a huge impersonal Cathedral, it's home. But you? No, you don't have to be exactly like them as long as you don't give up the search for fuller understanding!"

"Don't worry about that, Apu. I'm always searching. I want to be a Christian. Istvan knows that. We talk about everything. I don't feel the least bit restricted. The rest? It's too early to tell."

* * *

At the end of July, Eva's parents invited Kata to join them at Lake Balaton for a fortnight with the understanding that Istvan would spend a few days in a nearby boarding house. Her father hesitated, then gave Kata permission to go.

The newspapers spoke of Germany's military preparation. The survival of Poland was in danger. But the bright sun flooded the blue waters of Balaton, and the rest of the world was far away.

In the languid summer afternoons they lay side by side in a secluded spot of the garden surrounding the boarding-house, at first with book in hand. Then, the letters of the print were overwhelmed by the afternoon's brightness and their initial intent was swept away by the breeze coming from the water and the awareness that they lay close to each other. A smile, a touch, a furtive kiss in the afternoon's bright light.

Then, dusk, supper, music, walks, swimming in the moonlight. Joyous laughter as they tested the cool waves against their taut bodies. Kata and Istvan plunged in, swam, floated, played hide-and-seek and left in half-abated excitement.

Morning again, the sharply blue lake under a cloud-free sky, time for a walk.

"What is a real woman to you?" Kata asked, remembering an earlier comment of Istvan's. As she spoke she wished she could have retrieved her question. But Istvan did not laugh.

"A man needs a woman on whom he can count—I do, at least—a Solveig. Peer Gynt was a fortunate man to know there was a stable place of return, a place of understanding and acceptance."

For two weeks they had wonderful weather. No clouds reflected on the deep-blue water. No clouds interfered with their growing love. And as they returned to the city, they knew they were meant for each other.

* * *

"I don't like what's happening," Istvan said to her at the end of August.

"You mean the international scene?"

"Yes. Germany and Russia just signed a non-aggression pact. The two may still fight side by side. It would be a hard alliance to conquer."

"How do you see our chances here?" Kata tried to find a way out of the two dictatorships' orbit.

Istvan shrugged his shoulders. "Everything will affect us. Hungary, wedged in between the East and West—we are too small not to be affected. Further away, maybe."

He walked for a while in silence, twirling his moustache—a sign of his being absorbed in thought.

Finally he turned to her: "Kata, have you thought of leaving Hungary again?"

The question caught her unprepared.

"I don't know. Not really. My parents asked me to return at a time when so many others wouldn't have thought of it. I'm their only child. It's true, now father's disturbed, too, about the happenings, though he tends to underplay danger."

"Kata, I wrote to the New Zealand Consulate some time ago for information," Istvan spoke abruptly. "That country has many possibilities."

She nodded.

"They say it is breathtakingly beautiful," he continued. "Politically it has a socialist government, and economically it still has opportunities for immigrants. I would have to learn some practical trade, though, and English, fastest of all. Of course, you would have nothing to worry about in this respect. You have a tremendous asset!" he continued as if it had been the most natural thing to include Kata in the plan.

She smiled. "You could pick up the language easily, that may not be the main problem. But, isn't it far away?"

"Yes, and it would probably require a fortune, even if a visa could be obtained. But one must think of some way out while there's time. It may already be too late."

They were at her door.

"I'll call you tomorrow." He lifted her hand to his lips.

The warmth lingered while she walked up the stairs.

This was the germ of a proposal, she jubilantly recognized.

* * *

The following Friday World War II began.

At first, the developments were not clear. There was still a question of how the situation would differ from earlier German exploits. For a day or two the question was open: Would there be an international war or another cowering surrender?

The certainty came on Sunday. It was a hot day spent by Kata and Istvan in the spacious pool of Punkosfurdo twenty miles outside Budapest. With a group of friends, they took the electric commuter train in the morning to enjoy the last opportunity for water and sand before the cool of autumn. At the end of the day, pleasantly tired from the crowds, the swimming and the hot sun, they welcomed Zsuzsa's casual invitation for light supper.

The Venetian blinds closed all day had kept the apartment's living room reasonably cool, and within a short time they felt refreshed.

"Any new developments, I wonder?" Istvan said and rose, heading toward the radio.

"No interference, please," Zsuzsa steered him back to the sofa as she entered with a sandwich platter. "The news these days is not good for digestion. Let's eat first."

Istvan reluctantly took his seat. He could hardly wait for the supper to be over. Zsuzsa noted his mood. With the last tray emptied, she moved to Istvan. "Go ahead! The eight o'clock news'll be on in a few minutes."

The concluding cadences of gypsy music rang out. Then the thunderbolt they had been anticipating: "The Hungarian Telegraph Office announces—France and Britain are now at war!"

"My God! Finally they're acting!" someone cried out. "This is Hitler's end!"

"They will be liquidated in days; the bluffing is over!" Antal repeated excitedly.

"It may be longer than that, but something's happening at last! Chamberlain should have never pacified Hitler."

But Istvan was cautious: "I hope England is prepared. The pacifying may have had its reason."

There was an adventurous gleam in Zsuzsa's eyes: "We're living in dangerously exciting times."

Her comment was greeted by her friends' dubious looks.

"At least there's action, but think of all those who'll have to die!" Kata shuddered.

"Not here, thank God! We're fortunate."

"I wouldn't be so sure, Antal," Istvan contradicted. "A small nation like ours? Switzerland? Yes, she can be neutral. But Hungary? We never could in the past; what makes you think there will be an exception now?"

"Oh, but this is different," Gyuri said. "We're not caught between the East and West. That's been our downfall in the past. Now Germany and Russia are friends."

"That scares me even more. Of course, if Poland can resist—yes, it may then start Hitler's downfall. But we don't know yet. And the Poles, you know they are fierce anti-Semites, too."

"Come on," Antal turned on Istvan with annoyance now. "Don't be such a pessimist! At least here in Hungary the Jewish Laws were made only to please Hitler. The government pulls the rein tighter on Jews, Hitler loosens his grip on some territories. So Hungary gets back part of her own. If Germany is restrained? Well, why should we have any more problems? One can't live always thinking of the worst."

"What if?" It was hardly possible to entertain the thought.

* * *

The next few days prolonged the suspenseful wait. They expected miracles. In fact, the unimaginable happened.

On September 5, the Wehrmacht broke through the Vistula River and on September 7 Danzig fell. On September 17 Soviet troops crossed the Polish border and on the 27th Warsaw's fate was sealed. By October 10th, all of Poland surrendered.

And Hungary—Hungary grateful for the rewards of her alliance with Germany quietly regretted the fate of the Poles. Hungary and the Soviet resumed diplomatic relations on September 23.

Just before the end of the rapidly deteriorating military situation in Poland came Hitler's peace offer. Hours of throat-clenching anxiety filled the world. But Britain and France declined Hitler's overtures. The continuation of the war seemed to hold the only promise for the future.

In November the friends excitedly discussed the new event: "Have you heard, there was an attempt against Hitler!" The question as put was rhetorical. Hungarian newspapers were filled with demands for bloody retribution against the criminals, while the British broadcast found hope in the incident.

They speculated about hitherto undemonstrated English strength, or anticipated the United States' eventual involvement. But in the States, the Neutrality Act was signed.

"I got a note from New Zealand," Istvan brought the news to Kata. "It doesn't look promising. Yet, perhaps we shouldn't give up. I'll write back repeating my interest. Or even— How about some other country as a stepping stone?"

They both knew well that the plan was probably a dream.

"There are efforts to open up routes to Palestine," Antal informed his friends on a mid-November evening. But no one present was keen to review the possibilities. They were, on the whole, still Hungarians; fleeing to Palestine meant a decisive identification with a Jewish National goal.

But the topic cropped up in the following weeks.

"You know my cousin Tibor—you met him in the summer—he came up from the country to register for an *aliya*; he hopes to leave soon. He insists that I should go, too," Istvan said. "And you?" Kata asked with a frown.

"No! First of all, I would not want to leave you," Istvan reassured her. "Unless— You wouldn't consider it, would you?"

"Frankly, I've never thought of it. I don't think it would be easy. I can just see a new immigrant going to church!" She chuckled. Then, in seriousness: "Do you really feel one must leave?"

Istvan shrugged his shoulder. "Must? I don't know. I don't expect anything good here. But, to be honest, the thought of leaving becomes pressing when I think of us two, Kata." He was silent for a second then continued: "I love you. I never asked you to marry me in any seriousness—and I can't, not here! That's really the issue."

"You're such a worrier!"

"I don't think it's just worrying. The reality is bad!"

"Maybe. But there are always solutions. There must be, even here!"
Istvan shook his head. "Not here."

"Look," she said, taking a deep breath. "I'm much more confident.
But— All right, give it a try. I'll go with you, but only if that's the only
way for us two."

"You really would?" Istvan looked at her in amazement. "I love you,
Solveig!" And though they were on the street, he pulled her toward him
and placed the tenderest kiss on her hair.

The groups to Palestine did not receive their permits then. And both
Kata and Istvan were relieved. But after that, Istvan voiced fewer
questions.

They were becoming used to the constantly changing and deteriorating situation. They were shaken, defeated, despairing and impatient.
They were hopeful, poetic and in love. And, they tried to live as if they
had been two young people living at any other time.

"Incredible, I was able to write today," Istvan would announce during
an evening telephone call. "What a wonderful retreat into a land of
turmoil followed by perfect peace."

"You see! Things are not so bad!" Kata responded.

* * *

And when she received his Christmas gift—a short story with the
dedication: "To Kata with affection, Istvan."—she was tremendously
happy and proud.

"I loved it," she told him at their next encounter. "The story, the
characters, the quiet heroism of Dr. Pavlik, the unconditional love and
acceptance. Almost as if you had given it a Christian slant. Was that
your intention?"

"I don't know. Did I?"

"Of course, I was most intrigued by the family situation —mother
and son in an unspoken drama, its effect on husband and wife."

"You know, since my father died when I was twelve I often speculated what life would have been like had he stayed with us longer."

"Do you know what he was like?"

"Yes!" He halted for a moment. "Very bright, I understand. Not an
intellectual but he had originality. He built up the store from nothing
and it grew and grew."

"Isn't it interesting how creativity can be transmitted in a different form. Look, you're a writer!"

"That's true. Of course my mother is a great storyteller. But listen," he grasped her hand for a moment, then lit a cigarette. "Talking about my parents is an appropriate introduction to what I want to say. Let's talk now about ourselves."

"OK!" She agreed.

"The New Year is upon us, a time for resolutions."

"Yes?"

"I've been thinking about the future, our future, Kata."

She kept very quiet.

"Somehow that story—very different from problems we would encounter, still—the story as it was taking shape, made me feel there are happy endings to seemingly insoluble problems. And when I look at this world we live in, the doom that is hanging over our heads, I also think who knows, things may work out yet." He took her hand in both of his and looked straight at her. "Kata, will you marry me?"

"Istvan! So you have decided! I will! Of course I will. You should know that." He brought her hand to his lips and she felt a wonderful sweetness fill her.

Still holding on to her hands and looking at her intensely, he added: "It won't be easy, Kata. It may be terribly hard. But if you are not afraid, I've gathered courage. And I love you!"

"I love you, too, you know that," her eyes shining. "I can't contemplate all the horrible possibilities now. I don't want to. I want to be happy.

"Oh, Istvan, I want to make you happy—in every way. Not just physically either." She felt a little foolish saying this and was looking for words to explain what she meant. "I mean, I know there is so much to give, to share, to enjoy together. Even this afternoon: Talking about writing, I mean—life has so many facets. Sure, we don't know how the world will proceed but we can proceed, you can write, we can forge ahead. Don't you think?" She wanted to hear it from him, too.

"I believe we can achieve much together. I don't know how far we'll get. But I do love you and I want to have you in every way—body and soul. Will that be all right?" he asked with a smile.

Kata blushed as she nodded her assent.

* * *

Istvan saw her up to the apartment. She was surprised to find that her parents had gone out earlier and the note left for her indicated that they would be back at ten. It was nine-thirty.

Istvan helped her out of the coat and accepted her invitation to stay for a few more minutes. As they sat on the couch of the living room—presumably to continue planning for the future—Istvan's arms drew her near and the bony fingers sensuously moved back and forth, up and down her yielding body. He slowly unbuttoned the shirt-waist dress, and Kata seemed to lose herself as she passionately returned his kisses while those fingers went on and on, and now touched the nipples of her breasts. She tightened her body, then leaned back on the couch, lying there with arms above her head.

She became oblivious of the place and the hour and was unaware of anything but the electric current that Istvan touched off in her—a current she had never experienced before to this degree. It felt as if her extremities started to melt in this heat. She felt damp all over.

Their unchecked impulsiveness lasted but a short time, for Istvan remembered reality. After gently guiding her fingers to touch and explore his own excited body, he sat up, drew her to himself now with a quiet and wise kiss and pointed to the clock on the desk.

"Five to ten, my dear. Your parents will be here any minute. Let me come tomorrow or the day after to ask officially for your hand. I'm afraid I would not seem a very respectable suitor tonight." He got up and both began to laugh with embarrassment.

He quickly slid into his overcoat and waited until Kata returned from her room where the brush and swift hand on the dress effaced the traces of those exciting moments. Now she offered a light kiss.

"Good night, dear. Then you will call Father tomorrow? I will be seeing you then," she said.

A soft, almost accidental touch of the breasts as Istvan was opening the door, brought back the physical attraction she felt for him. As she closed the door behind Istvan, she thought with a smile of her statement earlier that she wanted to make Istvan happy, not "just" with satisfactions of the body.

How childish a comment, she thought. I hope he's not afraid of "just" the physical, she mused, as she started to undress in the privacy of her room.

* * *

Next morning, as she was gulping down her coffee, she excitedly told her mother: "Anyu, Istvan proposed! Can you imagine! At last!"

"Oh my!" Mrs. Vaghelyi embraced her laughing. "He's a nice young man, Kata, I like him. Good looking, intelligent—very pleasant. I'm fond of his mother, too. She is used to good things in life and is warmhearted, too. Your father is just washing up. Can you wait?"

"No, Anyu, I'd better not. If you want to, you can mention it to him while I'm at work. I'm sure Dad will have a lot of questions to ask."

Kata was happy her mother approved, but she expected that. The two of them had their battles at times but Kata could count on her mother's practicality. Father? He often had different considerations.

Indeed, what would her father say, she wondered several times during the day.

"Apu!" She burst into his study. "Did Mother tell you? Istvan wants to come over to ask for my hand!"

"Yes, I heard the news." Father gave her a solemn kiss. "Sit down, Kata," he motioned to the armchair. "When was all this decided?"

"Specifically, yesterday. You were not at home when we got back. But you know, Apu, I'd hoped for it for quite a while."

"So it's an accomplished fact?"

"Well, I wanted to talk to you but I did say 'Yes!' Apu, I'm tremendously happy, you must know that!"

Her father nodded. "An accomplished fact," he repeated. His features were drawn.

"Are you trying to dissuade me, Apu?"

"Kata, this is a serious matter. I can see you're in love; he is a bright young man, I've told you that before, but we should speak of a few things. Be patient!"

Kata sat back. All of a sudden her father seemed so old, so devoid of understanding.

"Yes?"

"Tell me about his plans."

"What plans? You know he is a partner—only partial it's true—but, he is a partner in the family store. It's not a gold mine any more but it brings an income. In the long run," she hesitated a moment, but decided not to skirt the issue, "in the long run it may be better than yours!"

She was aware of the sting. It only reflected her feelings of years' standing. And she was annoyed at the silly questioning about finances, questions by him, of all people.

"Apu, I don't understand you. You were always the one who under-played the importance of money!"

Her father nodded. "I still don't care for luxury. But that's not the point." He thought for a while and then almost apologetically said: "It's not easy to be a father at a moment like this. I may blunder in my questions, but look, I really want you tell me how you imagine your life. It's not the money at all. Tell me about Istvan's work, his goals."

"Well, it's true, he doesn't have a significant part of the business. I've told you, it's not as if this were his goal in life. Apu, he writes. He's very talented, I have no doubt. I showed you a sample the other day. And now, he gave me that short story for Christmas. It's beautiful. You see, he's rich. You should understand that!"

"I do. I have no questions about his intellect, Kata, even his literary talent. But, I'm sure you realize, not all depends on his talents alone. It may be rough, quite rough. It's nice he has some income, but it is a hard road to be an artist. Are you ready to share it? You tend to put emphasis on success."

Her father knew her well. Maybe it was natural for him to ask. Before she had met Istvan, Father and she used to discuss everything.

"Look, Apu, if the war ends well, if we manage here in Hungary without any major disaster, I have to trust Istvan will be successful. Even in business. Perhaps we can start something together. My English—it should be helpful even there. But, of course, we hope for the possibility of publishing. If not—if the war concludes in a disaster," she threw up her hand, "at least I can say I shared my life with a brilliant and gifted man. But this is only one part, believe me. Shall I say I love him? Well, that's obvious," she laughed. "He's really a wonderful, understanding, very good man."

"I think so, too."

"Well then?"

Dr. Vaghelyi looked at her fondly. "You didn't expect me to forbid you, did you?"

Kata sighed. "It took you a long time. Seriously, I was afraid of what you might say. Not about his work, but, you did want me to marry a Christian, didn't you?"

Her father became quiet. "You know that well. I don't mean the formalities. That's not important. With my ideas, how could I insist on that? Anyhow, the laws these days are so confusing. But tell me, how do you feel about it? And, what if you have children?"

Kata nodded. "I wanted to talk to you about this, Apu. It was something I had to think through, too. But one of the nicest things in Istvan, after his obvious assets, is that he doesn't mind my Christianity. Maybe, maybe if I'd be more dogmatic, more definite in every tenet, it might be a problem. But I have my own unanswered questions." She shrugged. "I have questions, but still, Jesus is very important to me. And Istvan likes that. He would like his children to believe, too. And by no means is he a narrowly thinking Jew or a die-hard agnostic."

Dr. Vaghelyi nodded. "All I can say then is that I pray that you both grow in faith along with the love for each other. Let's call in your mother!"

Mrs. Vaghelyi was beaming as she came into the room with Kata. "I hope you gave your consent, Erno! Istvan will make a good husband. Only the war, I only hope it will end soon," she added.

"We're in God's hands," her husband said thoughtfully. "Terrible things are happening and who knows—they may happen here, too. We can't foretell. We must live every day doing our best. Strength comes from within. It has been known for a long time. Let me read you something. Where is it?" And he took out his battered *Today* of Tolstoy, offering aphorisms from the sayings of the great, readings for each day.

"Yes, here it is: 'Man always has a refuge from every trouble. His soul is that refuge.' Marcus Aurelius—a great Roman Emperor—not even Christian in form, but in many ways, in spirit."

"Your Tolstoy!" Mrs. Vaghelyi exclaimed. "When can Istvan come? Tomorrow?"

CHAPTER 5

MARRIED LIFE

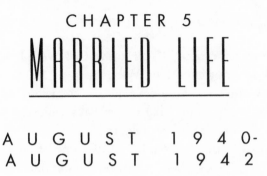

AUGUST 1940-
AUGUST 1942

They had a quiet wedding.

There were many military call-ups in August 1940 and they changed their honeymoon plans from a fortnight in the Matra Mountains to a long weekend at nearby Svabhegy.

It was good to start with a walk and to begin their life together by expressing what the day meant for them: The informal short pastoral blessing of the morning in the presence of the immediate family, the commitment they made to each other, the new dreams arising from their words "I do." And now, they talked of the future with children, with years of work and fun together, with fulfillment awaiting them in every sense.

Svabhegy towered proudly over the hilly slopes of the Buda mountains and the flatland of Pest.

Now, the twinkling house and street lights reached up from below to the stars as the horizon bent and formed a cupola above their heads.

They went up to their room and continued for a short while to admire the city from the balcony of their suite, feeling the beauty of the summer night, the majesty of the firmament and the hope that the God in whom Kata believed and in whose existence Istvan vaguely hoped would guide and protect them whatever might come.

"Let's go in, Sweetheart," Istvan kissed her gently.

"I'll be right with you," Kata whispered and disappeared behind the door near the entrance.

As she re-entered the room the cigarette stub a few steps away quickly lost its glow. In a moment she was held tightly in her husband's arms.

The first night!

The hours to come were full of embraces. Little cries of pain, gruffer sighs of contentment, thrills of rapture in being so close, to penetrate, to receive, to unite—one flesh.

So this is how it was.

And while she knew that for her this was only a foretaste, she reveled in the thought that he loved her, that he had wanted her over and over again. Her thrill came from the yielding and the pride of having become a woman—his woman.

Istvan was exhausted and looked a little surprised. He grinned. "Can I still be this vigorous at thirty-one? What a delight! To possess a woman, not just for the night, or for a weekly rendezvous, but for life. My wife! To love, to love, to love!"

They embraced and slept, made love and napped, then talked. Made love and dreamt. Soon, the morning dawn gave way to the rising yellow globe. Istvan opened the Venetian blinds to let in the morning air. The golden rays of the sun witnessed their new embrace.

It was a long night. It was a beautiful night.

* * *

They returned to the city Tuesday evening. Istvan picked up Kata and carried her across the threshold of the little apartment. They silently moved on toward the bedroom.

Then, they saw the envelope.

Istvan glanced at it, raised his eyebrows, then slowly reached for it. Kata watched as he handed it to her. She anticipated its contents:

Istvan was to report for service on September 10.

The honeymoon was truly over. With sadness, she reached for his hand and squeezed it wordlessly. He drew her to him, put his face in her hair, and said, "I have been so happy!"

She tried to lighten the moment. "And didn't you expect to be?"

He smiled wanly and said, "Of course. But these days have been idyllic. Blissful!"

She nodded. "For me, too, darling."

* * *

For the next months, he was in a labor camp. The re-annexation of Northern Transylvania to Hungary required a partial military alert. But no longer were Jewish recruits called up as uniformed members of the military. Rather, they were assigned to manual work, as yet not impossibly hard. Visits by wives and relatives were possible and after the initial fright, the venture gave the false illusion of a delayed scouts' jamboree. Istvan's unit stayed around the city for several weeks, before being moved to a distance of about a hundred miles. But even there, families could visit.

Kata took the train along with other women for a weekend in Hodmezo, in the middle of the Hungarian Plains. Of course, life was restricted. But Istvan, like others of his companions, had been able to rent a little room, and its sinking mattress with the fully stuffed eiderdown enveloped him, and on this occasion both of them, with temporary comfort and security that anyone would want. For Kata the weekend was memorable. For the first time her physical union with Istvan became a complete experience for her. And as the morning broke and she looked around at the embroidered pillows, colored pottery and the dried corn cobs hanging from the ceiling, she felt that life still had much to offer and that this labor camp did not take away the joyful love she felt.

Lovely, lovely little room. Wonderful, wonderful eiderdown to cover you after lovemaking, from the crushing November cold. Beautiful little town of Hodmezo!

"I still love this country, and things will work out."

Indeed, Istvan was back home in December.

* * *

Istvan continued to attend to his desk tucked away in the upper gallery of the store. The bookkeeping work was tedious as ever. And Kata worked, too, of course. Though her former job in the law firm had ended soon after their engagement (the partners had decided not to return from abroad), she was fortunate to be hired by a small export-import agency. By a chance encounter on the street she had learned of the impending emigration to Argentina of a former classmate of hers who worked in a one-person office. With the drastically reduced employment quota for Jews, only such replacements were possible. She applied and she got the job.

"Isn't this great!" she announced the news to Istvan.

She had work and a reasonable salary, and now they could count on some stability.

They were aware that any stability was tentative. And yet, the real meaning of the war and the many restrictions that came in its wake unfolded only gradually.

The Hungarian press and radio forewarned the annihilation of Britain and impending total German victory. A frightening thought! After Hitler's accomplishments in the one year of the war, one could not easily dismiss his works. And even the British broadcasts spoke of material destruction and the death of tens of thousands in the wake of attacks by the Luftwaffe. Greece was assaulted. Hungary joined the Tripartite Pact. The rumors of actions against Jews in every new land occupied filled Kata with helpless dread. And yet, she, like everyone, wanted to believe that the nightmare would pass and she grasped at the least sign of delay, or turnabout, or gesture of defiance to bolster such belief. After all, no landing had been attempted by Germany on the British Isles so far! And even within the country, in spite of voiced loyalty to the cause of Hitler, channels were kept open and even cultivated with the West. The spirit of Hungarian honor was still manifest.

"Look, Premier Count Teleki committed suicide!" A hush spread over the city when the scion of the aristocratic family made his stand in April 1941 against his country's involvement in German aggression against Yugoslavia, a neighboring country, with which Hungary had signed an "Eternal" Friendship Pact only four months before.

And theaters, movies, nightclubs and most other recreational spots were still open to all; though the impact of the Jewish Laws began to be felt, there were ways of overcoming at least their economic provisions with some planning and foresight.

And so in the first year of their marriage there was not much change in their lives—work, an occasional play, dinner out with friends from time to time, and visits with family.

Istvan's mother was an excellent cook and her meals a treat even during the war. Besides, she had a knack for storytelling. "Boske, talk," her children would teasingly goad her into revelations of family gossip which she presented with humor and vividly simple portrayals of the people involved. Istvan's sister and her husband made a habit of visiting the same night. Kata, as the only child, found it fascinating to observe intimately the interaction of brother and sister.

"Still writing?" Irene would inquire from time to time. She seemed both impressed and puzzled by her brother's literary interests. "Don't you think these days it's a futile attempt?" Istvan shrugged his shoulders.

Irene's inability to conceive after five years of marriage tended to make her increasingly emphasize the more aggressive side of life. A sensitive and bright woman, she vacillated between a wish for domesticity and the need to support her husband's business endeavors.

On the occasions of family dinners, Istvan's stepfather, Jeno Kalmar, would usually sit with the family for the main course but then quickly disappear to spend the evening at the corner cafe in the company of neighborhood old-timers.

"An interesting contrast!" Kata commented when back in their own place. "Irene, you of course, and your mother—you could talk for hours. You're all very good conversationalists."

Istvan nodded. "My stepfather—I told you he has a good heart. But, beyond that, at times I wonder about my mother. Well, anyhow, it has freed me from responsibilities. She is taken care of. Papa has always cared for her, I must say. In fact, he has cared for us, too, quite a bit. He likes to brag about his children."

And then there were the Sundays with her parents.

Kata was used to her mother's hovering and it was nice to receive the remnants of her baking after the weekend meal. The scene was familiar and she liked the broad aspect of discussions, which ran from her mother's reporting on minor news items in the neighborhood to the more potent subjects of politics, religion, justice and the destiny of man.

At times an old friend of the family, Dr. Tanar, was also present. He and Kata's father were similar in many ways. They had been companions from their university days, had made their pilgrimage of faith together and both were active in the church. Tanar was a widower and was often invited for meals.

"Where will this lead?" Kata anxiously asked the men after the news of Germany's turning against Russia. Hungary had followed suit.

"Germany is bound to lose," her father reasserted his conviction. "You know my belief—tyranny never lasts."

"But when?" Kata was impatient.

"We're getting deeper and deeper into the struggle, it's true, but Russia cannot be defeated. An immense country like that!" Dr. Tanar liked to look at things realistically.

They all remembered Napoleon in the bitter Russian winter. But now—it was only September.

"Hitler expects to roll up Russia in a few weeks. Incredible! Look at Minsk, Smolensk, Kiev!" Istvan just couldn't help pointing to the latest German conquests. "It's enough to make you wonder.

"Only if America intervenes—then, there may be a chance. How could Germany combat all that wealth!" Istvan, too, was searching for some hopeful signs. "Not that they are so keen on getting involved directly, but still, there are the naval operations, lend-lease and now the Atlantic Charter."

They all contemplated the possible impact of these steps.

"By the way, what do you think of it?" Istvan asked Dr. Tanar. "Have you had a chance to listen to broadcasts?"

"We're not so rich to have a short-wave radio like the Fogarases," Dr. Tanar kiddingly admitted his lack of direct access to the British news. "But from what I read about it, it's a promising document!"

Dr. Vaghelyi nodded. He got his news from the Sunday scanning of Swiss papers.

The *Zuricher Zeitung* was the secular counterpart of the Bible reading. "Church service from ten to eleven—news research right thereafter. It's father's mixed aperitif," Kata said.

"Your father couldn't eat his dinner if it weren't preceded by newspaper reading." Mrs. Vaghelyi called the hobby of her husband an excusable "weakness of the stronger sex."

Kata broke into laughter. "Mother, Istvan's also addicted to the news. He's glued to those broadcasts every night at eight, whether supper is on the table or not. My greatest competitor! And imagine, it's a man! 'Itt MacCartney Elemer beszel,' " Kata mimicked the English accent of the British historian giving his nightly newscap in Hungarian.

Istvan smiled. "Sweetheart, a life-giving competitor I must say. It's only words, but still—" They all knew that without the Western news they would indeed long ago have given up hope.

"The Atlantic Charter?" Her father returned to Istvan's question. "You'll see, this is where Germany will fall. This is my hope—the ideals of nations. Winter in Russia, money from the U.S., surely! But above all, I believe justice will prevail in the end."

"I agree," Dr. Tanar added. "But justice moves at a snail's crawl at times. Kata has a point."

And so the conversations went. Both Kata and Istvan enjoyed the discussions around the table but if the invitation was for Sunday, they liked to leave in a rather short time.

The day had its routine: church in the morning for Kata, on to her parents, dinner together and then back home soon. A delightful routine at that. Because during these years when war raged and its immediate as well as long-range impact were constantly on their minds, the Sunday afternoons represented the oasis.

They would get back to their home around four. Often love-making led them from the world outside into a terrain which was their very own.

Then they would sleep.

Upon awakening Istvan would bring out his writings. Still lounging in bed they now together entered his creative universe and laughed and cried, cheered and mourned over the fate of those characters coming alive on the pages.

The horizon became limitless.

Istvan planned to write a book about Michelangelo—the glories, struggle, embitterment and victories. A journey back into history, four hundred years in retrospect, came to life and helped to diffuse their own concerns.

But it was not only the review of gigantic historical figures that lightened their burden. Kata loved listening to Istvan's reading. One day the story about the girl with the violets—a walk in the woods, the upsurge of tender romance, the first kiss—with the tightly held bunch of purple heads slowly released as the girl yields to her lover's embrace in the early spring forest.

"Do you recall Visegrad?" Istvan put his arm around her.

Kata snuggled closer in memory of the Easter weekend.

During the reading, gentle words and tender kisses mixed and suffused into the now chilly room.

"Let me revive the fire," and Istvan got up to feed the cooling iron stove of their bedroom with a fresh shovel of coals. The melodious crackling of the flames made the room cozy again.

Then back to the stories!

"Here's another one—about 'Madame Golovan.' " And Kata listened with breathless attention to the sad attachment of the aging woman to her young office help, Lilla. Tender hovering over the girl, timid overtures for a companionship sustained beyond those short business hours, generous offers of privileges—and then? The girl announces her forthcoming marriage. How well one could see Madame Golovan sitting forlornly in her small apartment, the bright lights of the neighboring movie house finding their way into the dark room where she is struggling with her desperate wish to love and be loved.

What a relief it was after commiserating with this tragic figure to turn toward each other.

Beyond their twosome and the immediate family they still had their circle of friends, though it was gradually dwindling. A year ago Eva had surreptitiously met an Englishman, an airline pilot. A brief whirlwind courtship followed. And before one knew it, Eva was married and off to Britain.

They did not see Zsuzsa any more. She and Gyuri married in spite of Zsuzsa's ambitious plans for a rich husband. Gyuri was among those who was kept in service well beyond the other first-timers.

And the remnant of the group? They met on weekends—more and more only in each other's homes. Public places were still accessible and there were many who plunged into the glamorous entertainments of night life. *Carpe diem!*—and *carpe noctim*, too. But it was not for Istvan.

"I'm not going to the opera any more," he announced at the time all Jewish artists were dismissed. "How can one enjoy listening to their replacements? We have our records."

Istvan gave up cigarettes, too. Tobacco was a state monopoly. "I know it sounds foolish—the price of a few cigarettes. And yet, there is so little we can do. It's a way of showing some resistance. I wish we had the guts to stand up and fight back."

"Open revolt can only end in bloodshed," Kata expressed the general point of view.

"I know. And without it?"

How could one answer? There were surely dangers. There was also the double-edged foreign policy of the country: One arm stretched out to Hitler with a fistful of concessions—military and material; the other extended towards Britain assuring her of Hungary's friendly interest. This was before the official state of war occurred between the two countries on December 6, 1941. And there was ambivalence about the Jewish question too: strong words in Parliament about the excess of Jewish wealth and position, and drastic legal steps toward their curtailment—and then protective silence and the closing of eyes to the increasing number of Jewish refugees smuggled through the northern borders. Indeed, for a long while Hungary served as partial haven for many Polish and then Slovak Jews fleeing Hitler.

* * *

Kata wished for a child. Yet, they both felt it would be a bold and irresponsible step. Everything was utterly uncertain.

A call-up was the immediate threat. By now those who went faced grave dangers. Hungary was at war!

And yet, the more Kata thought of possible separation from Istvan, and the danger of losing him, the more she was obsessed with the idea of a baby. Something to remain from their bond to each other.

But Istvan would not hear of it. And indeed the order to report for labor service arrived. The date was set—February 1, 1942.

The initial shock of the long-feared event now becoming reality was followed by a false sigh of relief. Certainty seemed better than suspense. But it was an insanity to be part of a military unit fighting for German victory. To risk life for his own ultimate destruction? Istvan could not be rid of the thought.

"Oh, God, why should I?" But what chances did he have not to go? "What if I were sick?" he wondered.

Kata smiled sadly. "Sweetheart, there's nothing wrong with you, I'm afraid."

Istvan was not so certain. He tired easily. He was thin and coughed on occasion. He used to think it was the cigarettes. But he had not been smoking for months.

"I think I'll have a checkup before I appear at the draft board," he announced.

Istvan went to the Clinic in order to evade the thought fixed in his consciousness from the moment the call had arrived—the thought that life was drawing to an end, or at least was drawing towards a road from which return was dubious. He had been thinking about this for the last two years. He had told Kata how happy he was, how wonderful a woman she was and how, until now, it had been easy to push away morbid fantasies. But now that the letter had come, not Kata's love, not the friendliness of the three-room apartment, nor the solace from their record player or his writing could make him forget what was coming. Within two weeks his fate would be sealed.

When he mentioned his plan for a medical checkup to his friend Bodo, still at the University Clinic, the latter smiled. "There are many who are trying to find a way out, Istvan. It doesn't work."

"What if there's really something wrong?" Istvan insisted.

"If you have no more serious symptoms than those you mentioned, I don't think there is any chance of anything being wrong. I certainly could not do anything for you, Istvan, not in this clinic. You'll understand."

"Yes," Istvan understood that.

"But I want to feel that at least I explored all avenues," he told Kata. "I made an appointment with Dr. Goldstein for tomorrow. He used to treat my uncle. I prefer to go to someone I know."

"So you are Boske Steiner's son." Dr. Goldstein greeted Istvan the next day.

He listened carefully as Istvan told him of his predicament. There was nothing extraordinary in hearing that somebody would go to a labor camp or that he would have to leave his wife and even children. There was nothing special in Istvan's situation. Yet, Dr. Goldstein knew the family and he found himself touched by Istvan's description of marital bliss. As a bachelor of sixty-five, Dr. Goldstein was still a pursuer of lasting romance which had always eluded him.

"I can examine you, Istvan—allow me to call you by your first name, after all I knew you as a child—but you know the military is quite strict when it comes to medical excuses and I really doubt you have a chance. But as long as you have come—"

Istvan felt uneasy as he got out of his jacket and shirt.

This is really ridiculous, taking up his time for nonexistent maladies, he thought.

He considered quietly leaving the dressing room, but then he knew the doctor would phone him and an explanation would be embarrassing.

"I'd better go through with it."

Dr. Goldstein touched his head, neck, looked into his eyes, then down his throat. He took his blood pressure and his pulse, tested the knee reflexes. He thoughtfully tapped his chest. He shifted the stethoscope here to there. His movement followed a broad sweep. Then he became more meticulous and listened intently.

"You know, I seem to hear some unusual sound," he told Istvan. "I think I want to take an X-ray. Wait in the other room."

He started with fluoroscopy of the chest to get a quick glimpse of its contents. He muttered something and then proceeded with a full X-ray. He told Istvan he would let him know the next day.

When Istvan called, he could hardly believe Dr. Goldstein's words:

"You have definite involvement of the lung and we must proceed with further examinations. Be at the sanatorium tomorrow at eight in the morning."

Needless to say, Istvan's reactions were mixed. On the one hand, there was now some hope of escape from the labor camp. But tuberculosis was a deadly disease.

"Oh God, what did I bargain for?"

The conclusive tests showed rather extensive infiltration, but no cavity. The sputum was negative for contagious germs and Istvan ran no fever. Nevertheless, Dr. Goldstein recommended hospitalization.

"If we can collapse the lung with air, a pneumothorax, you might be able to manage fairly well without other drastic measures," he assured Istvan.

It took a week to see whether the regimen could be implemented. The pneumothorax treatment proceeded with good results.

Istvan was in the sanatorium three months. When he was released, Dr. Goldstein congratulated him. Medically he was in pretty good shape; the disease had been arrested.

"Of course, you must be careful and we shall have to check you regularly from time to time. At the moment, there is no danger of contagion."

Istvan got a one-year exemption from the Army.

"One year is a tremendouly long time!" he told Kata, as he twirled her around the room. "Many things may happen before then." Indeed, the fate of the British position in Africa was soon to take a different turn.

* * *

"Istvan, I want to have a child," Kata returned to the issue. "You were allowed to stay home!"

"It's only a year. And look what's happening in Czechoslovakia!"

Rumors had it that the Jews in Czechoslovakia would be relocated soon. And indeed Kata's father had received a mysterious note from his older sister in Bratislava. "I and the family here love you and have faith in you," his sister Marie's scribble stated. It was touching to receive her fond message after many months of silence. But what did it mean?

Within the next week, two teenagers rang the bell of the Vaghelyi apartment. "Magda, Karcsi!" Mrs. Vaghelyi exclaimed as she ushered the visitors into the safety of their bedroom.

"Come, Erno, look!" she breathlessly called her husband from his study.

Dr. Vaghelyi embraced his sister's grandchildren with tears in his eyes. "So that's what your grandmother meant in her note. How is she?"

The children had a long story to tell about their parents, grandmother and the rest of the family, but even more about the excitement of their having been smuggled through the Hungarian border. Grandmother was sure, once they reached Budapest, Uncle Erno would take care of them.

By now there were many refugees from Czechoslovakia. So far the Hungarian Government seemed to ignore the influx—but, for how long? One had to be careful. It was forbidden to shelter illegal immigrants.

"Look, we haven't had a maid for a while," Mrs. Vaghelyi began to speculate. "It's time that I have some help. Magda, you have a job!" They felt it was a solution for the time being. Magda was eighteen, had blond hair, blue eyes. "As long as you don't go out much, I think you'll pass."

Brother Karcsi was more of a problem. How could one justify the sudden presence of a thirteen-year-old?

Magda stayed with the Vaghelyis for a month until the appropriate documents could be procured and she could set out on her own. The

organization that had arranged for them to be smuggled into the
country, had a place for Karcsi in an orphanage. Was it safe? Who could
be sure? Nothing was sure. But at least these children now had newly
assumed identities and they came from time to time—preferably sepa-
rately—to visit their great uncle and often the young Fogarases.

In late spring 1942 the final phase of liquidation started in Slovakia.
Uneasy whispers reached Budapest, still in the form of questions, as to
the destination of those trains packed with old and young, healthy and
sick. What was happening to them? Surely not what some of the
frightening rumors implied!

They and their friends bemoaned the events when talking about
them. Everybody had family members in Czechoslovakia. After all, one
third of it had belonged to Hungary for centuries.

"At least in this country things are not deteriorating," Antal stated
in a reunion of the friends. "They say Kallay, the new Minister of the
Interior, is a decent man."

"Let's have a child now," Kata pleaded with Istvan, bringing back the
issue that occupied her thoughts.

"Sweetheart, we can't ignore the terrible things that are happening
just across the border! They say thousands of refugees are being sent
back. And what is happening to them?"

"That was earlier, wasn't it? And they were unable to obtain their
Hungarian citizenship. Our status is different!"

Istvan shrugged his shoulder. "Who knows? And besides, there's my
TB."

"Let's talk to Dr. Goldstein," Kata coaxed. "Let's see whether he
considers it wise to have a child."

At the consultation, the doctor referred to the negative sputum and
underscored the arrested state of the illness.

"There is nothing I could say about the impact of the war on baby
and family," he wryly added. "It would be a great decision with many
risks. I guess I'm too old to consider risks and I'd better stop at that."

"You see!" Kata triumphantly stated after the visit.

"There's no reason to wait."

Istvan was tempted. He was often touched by a longing to leave
some tangible legacy. It was dreadful to think of personal annihilation.
To cease, to be done with—if he only had faith! Christianity was a

beautiful code of ethics to live by and if they had a child he would want him to follow the proclamations of Jesus for love and peace. But life eternal? It was a vague mystical promise that was beyond his grasp. To have his seed come to life—that was more tangible, a stronger promise of eternity. Provided the child survived.

It was the end of summer. A sultry night had kept them awake for quite a while. The Sunday morning brought a fresh breeze and they decided to stay in bed to catch up on sleep. Kata discarded the thought of church for the day. Today they would eat at home and have a day just for themselves.

She woke up about nine to find Istvan aroused in his sleep. She touched him. He sleepily responded to the caressing hands on his cheek, arms and legs. His eyes opened now; his langorous mood lifted. There was a faint recollection of longing in his dream, of Kata beside him and a family playing in the garden. He could not recall whose family it was but he vaguely remembered the joy of watching the idyllic scene. But this was no moment for dreams. Here was the real Kata pressing her naked body against him. He began savoring her—her skin, even with the fragment of sweat on it, her rounded breasts, the shape of her hips as his hands followed their curves. He kissed her all over.

Was it the hot night, the sleepy awakening, the unconscious wish for continuity that dispelled his caution? He wanted her, was pressing her, was beginning to possess her and she yielded.

She responded with a freedom she had never known before. She clutched him with her arms, with her thighs, locking his body and pelvis in a prison of fulfillment. His excitement rose swiftly. He loved her, he wanted her, he must have her this very minute.

"Victory, victory, victory," he cried as his semen poured into her.

BOOK TWO
SURVIVAL ?

CHAPTER 6
THE GERMANS

SEPTEMBER 1942-
JUNE 1944

It was impending fatherhood that forced Istvan to a decision about the church. He had been attending services with Kata here and there, trying to anchor himself to the message of love and forgiveness. But the abyss between what was preached and practiced was forever widening.

And yet, as they were making plans for the coming of their child, the issue of religion had to be dealt with. If it were a boy, he would have to follow the religion of his father.

"I wish I had joined the church earlier, it would have been simpler. But now, it's desertion."

"You've changed your mind?" Kata asked in pained surprise. She had thought the issue settled long before.

"Kata, please understand, I'm not reneging on our agreement," Istvan protested. "It's just the formalities!"

His conflict was obvious not only to Kata but to his family as well. His sister Irene soberly commented, "Istvan, thousands of Jews are joining churches."

"I know. This is what makes it harder. It looks as though it's just for escape, rather than commitment."

For some weeks they suspended talking of the matter.

Early in October, frightening rumors were spread. Prime Minister Kallay had been summoned by Ribbentropp. The urgent liquidation of Hungary's Jewry was demanded. After all, the surrounding countries had already acted!

But the panic was relieved as suddenly as it came. Kallay said, "No!" Hungarian law did not allow for the destruction of innocents. Now, there was a man who dared!

About two weeks later Istvan came home in a relaxed mood. "I had a long talk with your father's friend, Dr. Tanar, today."

"You did? And?" Kata was happy to see Istvan less depressed, more decisive.

He was pacing up and down the room: "Tanar asked how I really felt about the religious upringing of our child. I told him I never had any question about it right from the beginning: I want him to be Christian. Tanar said this was the crux of the matter. If that's the way I felt, the decision has been made. And it has!"

He lifted her chin, looked into her eyes and gave her a loving hug. "Whether a girl or a boy, we will register the baby as Christian."

She felt elated.

So Istvan joined the church of Dr. Sarossy in the neighborhood and Jancsi was duly baptized by him. They even had a small party to celebrate the event.

Things seemed almost normal.

* * *

Little Janos, called Jancsi, was a beautiful baby, with a wonderfully sturdy body. A dark mop of hair showed in the cradle even in the hospital. The deep blue eyes roved aimlessly at first between mother's breast and the white walls of the ward. Then, as the weeks passed, they began to fix on her face—he knew her!—her heart filled with joy. The red circle of his mouth opened and closed groping for its target; then it chewed on her nipples giving Kata a sweet mixture of pain and elation. After a while the sucking stopped. His head rested with confidence in his mother's encircling arms. She looked at her child with pride.

The efforts of the little fellow varied from an impatient search for satisfaction to relaxed sleep while the muscles of his mouth slowly released the coveted faucet. The moment Kata was ready to put him back in the crib, he would greedily turn toward her again. It was a game and a bit of a struggle. Finally, Jancsi's need for sleep would win out.

Istvan spent time with his son. In the evenings he could hardly wait to have his share in the feeding ceremony—placing him on the scale, bringing him back to Kata, watching the work of his lips and the snuggling turn of his body.

He played with him, too. He brought home toys and Jancsi enjoyed the flying celluloid bird attached to the slots of the crib, enjoyed poking at the glass eyes of his Teddy bear. Istvan helped him, later, to the first shaky steps around the walker. He taught him the first words: "Ma-ma, mama." He wanted to savor fatherhood fully, to relish it to the limit while it lasted.

In this period of domestic basking, an unexpected event brightened the future. A publishing house for foreign books responded to Kata's long-submitted application and awarded her the translation of an English novel into Hungarian. This could not be considered a literary feat but it did seem to open the door into the circle of artists whose talents she had so admired. She had never thought of herself as a writer, leaving such claims to Istvan. Until now, only through him had she dreamt of having any claim to literary ascent.

The advance she received was not large, but it brought a message of hope—hope beyond survival. In a way it was peculiar, Kata felt, that such a promise came to her, rather than to her husband. She had her fulfillment with Jancsi even if she were to accomplish nothing else. Would Istvan be sensitive about her opportunity? But Istvan seemed happy over it. And she was doubly touched and grateful when he surprised her with a pot of flowers bearing the sign: "To the great literary contributor of the future" (in big printed letters) "from her small husband" (here the words needed eyeglasses to be seen).

The pot of geraniums was in the center of the table as Kata toasted Istvan's literary future with the champagne they purchased from the translation advance.

* * *

Two weeks later, ten-month old Jancsi developed a cold. The Fogarases usually took such events in stride, particularly as they wanted to avoid Mrs. Vaghelyi's overexcitement whenever the least bit of sneezing threatened her first grandchild. They were not worried; the fever was low and a telephone call to the pediatrician assured them that a small dose of aspirin should do the trick. But the cold lingered. After another call in the beginning of the second week, Dr. Molnar suggested that they bring Jancsi to be examined that Friday if he had no fever to speak of.

Wednesday was March 15, a Hungarian National Holiday. Both Kata and Istvan were home. They awoke late and Kata guiltily rushed to the crib to offer her son a delayed breakfast. Janos lay quietly. She picked him up cheerfully, announcing the food to come soon. But the child would not respond. His face was drawn, thin, eyes hardly opened. Kata touched his forehead—it was hot.

By now Istvan was up and they both looked down at the boy with perplexity. What had happened to the cold? Their glances met, conveying fear.

Dr. Molnar seemed concerned as Kata announced the rising fever over the phone. He could not come right away but would be there late that afternoon, he promised.

In the meantime, the child refused to eat. He seemed to have real difficulty with swallowing and he was lying listlessly. Kata was frightened and grew more so as the hours passed. Istvan tried to calm her fears, but she detected his own tension.

Finally, Dr. Molnar arrived. He took a quick look, touched the child's neck, opened his mouth and with swift resolution announced: "Fortunately I have my car here; we'll have to take him to the hospital at once. It's diphtheria."

Kata and Istvan were stunned.

"But he has had hardly any temperature for several days! How is this possible?" The doctor had no time to waste with explanations then. But in the car, on their way to the clinic, he speculated that nasal diphtheria, a relatively harmless disease, had spread to the throat, and real diphtheria, of course, presented a powerful danger. Even death.

Once at admission, everything went quickly. They signed permission for the necessary medical interventions. Jancsi was wheeled into an isolation ward and the parents were sent home. They arrived in silence at the empty apartment.

The withering leaves of the geranium were still on the table.

Kata and Istvan clung to each other during the night. Diphtheria had killed many a child.

Like many Hungarian families they did not even have a phone in their apartment!

They rose at five and struggled to the phone booth around the corner.

It was Istvan who made the call. Kata's eyes were glued to his face, but she could not read it.

"The doctor says there's nothing we can do," Istvan reported when he'd hung up. "He says for us to go home and rest for now."

"Rest! I can't rest, not knowing."

Istvan took her arm and guided her back to the apartment. "He says the crisis is coming. If Jancsi can make it through, then he'll recover."

"Oh dear, poor little boy! He must be suffering! I just can't face this. And Mother! If anything should happen—" her voice trailed off. She looked up at Istvan, taking his arm: "Darling, I wish we could pray together. Would you?"

Istvan nodded. They moved to the sofa, sat down and he put his arm around her. "I feel enormous gratitude for our little child," he said in a quiet voice, then added: "I must put my trust in a Creator who gave us such a gift. With all my heart I want my son to live! Sweetheart, you say the rest."

"Heavenly Father, we thank you for the gift of our little boy. We beg you, we beseech you, restore Jancsi to health!" Kata pleaded. "Please, please, let him live!" She squeezed Istvan's hand and they sat silently for a few more minutes holding each other close.

The hours passed slowly. At eleven, they decided to telephone again. Their hearts were heavy, yet they tried to cling to hope.

This time, when the doctor was reached, Istvan broke into a grin.

"The crisis is over and we can go visit!" he told her. "Thank God!"

He embraced her tenderly there in the glass-covered privacy of the booth.

"Oh, God, thank you, thank you forever!" she repeatedly exclaimed.

* * *

Thursday, Friday and Saturday the child improved greatly. At first they could only view him through the oxygen tent and then through the glass window of the ward. But once the crisis was over, Dr. Molnar felt the boy would be better off at home.

A smiling and confident Kata walked on her husband's arm as they entered the hospital corridor the morning of Sunday, March 19. They arrived early and were asked to wait on the bench in the hallway until bathing and second feeding was over. They chatted in a relieved mood. The doctors dashing by here and there seemed aloof. A tall, white-clad man—"he looks like the famous Professor Hennessy," Istvan commented—was discussing something earnestly with a group of younger men surrounding him in the far corner.

At last they could take Jancsi! As they were walking out they were dimly aware of animated conversations around them.

"I wonder what they're all so excited about?" Kata asked but without waiting for any answer they hailed a cab, settled in it and headed toward home.

Istvan's sister lived just opposite the Fogarases and they decided to drop in for a moment with the baby.

The Banats had moved to the neighborhood not long before and since then they had seen each other frequently. Irene had been fascinated with Jancsi ever since his birth and she was shaken almost as badly as the parents when she first heard of the child's critical condition. It was only right to share the joy of recovery with her.

They rang the bell.

Imre opened the door. His grim face softened slightly at the sight of Jancsi, then waved them towards the living room without a word beyond the quiet "Hi!"

His brother Laszlo was there, too, immersed in some topic with Irene. The visitors were almost in front of her when she finally rose and with a peculiarly strained smile, and an exceptionally warm and tender embrace, welcomed her nephew. Still she said nothing.

"I thought you'd like to see the baby." Istvan said.

"I'm glad you came!" Another kiss and a long sigh followed. She handed Jancsi back to his father and pointed to the armchairs.

"Is something the matter?" Istvan seemed puzzled by the restrained response on the part of this usually animated couple, and even Laszlo Banat, an articulate lawyer.

"The matter?" They looked at the Fogarases startled.

"The matter?" they repeated. "Don't you know, haven't you heard?"

"Heard what?" Istvan viewed them with bewilderment. "No, we haven't heard anything this morning except the good news that Jancsi is well. We dropped in here to have you share in the joy. Is anything wrong?" He wasn't sure whether to be touchy or perhaps worried.

Irene looked at them with weary understanding as she rose to turn on the radio.

"We are repeating the special news," the broadcaster started in a wooden voice: "As stated in our earlier bulletin, German troops entered our country this morning to enhance the fullest cooperation against our mutual enemy, the Red Army. The action took place in agreement with Admiral Horthy, who will continue as Regent of Sovereign Hungary."

The knob clicked again.

"Now you know," Irene said quietly. Her lips quivered.

At first Kata and Istvan sat in stunned silence.

"German soldiers in Hungary?" Kata's voice came in a husky whisper. She shook her head, feeling incredulous. "Germans here now? When the Allies are making steady gains? Now this would happen here?" She kept repeating the question.

They all looked confounded.

"So it was too good to be true.." Istvan's quiet words sounded powerfully ominous against the anguish-filled silence.

"A disaster, a real disaster," Imre muttered.

Jancsi began to whimper.

"Look, we'd better go home. The child needs a nap."

"Keep in touch!"

They kissed each other fondly.

Istvan, Kata and the baby entered their apartment they had lovingly prepared earlier for the child's return. A bunch of violets scented the corner near the crib. It reigned over the room like a queen greeting a home-coming delegation, a symbol of beauty and unmistakable presence. But it was too much for Kata.

"Beauty and joy! Over!" And she broke into uncontrollable sobbing. Jancsi picked up her distress and began to scream.

"Sorry, Darling. Take him!"

Istvan took the boy and held him tightly. He looked at the tear-drenched face with infinite tenderness, patted the child's bottom until he was quiet, and rested his lips for a while on the silky head.

"All right, sweetheart," he whispered as he lowered Jancsi into the crib. "Sleep now, here's Teddy Bear."

The child turned toward it with recognition. His mother's soothing palm over his face and head assured him also of her presence beside the crib and a smile broke through the features so unhappy just a little while ago. He clutched the bear. The discovery of a lost friend prompted him to incomprehensible noises of communication which also faded soon as he sank into a nap.

Istvan's arm sheltered Kata as he led her now to the sofa, helped her to get comfortable, spread a blanket over her, and sat there holding her hand. Then, with the other hand, he quietly began stroking the chestnut hair. There were no words. Germans in Hungary! The news was too shocking for talk.

She closed her eyes, cuddled up against the sitting figure and let his tender fingers hypnotize her to sleep.

* * *

"They took Mr. Goldfarb!" Istvan told her the next day.

"What?" Kata let out a cry of disbelief.

"He's gone!"

Lajos Goldfarb owned the fur store beside the Fogarases for many years. During the winter he often met Istvan's stepfather after supper at the coffee house. But not during the summer—at least not on weekends. Mr. Goldfarb, a man in his late fifties, loved the countryside and took every opportunity to enjoy the budding spring even before the snow melted.

"On March 21st, spring arrives," he used to say, "and I want to find the first snowdrops in my garden!"

He and Mrs. Goldfarb spent their weekends in the country as soon as they were able to shed their winter coats. This year they had taken advantage of the national holiday in the middle of the week and entrusted their store to their salesman and had started preparing their country home for Easter, when their children would join them for the two-day holiday. After she had supervised the cleaning woman for a couple of days, Mrs. Goldfarb decided she needed to get new curtains.

"I'm going back to the city Saturday morning," she announced. "I can take the train back Saturday night."

Mr. Goldfarb wondered whether it would be worthwhile for her to come back for one day. And after all, he deserved to be a grass widow for a day or two.

So Mrs. Goldfarb did her shopping in Budapest, was satisfied that everything would be ready in two weeks and had a good night's sleep. When she awoke Sunday, she felt as though she was coming down with a cold and decided against a visit with her grandchildren that afternoon. "They don't know I'm back, anyhow," she rationalized. Shutting herself off from the world with Vicky Baum's latest book, she had a pleasant afternoon with a nap, some sentimental records and the remnant of a box of chocolates left there by their last week's supper guests. After a while she felt well rested and became ambitious; she reorganized her bedroom drawers. Working for an hour made her drowsy; she had a light supper and went to bed early.

"I'd better open the store before Lajos gets in," she thought, making her plans for the morning.

When she walked toward the store next day she sensed something strange around her. It seemed to her as if the city had changed. Were there more soldiers on the street? Yes, she saw some German uniforms! She opened the store surprised that the salesman was not there before her. Sam was a faithful soul who had worked for them for thirty years and was always awaiting the couple at the store door. Today, he was late.

Mrs. Goldfarb entered and settled down in the expectation that at any moment Sam and even her husband would be there. Minutes passed and it was soon nine-thirty. This is strange, she thought. She called up her daughter and began cheerfully telling her about the beauty of the Danube shore and their joy in anticipating Easter vacation when Magda and the children would join them. Magda responded with curt politeness, and Mrs. Goldfarb could not understand what had happened to her daughter.

"Did you have a pleasant weekend?" she asked, trying to skip over the fact that she herself had been in town for forty-eight hours without making this known to her children. Magda muttered something incomprehensible and asked for her father.

"He's coming in this morning, by train."

"By train? Oh my God, I'll be right over!"

What on earth has happened to the girl? Mrs. Goldfarb wondered and she became somewhat impatient with the world. Magda was almost rude, Sam inexcusably late and even Lajos should have been here by now.

She was really surprised when she saw her daughter arrive. "Rather untidy I must say," she noted. Magda's hair was covered with a kerchief, country style; she was wearing no make-up and seemed to have been in a hurry.

"Why did you have to come here?" Mrs. Goldfarb asked and she was about to reproach Magda for leaving the children so early with the maid. Then her pupils began to dilate as she spotted the news staring from the morning paper under her daughter's arm:

"The Germans are welcome in the Capital. This is a Day of Celebration!"

She grasped the desk and sat down. She wanted to ask questions but found herself speechless, and instead stared at her daughter.

"Mother," Magda touched her shoulder, "didn't you know? Doesn't Father know? When do you expect him?"

Mrs. Goldfarb took the paper but found it hard to read. Her shaking hands went back and forth between her glasses and the crumpled sheet, then automatically smoothed her hair, and adjusted the glasses again as if hoping that once the lenses were properly set they would reflect some other kind of news. This went on for about five minutes—no sensible conversation, only a word here and there, a question and unheard answer. Then Sam arrived. He looked pale and worn out, but appeared to be delighted to see Mrs. Goldfarb.

"I'm glad you and the Mister are here," he broke into a grin. "Oh, how glad I am; I hear they are picking up people at the station and I was so worried. How good you got in safely," he tensely rattled on without really taking notice of the fact that not the couple, but mother and daughter were in front of him. Then, he posed the question, at last. "Where is Mr. Goldfarb?"

"I don't know, Sam. The train was to get in at nine. It's nine-fifty now; he should have been here. What did you say about trains?"

Sam tried to amend his earlier story about a certain train from Szeged where some of the passengers were screened and the Jews were asked for their identification papers.

"This was just one train," he assured his mistress.

The minutes were ticking away. No customer came to the store and there was no Mr. Goldfarb. Magda asked her mother to leave with her, to come to her place. Sam could call them as soon as he heard from Father.

Later, Mrs. Goldfarb nervously tried to play with the children. Their presence, hitherto a great joy to grandmother's heart, was now a nuisance. Mrs. Goldfarb impatiently reminded little Joska to be careful, not to step on toes. The boy looked at Nagymama in amazement and started to cry.

"All right dear, all right, grandmother loves you," she reassured the little fellow and went into the other room to correct her temper.

At around eleven Magda received a telephone call from her husband. Mrs. Goldfarb wanted to know what it was all about, but Magda brushed it off impatiently saying that Otto was coming home for lunch. This was unusual. Otto's legal practice kept him in the office during most of the day and the family had a meal together only in the evening. It was hardly twelve and Otto was home! He quickly greeted his mother-in-law, then drew Magda into the bedroom. They were there for a long time.

When they emerged, Mrs. Goldfarb knew that there was something really wrong.

"What is it?" She anticipated their news.

Otto came over and kissed her. So did Magda. Her daughter began to cry.

"What is it then? Tell me!"

Otto sat down in front of her and made as light as he could of the story about the train from Goed having been screened upon arrival at Nyugati station; all the people whose identification showed they were Jewish were taken to headquarters for checking and he was sure Mr. Goldfarb would be among the first to come home. After all, he was an elderly man, and all they were looking for were draft dodgers. "I'm sure he will be here any minute, Mama." He feebly and unconvincingly tried to calm his mother-in-law.

They waited and waited, but Mr. Goldfarb never came back.

* * *

"Mr. Goldfarb has never come back," Istvan told Kata. "Anyone can just disappear!" He added, "And we? What are we to do?"

Istvan posed the question again and again.

The decree was posted at the end of March, ordering the Jews of Hungary to wear the David's Star. This was to "clarify" their position. It would be easier for the police to defend them in case of unprovoked molestation by the population, which—as the papers reported—had become more and more impatient with Jewish imperialism and world power in the service of the wealthy Americans.

The change to total German domination had come with unexpected swiftness.

At this point of history, when the war seemed to be moving toward a conclusion against the Germans, it was particularly hard to face the emerging reality, a reality coming into their personal lives. It was no longer at a distance, happening to someone else. It was now their reality.

And so now when one had to act, or at least to think through what was ahead and whether by some means tragedy could not be averted, it was especially difficult to assess the meaning specifically for them.

The churches began to stir, to make new efforts to save their flock. The sporadic and weak protests of the past had had only minimal effects in protecting even their own membership of Jewish background, let alone the Jewish community as a whole. Still, there was a chance that Dr. Vaghelyi and his wife might be exempted. Priests, ministers, church officers—perhaps. But Kata's legal situation was clearly questionable, Istvan's definitely dangerous and Janos as a baby would be viewed the way his parents were, certainly as long as he was with them.

Whatever their own status and fate, their main concern was for the child.

"Kata, there may be a chance." Her father brought the news. "Dr. Csegey may be able to help to find a safe home for Jancsi."

"Csegey? He's an important man. His daughter was in school with me. For a while we attended Sunday School together, too," she explained to Istvan.

"I went to see him yesterday," Dr. Vaghelyi continued. "He was as friendly as ever and promised to see what he could do through his entry into church administration. He's highly regarded there."

Kata nodded. "At times I'm amazed, a man with his political views in church positions! It's one thing to be a revisionist, but such an admirer of Hitler! But he's willing?"

"It would be a wonderful solution, Papa," Istvan turned to his father-in-law. "It would be so much easier to take everything, if I knew that Jancsi would be safe."

And so, after a time of waiting anxiously, the message came that a place had been found for Jancsi in the Tiszantul, east of the Tisza river. Both grandmothers shed tears and both prayed that all would go well with the child.

"Nobody will ask about him in the country," Csegey assured Kata as she went personally to him. "The lady of the house has always had a couple of orphans in her home. She has been a widow for years who provided a foster home to church-affiliated orphans, and the local authorities will find it quite natural that another baby should find his way to her door. In any case, Jancsi's birth certificate indicates his registration in the Reformed Church, born to parents of the Reformed faith."

Kata expressed their gratitude. Even so, she was greatly disturbed. On the desk of their benefactor she had seen the newspaper *Virradat*. How could he read that vicious, anti-Semitic filth?

Istvan paced the room. "It's so tragic—a bright man, an educated man, you say a believer! Blind! Blind! Sinfully blind! And the same man who is willing to save our son!"

"You can be certain, Erno," Dr. Csegey himself reassured Dr. Vaghelyi later, "your grandchild will be in good hands."

It was a wrenching decision to make. Kata and Istvan talked about it at length, weighing the pros and cons. Not only that the home would be so quiet without the child but they had to trust him to a stranger. Far away! But Jancsi's safety seemed to require drastic measures. They'd better let him go.

And so at the end of April, when Janos was not quite a year old, an unknown woman took him in the dark of the night and traveled with the boy a hundred miles—a considerable distance in a small country. They knew they could not have any direct contacts with Mrs. Kovacs. But they heard indirectly that Janos had arrived safely at his foster mother's home.

After the baby left—and they made some feeble explanation to the concierge and a large gift of money as consolation for the burden of secrecy—they lived as if they had never had a child. Because their home was in a private house located in the back of the garden, a two-family house owned by a distant relative of Istvan's, they were less exposed to questions as to their movements by neighbors. In an apartment house with many tenants, it would have been much more difficult to account for the child's disappearance.

* * *

From the middle of April they had been aware of the ghettos in the
provinces. As always, some "plausible" reason was given. If not to
"repatriate" refugees, or fairly new residents, now the stated goal was
to clear the newly declared military operational zone near the eastern
border of potentially "dangerous elements."

It was not only those who were recent residents of the country or
those residing in sensitive security regions, but the concentrating of all
Jews started in one zone after another, orders to leave home, to report
to the appointed center, to be put up in ghettos—a "brick factory," a
roof above four pillars, with no protective walls. The ghettos? To what
end?

"They need quarters for Gentiles. The bombings demolished many
homes," came the seemingly reasonable explanation.

"And those disappearing? Deported?"

"There's a war; manpower is needed. If you're healthy and willing,
you can survive," one Jew tried to convince the other.

And yet, the way the Jews were collected in the Hungarian provinces
and the conditions of their travel, forced one to wonder.

"Have you heard? A knock on the door at night, a few minutes to
pack, a change of underwear, a valise to contain the needs of a household! Then, the march to the local collection center. From there, to the
ghettos!"

Chilly nights of April and May. Rain and wind gusting into the
huddled mass of men and women, old and young, sick and helpless.

And then, whispered rumors from the Security Zones—seventy,
eighty, a hundred people jammed into freight cars. One pail of water for
drink, one pail for waste.

Sealed cars, no windows, no air—they roll on.

In Budapest? Events evolved in a more fragmented manner. There
were only haphazard, though alarmingly increasing instances of individuals disappearing. It started with the raid on trains. Poor Mr.
Goldfarb was among the first victims. It did not take long to realize the
dangers of travel for Jews.

In any case, the whole issue of travel soon became illusory. The new
restrictive measures did not allow for any move without the knowledge
of the authorities; they hardly allowed for anything at all.

Within days of the German occupation, stores owned by Jews were closed, even in Budapest, and their contents expropriated. Professionals were disbarred from their licenses. Food rations were reduced to a minimum and items such as butter, eggs and rice withdrawn from Jewish consumption altogether. Jewish shopping in Budapest was limited to specified hours. No telephones, no cars, no cabs, no buses—Jews could use only streetcars. Valuables had to be surrendered: jewelry, gold and cash above a limited sum; art objects, of course, and books; and perhaps most painful of all, any radio equipped to carry foreign broadcasts. The magic lifeline to the free world, long-forbidden but still available, had now been irretrievably cut.

And while all these material deprivations and prohibitions were duly implemented, the unannounced and unheralded steps continued affecting—in increasing numbers—certain individuals here and there. It was still individuals only in Budapest, mostly people of special importance. Dr. Bodo was arrested.

"Goodness! Why?" It was foolish to expect an answer.

The rulings and orders came one after the other with paralyzing effect. The so-called Jewish Council, headed by Jewish leaders, was the appointed arm of the Nazis—and they called for compliance. They promised no harm!

So, one complied and waited.

Kata took in the news and felt terror. "Istvan, are we just waiting? Helpless? Shouldn't we plan?" Kata pleaded.

"Plan? We're trapped!"

"Istvan, please, let's not give up. We can't fool ourselves any more."

Istvan looked at her sadly. "I've never been fooled. Shall I burden you with my despair and rage?"

Kata's eyes welled with tears. No, Istvan had never been fooled. It was he who from the very beginning had recognized the unmistakable handwriting, spelling out death. It was he who had been tortured by the impotence with which Jewry marched toward the inevitable. It was he who had kept asking the unanswerable question: "Isn't there a way to take fate into our hands?" But now, just as then, the barriers loomed indestructible.

"Still, don't you think we should try? Get papers, go underground?" Kata persisted.

"We can't. Not now, you know that. My next draft appearance is on the first of July. I must keep the date. A deserter, Jew or Gentile, would immediately be shot if discovered."

"That's true," Kata responded with tears.

"Look, dear," he embraced her. "Look, let's see what happens with the military. I can't imagine they would let me go this time. If they do, we may try to explore the impossible. Or you, alone, you might move with greater ease. But a man of my age?"

So they waited. It was the last week of May.

May twenty five, twenty six . . . thirty one . . . June 1 . . . One more month to go!

But on June 1st, Istvan received a strange notice. He was to report to the Hotel Majestic on Svabhegy on June 6th. The hotel was now German Headquarters. No reason was given.

Frightening, and yet, it was just a card. Still, why was it sent?

"I'm surely not an important personage," Istvan said trying to rule out some possible basis for the special treatment.

"Could it be the British broadcasts?" Kata raised the possibility. "Or Jancsi?" She felt frightened.

But Istvan remained fairly calm. "Look, we turned the radio in weeks ago. Of course, someone may have reported me before that. And Jancsi? No! They would not bother with a card. It must be the military. It's true, I'm not due for another month. But would they give me a week to 'prepare' if they had drastic measures in mind? It sounds more like some official routine."

Kata sighed. Routine indeed! And ironically, at the Hotel Majestic, where their honeymoon had been.

They spent an anxiety filled week. Still, Istvan did not lose heart. By now they were so used to the ever-present danger, so accustomed to sleeping with fear at night and waking with a start at every truck noise screeching in the silence of the dark, that a call-up to the Svabhegy was another hurdle to overcome until the draft status was clarified. And most likely, this would be the clarification.

He had a vague notion of inquiring at the draft board, but then decided against it. It was better not to make oneself conspicuous.

So he went the following Tuesday.

"I'll see you tonight," he said almost casually as he left the house.

But he did not come home that night. Kata spent a fear- filled night, tossing in the lonely bed, her thoughts churning.

He came the following day. "Somebody denounced me," he said, dejected.

"Who? Why?" Kata felt shaken.

Istvan shrugged his shoulder. "They don't tell you. But it was a denunciation. And, they ordered me to be back in twenty-four hours. I can pick up some clothing, they said."

"And—where? Where are you going?" she hardly dared to ask. "Labor unit?"

"No, concentration camp—Ujpest."

Her hands flew to her face. "Oh, Lord," Kata moaned.

"Couldn't you disappear?" the family suggested. "Take this opportunity provided for saying goodby and not return?" His stepfather particularly begged him not to go. "There's a small note in the papers, the Allies have landed in France. The whole thing may not last long."

Istvan waved his hand. "They landed in Italy, too. It was a year ago and look what happened after. No, I can't disappear. They may look for me and take others instead. Kata, Irene across the street, who knows, maybe Mother. But worst of all, they may find out about the child. No, I don't want them to come and look for me here. Oh, what's the difference? It cannot be worse than the formal call-up in July. I'm sure they would not let me off at this point of the war."

The night came—time to take leave from each other.

"Good-bye my sweetheart, my treasure, my love!" He kissed her tenderly now, without passion. "We've had four wonderful years together!" A long pause. "And what a glorious year with our little boy!" He held her tighter. "Take care of him! I know, you will take good care of him," he said with a broken voice.

Kata's tears were flowing steadily. She swallowed frequently and turned her head. What was the use of making Istvan more miserable?

Istvan, too, was struggling with despair. He must not be overwhelmed.

So he recalled all the memories of their married years and mentioned them one by one as they lay awake all night awaiting the morning.

There was a last embrace, a last pledge of loyalty and faithfulness.

Then, Istvan rose, dressed and left early before the rest of the family on the block had a chance to assemble. Kata watched from the window until the man she loved so was gone from view. A dreadful loneliness came over her immediately, a loneliness she had never known before. The apartment seemed hollow, echoing with emptiness.

CHAPTER 7
SUMMER 1944

JUNE-
OCTOBER 1944

June 20, 1944

Dearest:

I don't know where you are and I must talk to you. Many people have gotten cards—from Waldsee. Where is Waldsee? Nothing has come from you. Is that a good sign?

Since you left the house is unbearably empty. Three of us three months ago—now I'm alone. I miss you, I miss you terribly.

Obviously I have no address to which to send a letter, but I will give our news from time to time—to have it ready when you write, or to have you read it when you return.

God bless you! Good night!

June 25, 1944

Dearest—The first move toward relocation has started in Budapest. Jewish houses have been designated for us. They bear a big yellow star.

Fortunately, I did not have to move. Since this is a private house with only three tenants—all of whom count as Jews—this house now carries a yellow star. The same happened to Irene. Your mother and father moved in with them. At least we are near one another.

There is a chance my parents will be exempt. There are indications that priests, ministers, church officials will not be affected. But it is only rumor so far. Until it becomes true, they had no choice but to move into a Jewish house, too. They share an apartment with the Markos family. We felt it was better for them and for us to be independent from each other. But I try to see them every day. Since we are deprived of phones, we must keep in touch in person.

I love you!

July 5, 1944

Dearest—Frightening rumors are spreading! Baky's gendarme unit arrived in Budapest. It's a matter of days they say and we will be deported. But why do I say this to you? Who knows where you are? Still, I dream that should I be taken, I might at least be with you! Crazy thoughts. I am scared. Alone at night, I open the Bible and try to draw comfort from its words: "I have mercy on whom I have mercy and I will have compassion on whom I have compassion," I read. "It is not of him who wills it nor of him who runs, but of God who shows mercy." I want to run!

July 9, 1944

Sweetheart—a miracle happened! The churches finally woke up. The Primate Seredy threatened a pastoral letter condemning the deportation of Budapest's Jewry. The threat was effective. The government promised to hold off. Some of the pastoral letters were actually read at the pulpit, they say. A few hundred were mailed against the Government's warning. And the Protestant churches seem to have joined the effort. The gendarmes left. I can't believe it. It was a last-minute decision.

As always, I am dreaming of solutions. I look at the last note: how ugly, how desperate. I'm tempted to destroy it. But no, you should know. And now, I am confident, we will survive!

And you? Still no word from you. There's so little mail these days. Yet, I am waiting and waiting every morning.

July 18, 1944

Dearest—Can you imagine, I'm working and in an office job? You must think this is a joke. No! Finally there was a new organization formed: The Association for the Interests of Jews of Christian Faith. I volunteered my services. There is much need to visit people in congested quarters, to arrange for an additional room or an additional tenant. At times I can be of help, we all discuss the future and we nurture hope. There is some cause for it, too. My parents did get their exemption, on account of father's being a deacon of the church. They say all Christian Jews might be exempt. By the way, Mother and Father stayed in the apartment where they are. It's better not to move around much. But they don't have to wear the yellow star any more. Isn't this wonderful!

August 10, 1944,

My Darling: It's three weeks since I wrote. Looking at the note, I was hopeful then. And now? I really don't know. The rumors are unbearable. They speak of deportations being on the agenda again; of negotiations with the Germans to save Jewish lives; even of letting Jews leave the country, to emigrate; of giving exemption to all those baptized.

Everything is confusing except for news on the military front. The Russians are advancing. It cannot, it cannot last much longer.

I go to bed and my head is full of memories, dreams, agonies, hope. I want to be near you. I want to be with J. I want the war to be over and to live in peace. Crazy, crazy thoughts. And you? Maybe you are walking in the Valley of Death. I will myself to say: "The Lord is my Shepherd."

August 20, 1944

Dearest—I obtained a certificate of protection from the Swedish Government. I don't know how effective it will be. But everyone who can tries to procure one of these exemptions. The greatest number is from the Papal Nunciature. But since we are not Catholics— In any case, through my former work, there was a link to Sweden. If nothing else, the paper gives a sense of safety.

Wherever you are, are you aware of military developments? A few days ago, Rumania capitulated. And here, a new government has been formed. Shall I dare to say things may change at last?

Keep well my darling. It may not last long!

October 10, 1944

Sweetheart—Yes, the Russians are in Hungary. I understand they occupied some southern parts. It is said truce will be here soon. We are breathing much easier now. The last three months were full of dramatic ups and downs—seeming immediate danger, sudden retreat of the gendarmes of death; bombings and long hours spent in shelters; some tragedies, then gradual overall improvements.

On the personal front, Father had an automobile accident. As he crossed the street in front of the house, he was hit by a car. He's in the hospital and mother is heartbroken. But this seems such a minor problem. It's true his ribs are broken. But who knows, he might be best off there.

Darling, oh how I wish, I wish you would write. I pray every night, so fervently I pray for God to allow you to return. There are so many people to pray for. Is it a sin to keep mostly you and J. in mind?

October 15, 1944—12:30 P.M.

Hurrah! Hurrah! Hurrah! Horthy announced Armistice negotiations today at noon.

October 15, 1944—10 P.M.

Tragedy—worse than ever. Szalasi and the Arrow Cross Party have taken over.

God help us! Arrow Cross—that hateful bunch of Hungarian Nazis! The very name strikes terror in the heart.

CHAPTER 8
HIDING

OCTOBER 1944

Kata was settled in the choir loft of her church. It was hard to move wedged in the tight space where she lay crouched between the organ and the nearest choir stall. But the place offered a wonderful refuge, transient though it might be, from the cataclysmic turmoil of the last two days.

She had decided, with Irene's firm encouragement and final push, to abandon her home. The decision to do so had in itself been agonizing. She was taking action—action that could affect her life, or bring death. Every move from now on could be fatal.

* * *

When Kata finally slipped out of her home on the morning of October 16th, 1944, the home which first Jancsi, then Istvan and now she had left, she decided to go to her mother first of all. "Let's try to find a hiding place together, Anyu," she coaxed. But Mrs. Vaghelyi would not try.

"I can't go. Your father is in the hospital, how can I abandon him? Besides, I have an exemption of sorts. You go yourself. I'm deadly worried for you, but you must! God be with you!" her mother said with tears in her eyes "Are you sure?" Kata asked again. Her mother nodded. "Yes, I am."

They embraced. "Give my love to Father if you see him. Let's hope it's just for a few days," Kata added.

With a heavy heart Kata's steps took her to Mrs. Gondos.

Mrs. Gondos was a simple woman believing in right and wrong, thoroughly confounded by the incomprehensible provisions of the war years regarding some citizens. She could not understand how such provisions could affect the Vaghelyis. The good man had tried to help when her son Lali had got into his many scrapes. And such fine Christians, too. Dr. Vaghelyi: a deacon of the church, a lay preacher—any step against them was nonsense! She would always be happy to do whatever she could for the family. After all, she lived alone—somebody could even stay with her. And she repeatedly mentioned the possibility.

Now the woman received her unexpected visitor with warm concern but some fluster.

"Mrs. Fogaras," (since Kata had married, Mrs. Gondos more often than not addressed her in this more formal way) "make yourself comfortable," she nervously offered as she dusted off a wooden chair with her apron and apologized for not having had a chance to fix her daybed. "I had a sleepless night."

She busied herself with tidying up the room. This done, she finally sat down with her visitor.

"How is Dr. Vaghelyi?" She inquired anxiously. "I heard about the accident. What a terrible thing!"

Kata reassured her of her father's improving health. Mrs. Gondos launched into lengthy recollections about similar conditions in her own family and commiserated about the length of time fractures took to heal. She surely hoped Mrs. Vaghelyi was bearing up well under the need to visit the hospital daily.

Kata sat tensely forward in her chair. At last she edged in a word: "Mrs. Gondos, what if neighbors come?" she looked around the compact room.

"Maybe nobody will come today, it's Monday." The woman had not grasped what her offer of help would involve. Of course, Kata, too, counted on the quick resolution of the Szalasi coup, but still—

"It's a small apartment, isn't it?" Kata probed further.

"One room and a kitchen. Adequate," Mrs. Gondos commented with some pride. She was glad to live in a decent neighborhood. "It's all I need."

The statement led Mrs. Gondos to think of other needs. "Let me go and prepare some lunch," she offered. "Move over to the sofa, Mrs. Fogaras, it's so much more comfortable," she coaxed her visitor on her way to the kitchen.

Kata complied. She pulled herself up to the cushions propped against the wall and continued weighing the situation. She could see that Mrs. Gondos was not aware of many things.

In the meantime, while tinkering with pots and pans, Mrs. Gondos kept up conversation from the kitchen. Food was so scarce! One needed so much ingenuity to manage. The ration card for a person was just not sufficient at all.

Another problem, Kata thought, was that she couldn't use her ration card with the special "Jewish" designation here, for sure. And the woman didn't have much reserve. In any case, her confidence seemed to cover "today" only.

What time span might she need? Surely, the Szalasi regime would not last! That was her only chance. But, could it all be over by tomorrow?

The announcement on the radio—Mrs. Gondos had turned the knob to keep Kata company while she was preparing the soup—arrogantly spoke of the Arrow Cross entrenchment, solidly accomplished in one day. The speaker rattled off plans for the day, the next day, the week— until unquestionable German victory! The first step was to control the inner enemy: the Jews.

"All Jews must be in their homes by six o'clock tonight. Transgressors will be subject to the strictest punishment," the announcer continued. "Anyone giving refuge to Jews will be treated as one of them.

"It's a warning that we must repeat: Anyone giving refuge to Jews will be treated as one of them!"

"My God! So it has started." Kata drew in a sharp breath as she realized the new feature of the broadcast. Had Mrs. Gondos heard this?

The dishes clattered noisily in the kitchen.

Kata was trying to formulate some new decision. Her coming to Mrs. Gondos might have been a mistake. The nature of the forewarned punishment had not been defined. But the tone of the broadcast— Her stomach tightened into a knot.

She asked for the bathroom.

"I use the common lavatory shared by the floor's tenants," Mrs. Gondos explained. "One-room apartments have no private facilities in this building."

My Lord, common lavatory! Kata moaned to herself. To walk through the corridor open to the inner courtyard in view of unknown curious eyes? How many tenants—sixty pairs of eyes, forty, twenty, even ten,—watching and wondering, asking questions, or taking action. They must have heard the warning, too! It was clear: By hiding Jews, you became an accomplice, sharing their fate.

Mrs. Gondos came in for a chair to seat two at the kitchen table. Kata intercepted her efforts.

"Don't bother, Mrs. Gondos. This won't work."

She stopped. The radio was now repeating the earlier announcement. Mrs. Gondos listened with frowning attention in an effort to understand the impact of the message.

"My God! Those people are crazy, wicked sinners," she burst out in despair. The gravity of the situation had apparently hit her at last. She was clutching the dish towel as if seeking some clue from its comforting familiarity.

"Look, Mrs. Gondos, I'm going to leave. It's too complicated." Kata's tone was decisive, thinly masking defeat.

"But, where? Maybe——," Mrs. Gondos stammered.

Kata patted her back. There was no question about it, she had to go.

"Perhaps home, perhaps some other place; I'll be on the way." She reached for her coat. "Thank you, Mrs. Gondos. I know you wanted to help. But, you can see, it is much more complicated than it seemed at first. It's impossible here."

Mrs. Gondos stared at her helplessly.

"Thank you, just the same," Kata repeated from the door.

The woman's sigh—a mixture of worry and relief—accompanied her as she was descending the stairs.

Where now?

Her legs carried her aimlessly. She strained to find another solution, but none occurred to her. Time was passing and the deadline to return to her home was six.

She moved on toward the big avenue where she would have to cross and turn.

At the corner, the red traffic light provided a natural pause. Kata rested her eyes on the familiar scene. The sight of the church a block away recaptured an earlier notion.

Would there be a possibility there?

She hardly dared to continue the thought. She had never seriously contemplated such a move. The church was too near—geographically within the boundaries of her own community. There had never been any encouragement either. And yet, what was there to lose by trying?

And as Kata reached the fence the decision was made: She would see if she could find the minister.

* * *

What wonder she had, that Sarossy had allowed her to find refuge in the church for the night.

The place was quiet. Now, in her cramped position, she wondered what the time could be. She must have forgotten to wind her watch. As far as she could see, it showed six. But she remembered she had heard the church bell chime six quite some time ago. It was surely much later now. The sanctuary was quite dark, except for the small light at the altar illuminating the bronze cross.

She heard the bang of the closing portals. It must be eight, then. An endless night to face.

She began to wonder how long she could stay in this position and how she could relieve herself.

She heard steps. She hardly dared breathe. Boots were treading the stairs.

Her heart raced. But, in a moment of clarity, she thought it must be the sexton.

Indeed, Mr. Szabo was up in the loft now.

"Hhh . . . " The withheld air forcefully escaped from her windpipe.

"Come on, Mrs. Fogaras," the man addressed her with quiet warmth. "Come, my wife has dinner on the table."

She accepted the helping hand. How good it was to be able to move!

"Are you sure?"

But the sexton waved away her worries.

"'He who finds his life will lose it, and he who loses his life for my sake will find it,' says the Lord," Mr. Szabo resolutely expressed his position while leading the way downstairs.

"It's wonderful of you," Kata repeated to Mrs. Szabo as the woman welcomed her with the steaming tureen in her hands. "I don't know how to thank you."

"Just some soup," Mrs. Szabo said, as she placed the bowl on the table.

For a while Mr. and Mrs. Szabo spooned their soup in silence. Kata fingered her spoon and brought it to her lips, but, though she felt pangs of hunger, she was unable to swallow. She tried it once or twice, then gave up.

"Maybe I'll be able to eat something later, or in the morning. It just won't go down now. Perhaps I should get back behind the organ soon," she offered. "Someone may search your quarters."

But the couple did not see how she could spend a night up there on the bare floor.

"It's getting cool, too, and while you are with us, let's see if we couldn't put up a cot in the parlor," Mrs. Szabo wondered. But Kata would not hear of that.

"You have a very small apartment, Mrs. Szabo; there is no place to hide here. No, I just cannot put you in such danger."

Mr. Szabo did not give up. He pondered her statement for a little then his face broke into a half-moon of smile.

"No place to hide, Mrs. Fogaras?" He almost teasingly uttered the question. "Well, perhaps not in the parlor. But, come with me!"

Kata obediently followed the man. He led the way into the back room, behind the pastor's office, opened a closet and pointed there, saying: "Here you are!"

The closet was full of beautifully laundered white tablecloths. On the upper shelf there was the silver chalice and a supply of candles. Mr. Szabo opened another closet which harbored warm blankets which the Sunday School children used for picnicking. He laid a blanket on the floor of the closet.

"You mean I could sleep in the closet, half hidden by the tablecloth?" Kata began to understand. "I wouldn't be exactly in your apartment and could claim—if anybody found me and believed me—that I myself had edged my way to this hiding place?"

Mr. Szabo nodded.

"Mr. Szabo! How wonderful! God bless you."

"You know, Mrs. Fogaras, the lavatory used by the Sunday School is right here. Also, in the morning you can have some coffee with us before you take up your place behind the organ. In the meantime we'll listen to the news and let you know if there is a break in this miserable situation. Who knows, it might be over by tomorrow. 'It's just a matter of days,' the Pastor said. After all, we did ask for the Armistice."

Kata crawled into the hiding place. Mr. Szabo closed the door of the closet halfway and turned off the light.

What about tomorrow? The disquieting thought lingered.

She tried to make some effort at planning but found herself unable to concentrate on any steps. She was not aware of the hunger she had felt earlier, either. Rather, she wrapped herself in the woolen blanket and lay in a bundle in the snug space. With her head resting once again on her sweater, her muscles relaxed. She was aware of the communion tablecloth drooping down from the rod above her head. The thought was luxuriously consoling. It made her feel like a guest at a dinner table—at the table hosted by the Lord. She felt in an almost festive mood as she touched the delicate lace in the dark.

I am a guest in God's Castle and am at the foot of His Table. The bread and the wine have not been served yet, the other guests are missing. But the tablecloth is here to remind me of the communion with the Host and His followers. "This do in remembrance of me!" She recalled the familiar words. Then, the thought of the crucified Christ came to her mind.

"After three days came resurrection." She grasped at the thought.

It was quite late, and she could no longer think clearly. She could feel only the warmth of the blanket, the reassuring nearness of the communion tablecloth, the trusted safety of God's House where she was, and sleep took over her worries and fears.

* * *

She woke feeling rested. She was even able to take a generous breakfast of coffee, bread and butter—butter was scarce these days. Then, she took up her position again on the balcony, just before Mr. Szabo opened the church door to welcome the day. According to him the news broadcasts were no different from those of the previous day.

As she settled herself on the balcony floor, the idea of getting to a Swedish House became pressing. She knew she could not possibly stay here long.

Nine o'clock came. The open portals below let in the morning noise of the street. Footsteps turned from the pavement into the sanctuary.

"Have you seen them dragged along Kiraly Street?" a young man asked the church secretary as they were crossing the nave.

"No, seen what? Whom?" the young secretary naively responded.

"Well, those Jews. They were being driven along by the Nyilas, guns loaded and fingers on the trigger as they were herding them, who knows where? My father says they will be executed because they are enemies of the nation. But then, I don't know. Would we have all those bullets to spare in a time of war?"

Kata could peer through the openings of wood and see the blond locks swing as the secretary turned towards the man. She stopped to understand him better.

"You mean, they'll all be killed?" Kata heard clearly as she spoke upward, facing the man.

"This is what my father says. My dad says things will change now that Szalasi took over. Now we can really help the Germans and the victory will be here soon. He is in the police, you know, and they hear a lot," the young man said. "My dad also says that they're arresting some fools who are giving refuge to Jews. I always knew Jews were sort of cowardly, aren't they? They want to hide."

"But, but—" The girl protested meekly as she resumed her steps. Then their voices became indistinguishable as they approached the back door, near the altar, a shortcut to the office.

So, Kata thought, they are herding Jews, and want to kill them. She pressed her palms hard against the floor to counteract their trembling. She could not just wait here!

What should she do now? Oh Lord, what should she do? she wondered, repeating the question with panicky compulsion as she looked at the gleaming cross on the altar down beyond, some ninety feet away. She suddenly realized the need for action. She could not stay here beyond one more day, if even that much. She could, of course, return home. But what then? They might even catch her right away. The police surely had an eye out for those who had left their homes.

They may not know, though, she continued her mental dialogue. Still, if I'm going to risk arrest, I might as well try to escape. But I'd better leave soon.

She decided to try the hostel a few blocks away, which the church was sponsoring for refugees from Russian-occupied territories of Hungary.

She listened to sounds within the church building, to time her departure well. Perhaps it would be safest at noon. The secretary would be out of the church on her midday break. But then, who might wander in during the lunch hour? There was no time to waste.

Kata sat up. Everything seemed quiet. She smoothed her hair, put on her sweater, rose and slowly descended the stairs. She stepped into the sanctuary. There she sat down quietly in the last row, head bent. A moment of grace—

The time had come!

She rose and swiftly stepped into the street, turning her steps toward the hostel.

Mr. Szabo and she had talked about this. The sexton himself thought the hostel might be a possibility for a few nights. The employees had been newly hired. People came and went, using it as a shelter for a few days, then leaving for more permanent quarters. And though she did not warn the Szabos about her leaving, he would probably remember their conversation. In any case, had she run into any problems up in the choir loft, the sexton could not have helped knowing about it.

Pushing her surging panic aside, she willed a calm front while checking the street numbers. The wide street harbored houses on one side only. Across there were empty lots and warehouses; besides some workers loading their cargo, there were not many passers-by.

She came to it! Sizing up the surroundings and cautiously anticipating the scene inside, she entered the hostel.

Kata managed to give a fairly plausible story to the receptionist, who waved her upstairs to speak to the matron. The bulging, loquacious little widow was busy just then and motioned her into a room where she might wait for her return.

Kata sat down in the small parlor. The windows opened to the street and brought the greeting of late autumn sunshine. With sweet-bitter memories she thought of Istvan, their hikes in the Buda Hills in autumn's haze, their shared love of nature. God, where is he now? And where am I heading? She hardly put the thought to herself when Pastor Sarossy entered the room. He closed the door behind him. Kata had not expected to see the minister there.

"You cannot stay here, Mrs. Fogaras," Sarossy came immediately to the point. "I just cannot be responsible for it." He had somewhat sanctimoniously become a man of duty—toward whom? "As long as you were in the sanctuary, I felt it was an appropriate refuge and that somehow I could explain it away, should they find you. But not here. You would not only jeopardize me—and surely the danger today is much greater than when we talked yesterday afternoon—but the police might close the hostel, take the matron and even the guests, in custody. No, I just cannot permit putting several people in danger, for one to escape. I'm sorry, but it is lasting longer than I had anticipated.

"I'm really sorry, maybe you can find some other solution," he added.

Kata nodded in acknowledgment of his difficulties, but she felt stunned. His gesture of yesterday had been so generous. Now, he seemed a different person. Tears welled.

She reminded herself that he had, after all, given her almost 24 hours; he had offered the church to spend the night in.

She managed to thank the minister and muttered something about trying to reach a friend of her father's and left.

She was once more on the street, in the bright, early-afternoon sunshine. What step to take next?

If I want to reach anybody at all, it must be before six. Either I find a place, or I'd better go home.

The latter course was so very tempting. Dangerous? Yes! But was not every move she was making dangerous? Pretending, lying, scheming, maneuvering. Lord, what a burden! To be constantly alert, to know that a false step might be fatal. And yet—at home? Surely, there would be less need for action. She could just sit—and wait! Wait for others to decide.

She must not do that! There was responsibility in living.

She decided to try once again to contact Dr. Garay.

* * *

Garay was a judge, a good friend of her father's and a devout Christian. He had abhorred the internal state of events in the country, even before Szalasi had taken over. He had felt penitent, he told his friend, about the sins of the nation, of every Hungarian.

She must try to talk to Garay. How?

She thought of a telephone call to the court. But, what if Garay's line was tapped? She must try to go to the court herself. Of course, traveling to the court would not be easy.

For a moment she thought of her mother, too. She must be quite anxious not knowing where Kata was. But there was really no way of communicating with her now and Kata relied on her mother's strength in situations requiring wit and faith.

She herself had to decide first of all what to do with the yellow star. If she let it be seen, she had no business going to the court. If she took it off—and she was strongly tempted to do so—she was providing unmistakable evidence that she had broken the law. She could be arrested, must be arrested, for screening people on the street had almost had to be expected in recent months.

She decided to leave the star on. But she covered it with the big flat purse she carried. That would be best.

Technically speaking, she was observing the rules. Well, almost. The star should have been displayed in full view.

She took the streetcar to her destination. She scouted her surroundings with seeming nonchalance. There were not many travelers.

The number 10 tram neared its last stop. It was a frightening moment.

How would she ever get to Dr. Garay's office? The court was beside the Marko Street prison with its policemen and guards. Perhaps the court itself had policemen on watch. She could never get in! Her mission seemed impossible to her now.

The car jolted to stop—end of the route. She had no choice. She had to get off.

The absurdity of her attempt struck her and she decided to return as she had come. But she would have to wait for the next tram; if she returned on the one which had brought her here, the conductor might become suspicious. He must see her walk away. There would be another car in about ten minutes.

She walked to the right. The street was quiet and showed few signs of the political uproar. But she did not want to loiter and thought perhaps she should go another block while she was marking time.

She was closer now to the prison and court. It still seemed quiet; perhaps she could continue. She moved on. With a lump in her throat and attempting to maintain a purposeful pace she passed the prison. The sentinels stood there at attention as always. Now she was standing opposite the court building. There was no guard at the entrance! She waited at the curb to cross the street.

"Hey, Miss, do you have the time?" Kata heard her pulse pounding her eardrums. She brushed back a lock of hair on her forehead and could feel the sudden sweat beneath. But she glanced casually at her wrist watch and turning to the man she looked straight into his eyes saying in a clear voice: "Ten past two."

The soldier studied her face for a moment then lifted his hand to his cap and moved on.

Kata forced herself to control her inner trembling as she crossed the street with deliberate steps, and carried by the momentum of the courage mustered in the encounter, walked through the gate head erect. She turned toward the stairway leading to the judge's chambers, which she remembered from an earlier visit with her father. She was aware that her heartbeat was still fast.

Because of her fear that the judge would be away, she could hardly believe the familiar "Come in," in response to her knock. As she opened the door, Dr. Garay rose in apparent surprise, reached out his hand in warm concern to meet her, made sure the door was closed behind her, and finally motioned her to the seat beside the big desk.

"Well, well, Kata, you're here! What brings you here in these terrible days? How is your father?" he inquired.

"Father? He's a little better. I last saw him Saturday. He said you had visited him in the hospital. And what am I doing here?"

She related to Garay her experience at the church, her desperate wish to escape and possibly find her way to a Swedish House. "Could you help?"

The same question—expressed in a bolder way.

Her father had always said Garay was a very good man and a real Christian. "He would give his life for others," Dr. Vaghelyi spoke of his friend with unquestionable conviction.

Garay did not hesitate. He did mention his wife who was a frightened woman throughout these years of war. Yet, he was sure she would understand her Christian duty and if Kata wanted to come with him that night—he had some official function to perform before that—he would be glad to offer her his home until they could plan for the next step.

Kata expressed her gratitude. She was somewhat concerned about

Mrs. Garay but hoped that the challenge of saving a life would help the judge's wife to overcome her fears. She needed at least one more day.

"Tomorrow this whole thing may be over."

They decided to meet at 5:30 at the number 4 streetcar station in front of the Vigszinhaz theater. She had two hours to spend until then. It was terrifying to think of the time lag. So many things could happen to her.

She walked toward a park not far from the court which was normally used as a playground. There was a bench with no one in the immediate vicinity and she could keep an eye on several approaches. But, it was deserted. There were no children playing there today and she decided it was safer to be on the move. Kata was on the street again. When she was a mere block away, she heard a police siren. She saw the car coming, bent down for a glove she had dropped and the car raced past her. She heard it screech and stop a half block down the street. She quickly turned into the next side street and wove her way toward busier Vilmos Csaszar Ut, then on to Margit Korut until the time had come to meet the judge.

The Garays lived in Obuda, an old landmark district of the capital, quite a distance from the court. By the time the judge and Kata got there, it was dark.

The judge let himself in and escorted Kata to the living room. He said he would be back shortly.

In a while, Mrs. Garay appeared. A tall, middle-aged woman with faded blond hair and lifeless complexion, her welcome was proper, but strained. She announced that dinner would be ready soon.

Mrs. Garay was indeed fearful. But the mention of dinner made Kata put her worries aside. In the last twenty-four hours she had had only coffee, bread and butter that morning and another chunk of bread that Mrs. Szabo had made her put into her purse right after breakfast. She could hardly wait to have something to eat now.

They sat down at the table. Kata relished the smell of the steaming potato soup. She dipped her spoon into the hot liquid and took it to her mouth but she could swallow it only with the greatest effort. This was no place to be sick.

How could she really eat? It was obvious Mrs. Garay was tense and frightened. She spoke of their two children in the university. They would be home shortly. Earlier in the day they had brought home two new friends—refugees from Miskolc. It might be best if Kata did not meet them. But, what if there was an air raid?

Kata herself had her concerns about meeting the younger set. They were more or less her contemporaries. There would be too many questions: where did she go to school, where did she work, who were her friends? How could she concoct any believable answer? And from Miskolc, too! She had wanted to claim she was coming from Miskolc as a refugee, if anybody inquired. That was the only place of the Russian-occupied parts of Hungary that she had known slightly. Miskolc was out.

"Could I stay in the apartment in case of a raid?" she asked in return to Mrs. Garay's question. "I think that would be best. I'm not concerned with that danger now."

But her hostess was worried. "You know, you're not supposed to stay upstairs. And, in case they find you here—"

She was unable to finish the sentence. The thought of the consequences horrified her beyond speech.

Kata nodded. "It's a problem, I can see that."

Dr. Garay himself was not shaken, though he recognized the realistic problem. "It's getting late. Kata must be exhausted. It's time to prepare for bed. Let us pray. Let us ask God's guidance."

The prayer seemed to fortify Mrs. Garay somewhat and she gave Kata a light kiss as she showed her to a small guest room.

"Try to sleep, my dear," she managed, in a softened tone.

In contrast to the previous night, Kata stayed awake for a long while. She thought of possible alternative steps to be taken the next day. She could not stay in the Garay home beyond the morning. Apart from the anxiety of her hostess—and this was an important factor to consider—she could not really avoid the student houseguests forever. And the Garay youngsters? Who knew, they might even be Szalasi supporters. It was not likely, in view of Garay's own attitude, but—

She must look for another place tomorrow. This was no solution.

How to get to the Swedish Embassy? On her own, with the terror spreading, she did not dare to venture to unknown places. She needed someone to make the contact first and Garay was not the person for that. Who else?

All of a sudden a name struck her: Laszlo Baumgarten. Her father considered him among his friends—someone to trust.

Baumgarten was also a minister. Kata had met him only once. He was fairly new to the city and she thought he lived with his family outside its confines. But his office—he was in church administration now, and had met Dr. Vaghelyi on "business"—his office was in Pest. On the way "home," Kata ironically recalled.

Baumgarten, her very last try! If that didn't work, then, back home. She had settled her steps then.

Once the decision was made, she fell asleep.

She was able to eat breakfast next morning after the college students left. By now, Dr. Garay had gone, too. Kata announced her decision to Mrs. Garay. The lady sighed with obvious relief, though she assured Kata of her concern.

* * *

It took Kata almost two hours—walking, changing trams and cautiously searching for the address—to arrive at Mr. Baumgarten's midtown office.

She wondered what he would say. In a way, it was foolish to approach a man she hardly knew. It was really stretching her efforts too far. But Father had mentioned the man several times. He had described him as warm, friendly, interested.

She felt he would not turn her in. And where else could she go?

It had started to rain. The dark clouds, the downpour, rendered a dramatic setting to the finale—the last try!

Kata was quite impressed by the simple and unmistakable welcome the minister offered her.

"A wonderful person, your father is," he exclaimed. "We have our business discussions, and then, we venture into many fields. He is quite a scholar!"

It was an encouraging introduction. But Kata did not have much time to lose; it was well past noon. A decision absolutely had to be made one way or the other.

Once again, Kata broached the question of the Swedish houses. Unfortunately, Baumgarten had no connections to the Swedish Embassy. He had heard, though, that those houses were full.

By now Kata did not really expect them to be her refuge. She had had to explore every avenue, but she had not counted on success.

"I'd better go, then." She was gathering her things.

Baumgarten shook the hand she reached out but hesitated: "Why don't you stay a little? The downpour's fierce!"

A downpour! A normal nuisance of everyday life. But his concern touched her.

"All right, I'll stay a little more," she decided. "Please, don't let me keep you, though."

Baumgarten nodded. "Make yourself comfortable. I have a few phone calls to make and then will be back." He stepped into another room.

Kata took off her raincoat.

She looked around, noted the simple furnishings, and the large atlas on one of the walls—a world not accessible to her for the last several years. It spurred her imagination about the beautiful places she had never had a chance to see and perhaps would never see. The world was closing in on her. The world? Her own country, her native city, her very life, narrowing.

She noted, too, a bunch of rusty leaves in a vase on the window sill. This touch of beauty she was still allowed to enjoy. It contrasted in a comforting way with the rain pounding on the window panes.

But even the rain was slowly diminishing. She sighed. The time had come to go home.

Baumgarten was back and she stood up.

"Thank you for the shelter and your kind words. I really think I must go now."

Her mouth quivered. She was fighting tears. The exertions of the last three days had been for nought. Baumgarten watched her intently. Then, he pulled a chair near to the desk and said: "Sit down, Kata, let's talk this over."

With eyebrows raised, she obeyed. She could stay for a few more minutes.

"I made some inquiries," Baumgarten explained. "But nothing worked out."

"It was very kind of you." Her voice trembled.

Baumgarten cleared his throat.

"Look, I can't let you go home. It would surely be the end."

"Well?" She looked at the minister askance. "What else can I do?"

"I've been thinking. Your father's a good friend of mine. He always talked proudly of you. He told me about the plans for your son and later about your husband's being denounced. No, I cannot let you just go home. Too dangerous! Listen, we moved out to the outskirts of Huvos-volgy when I was transferred to Budapest. It's a rather remote house in the midst of a big garden. My neighbors live behind closed doors, particularly as we're coming toward winter. We don't have many visitors and you can stay in one room if anyone comes. The house has one floor, with an entrance to the cellar from the kitchen, so that there's no need to seek public shelter in case of an air attack. Nobody would know you're there. I'd be glad to take you out there tonight."

Mr. Baumgarten sat back with the satisfaction of a man who had had a little debate with his conscience and had yielded to it. He actually seemed quite happy with his resolution.

"But what about your family?" Kata asked. "You have children. What do you want to tell them and how would your wife feel about it?"

"Oh, I thought you knew; my wife and children have gone to my parents in the West in the fear that the Russians might get here soon. Less harm could happen to the children over there. If needed, the family is ready to move on even further, but I couldn't leave my work, not yet. I'm working here at Headquarters performing a roving ministry; tending to the unhoused and unfed—bomb victims, evacuation victims, maybe Nazi victims," he smiled faintly as he looked at Kata.

"You're alone in the house then?" Kata asked with some awkwardness.

"Oh, no," Baumgarten quickly reassured her. "No, my brother is working in Budapest and has been staying with me. I'll have to explain to him who you are, but I expect him to be a man."

Kata did not know whether to laugh or cry.

"Oh, Mr. Baumgarten! You're willing to take the risk, to let me stay with you for more than one day. Is this what you said?" She wanted to be sure she understood him well.

"Let's face it, Kata, these are times of which many people will be deeply ashamed in the future. With the children around, I might not have been able to have you in our home. But as far as my risks are concerned, am I not God's minister?"

With this, he went into the other room of his office to work on his Sunday sermon.

At the end of the day Zoltan Baumgarten came to meet his brother. He was a fellow in his early twenties. The two men had a short conversation in the pastor's study. How the discussions went Kata did not know. His age worried her a little—would he have the state of mind to be on her side? But Baumgarten must know him.

Zoltan opened the door for her with natural chivalry and kept quiet most of the way; in fact he chose a back seat in the tram headed toward the suburbs and did not move to join Kata. Neither did Laszlo Baumgarten, when the thinning crowd would have allowed them to do so towards the end of the journey.

She followed a few steps behind them as they walked silently from the station to the home. She realized that each walking alone might evoke less attention than a group of three.

At seven-thirty Kata entered her new home in Hidegkut.

While she was washing up, the two men prepared a simple table and heated some stew left from the day before. It was the most savory meal Kata had had for a long time. In the quiet isolation of the house she was able at least to talk without fear of immediate danger and could think of the future with some hope. It was too late to make any kind of further plans, but for her, there was no pressure now. Whatever might happen, she had a home until Szalasi was overthrown. Of course, somebody might detect her. There was no perfect safety for her anywhere. But still, she could surely relax in this home and put her trust in God.

"The Lord is my shepherd, I do not fear," Mr. Baumgarten's evening devotion started. The words articulated the assurance Kata had felt moments ago.

"And I'm going to visit your father in the hospital tomorrow," Baumgarten said before retiring. "He should know where you are."

The door closed behind him as he said good night.

CHAPTER 9

OCTOBER-DECEMBER 1944

The following weeks proved to be the most domestic period in Kata's life. The two men started out early in the morning and she was left with the dishes, the cooking, the washing and the ironing.

Though within walking distance of the Budapest streetcar system, the house was more a country cottage than a year-round city abode. Its only claim to modern comforts was a small lavatory. While lighting came from the city's electric supply, cooking had to be done on an old iron stove.

Every morning Mr. Baumgarten stacked paper and kindling wood on the grate ready to be ignited later, but as soon as he had left, the fuel assumed a will of its own. The matches would shatter in Kata's fumbling fingers. The kindling seemed to move from its carefully ordered array and when flames finally wavered feebly, she had to watch every moment as she fed them with the daily coal ration. Those independent egg-shaped pieces more often than not extinguished the flames and the sparks generated earlier. And Kata had to begin all over again. The first day it was late morning before the fire started.

Though her frustration was great, as the days proceeded, Kata fought

106

her way through her apprenticeship in primitive housekeeping and eventually victoriously loaded the top of the stove with the stew or a pot of soup. The choice and quality of food were limited and the preparation of meals required ingenuity from any housewife, no less Kata. Yet, she enjoyed the hours spent in chores. They took her mind from too much speculation about her own circumstances, about Jancsi and Istvan. How she longed for them! And others— The list was endless.

"The situation is terrible in the city," Baumgarten reported a few days after her arrival.

"They say the Russians entered Miskolc; some men in the office are talking of resistance to the last, should they ever reach us," Zoltan said. "Everyone abhors the thought of the Reds in the city."

Kata kept her eyes on her plate. Of course, all of them would have preferred the British or Americans. But they were not the ones to liberate Hungary! And the Russians were in Miskolc? They could be here very soon, she silently exulted.

"But listen to what I saw today," Baumgarten exclaimed. "Lines of men and women—have you seen them? The Nyilas shouting and kicking them, pushing them back in place with their guns. And the most terrifying of all: I saw Erwin Moskowitz and his wife moving along, bent under their knapsacks. They were my parishioners. I tried to catch their eyes but they didn't notice me. And we Christians are doing this against God's chosen people!"

"You're not doing it!" Zoltan retorted.

"You really aren't," Kata chimed in.

"Should I participate actively? Some—look at the Slovak priest Tiso—shamelessly serve the Nazi Devil. Most of us, well, we just wait, and perhaps at times we seize enough courage to act. But God's commands are there, at all times. Let's clear the table and hear what He has to say about this."

They returned from the kitchen after everything was washed and dried. Baumgarten opened the Bible at Genesis Chapter 12. "Listen to this, you, too, Zoltan: 'Now the Lord said to Abraham . . . I will make of you a great nation, and I will bless you and make your name great, so that you will be a blessing. I will bless those who bless you and him who curses you I will curse; and by you all the families of the earth shall bless themselves.' To think of it, I gained salvation from the King of the Jews, Jesus Christ. And until now I have not had the courage to salvage one of his people." he said with a flushed face. "The Germans must go, one way or the other!"

* * *

During the first few weeks, while she thought that some change might come to pass soon, Kata stayed in day and night. The small house gave her a sense of safety; she was well-enclosed within its protective walls. And the view was a peaceful sight to look through the transparent curtains of the living room, to see and yet remain invisible, and rest her eyes on the withering beauty of autumn's plants and the firey foliage of the more distant hills. Janos Mountain in front of her beyond the intercepting valleys looked the same as ever, though it was probably now void of hikers. The change was more obvious in the evenings, the Observation Tower's peace-time illumination gone.

At times when the thought of Istvan and Jancsi emerged, a terrifying coldness gripped her. Knowing what was happening in Budapest, she could think only of horrors. Jancsi, probably Jancsi was all right. But Istvan? She could not even imagine the nightmare. Was he alive? "God, please guard him, please bring Jancsi and Istvan back!" she pleaded aloud in the empty house. Then, she went ahead with her chores. She must not dwell on horrors. To survive, she needed hope.

The evening was the social time of her day. There was even a married couple, Tibor and Elvira Szantos, good friends of Baumgarten, who were drawn into the secret and became an extension to the small family circle.

Of course, the mainstay of the household, by right and by character, was Pastor Baumgarten. He was in his mid-forties, brisk and vigorous, in some ways at the furthest end of the pendulum that might cover her contemporaries. Contemporaries? Kata was twenty-five and that made her twenty years the minister's junior. It was more appropriate to think of him as a sort of father. For one thing, he took care of her, providing for her board and safety. But more important, there was much in his thinking and beliefs that could have come from Dr. Vaghelyi. The latter was of course much older and had been fragile even before the accident. It was all the more fascinating for Kata to live in the home of a man who in some ways fitted into the picture of the wise senior, but whose seriousness was tempered by the sheer physical energy appropriate for his years. To think of him in this fatherly role was made easier by the fact that Zoltan looked upon Laszlo as his mentor.

Not until later did Kata find out that the two were half-brothers. Zoltan was the late fruit of his mother's remarriage after her first husband died. The younger boy had been reared at their country home. Zoltan had acquired from his own father the zest for open spaces, the interest in plants and trees. The two of them had gone for walks together and Zoltan shot his first hare under his father's tutelage.

Brother Laszlo—who had started at the Debrecen Theological Seminary when Zoltan was born and was a young minister when he came for vacations during the child's early years—brother Laszlo seemed in the boy's eyes to be the holder of different kinds of treasures than his father. Not that Zoltan eventually chose a life of intellect and spirit for himself. He became an agronomist. Nevertheless, brother Laszlo's ideas had opened new vistas to him, vistas which he hesitated to follow, but which broadened his world, and gave added dimensions to his life.

Zoltan had finished college the past year and his work at the Ministry of Public Works was temporary. He had gotten it through the manipulation of an uncle in the Division, who had yielded to his sister's plea to save her baby from the war. From Zoltan's point of view, deferment of military duty was a dubious triumph. However, he accepted his current situation to appease the anxieties of his mother and in the hope that his sojourn in the capital would provide ample opportunities to be with his brother. This was all the more appealing now that Laszlo's family had left. But then, Kata arrived. Things had changed. Now conversations with his brother almost always included her as well.

"I saw your father today, Kata," Mr. Baumgarten said. She looked at him with anticipation.

"Yes, he seemed much better," Baumgarten added. "Medically he might be ready for discharge in another four weeks."

Kata turned toward him startled.

"Out of the hospital? Oh, no! And then?"

"This is no time to think about what will happen in a month's time, Kata." Baumgarten realized the questionable value of improvement in Dr, Vaghelyi's health under the circumstances. "Four weeks is a long time; many things can happen before then. Many things indeed!" Baumgarten's words were meant to be consoling but they contained a note of defeat.

"What did you hear in the Ministry, Zoltan?" He turned to his brother in a wish to shift the conversation from Dr. Vaghelyi.

The young man was noncommital. It was just too confusing to talk about the war with this girl here.

"I saw Uncle Bela today; he just returned from a visit to Sopron," Zoltan felt safe enough to discuss the family.

"That's what I understand. I got a note from mother. This reminds me, Zoltan, you have mail, too." Baumgarten was patting his pockets to find it.

"Mother says some communication came from the Ministry of War about your deferment status and she wanted to warn us right away. That's what she explained in her letter to me. And here is yours." Baumgarten handed a sealed envelope to his brother.

Zoltan became engrossed in the news from home. His mother was not clear what the communication was about. It just set a date for him to report in Gyor, in three weeks, on December 1st.

"She says Father will undoubtedly try to find out more about it when he's back tomorrow. Well, the vacation may be over, Laszlo!" He shrugged his shoulder. "You know what, it may not be so bad. How can I just sit on my haunches waiting for the Russians to come? Too much is at stake, just too much. They need every able-bodied Hungarian." But in spite of his bravado, he looked quite tense.

"Let me finish this now, Laszlo, and maybe you and I could have some time together tonight," he said with a touch of reproach. The minister sighed and was about to answer when Zoltan reached the end of the note. He grew pale, his eyes glued to the notepaper.

"What is it, Zoltan?" his brother asked with anxiety. "Is there any special news in the letter?" Zoltan cleared his throat, his head hanging. Finally, when he spoke up his voice was weary and quiet.

"Jani Bekes died on the front, Mother just heard. Jani was my best friend, my very best friend. I have to go for a walk, I'm sorry," and he rose, going for his jacket.

"Would you want me to join you?" Baumgarten asked.

"Not now." His voice reflected an effort at bravery and the failure to muster it. The door closed quietly behind him as he left the house.

Kata and Baumgarten remained silent for a while. Then Kata burst out: "Poor Zoltan. He looked quite shaken. It must be hard to hear of your best friend's death. It's almost as if it happened to you."

She was thinking back to her teens. She had been in the sixth grade of the *gimnazium* when a classmate of hers had died. She told Baumgarten about it. "And we weren't even that close."

"But it affected you a lot, still, it seems," the minister said.

She nodded.

"You know, the whole class went to the funeral and we all filed before the open coffin. There was Borcsa, her long blond hair braided, placed peacefully on the satin pillow. The obvious thought came to me then, she is asleep. It was only that she was so young. I remembered her in the gym class jumping up and down only two years before, full of vitality, and it seemed the sleep was lasting too long—too long even for the duration of the half hour until the service began. Then the coffin was closed and all of a sudden I awoke to reality. Boriska's life was over and her sleep was to be forever. It shook me up for weeks.

"You know what was on my mind then?" she asked hesitantly.

"What was it?"

"I wondered whether she had ever been in love, whether anybody had ever kissed her. We were fifteen then. Wasn't it a peculiar concern?"

"Peculiar? I don't know. You wondered whether her life was fulfilled. Life was ahead of you, a mystery. You must have wondered whether she had gained any intimation of that mystery."

"I guess it was something like that," Kata agreed.

"Of course, there are many forms of fulfillment," he continued, "many other forms. But, oh, I understand."

"It's hard to take death when you're that young. By now I'm an expert," she wryly added. "Not that I've seen it happen right in front of me, thank God for that."

The door bell rang. Kata quickly retreated to her bedroom.

In a moment Mr. Baumgarten called her. It was Tibor Szantos. She came to greet him and asked about Elvira.

It was Baumgarten who answered.

"We're in a bit of trouble, Kata," he began. "Elvira was visiting the family in Budafok and Tibor got a message that her father, a diabetic, fell from his horse and is in a bad shape with a broken hip. They are planning to operate on him tomorrow, but he asked for me. He says he has much to settle and that he must talk to me." Baumgarten looked at Kata with concern.

"You want to see him?" she asked. "When are they going to operate? I guess it would take at least three hours to get there, wouldn't it?"

She was careful what she said.

"It's much easier at the break of dawn," she continued. "In daylight, you may even cut across the mountain, it would surely save time." She rushed her words as if to settle the issue of Baumgarten's leaving in the morning.

"Kata, I'm afraid I'll have to leave tonight. There is not enough time tomorrow morning."

A moment of frozen silence.

"Tonight? How? This late?" Her words carried forced calm but sounded hollow. "And here?—" She did not finish the sentence, just looked at the two men for some viable reply.

"There is no need to be so scared, Kata," Baumgarten rather limply tried to reassure her. "Zoltan is here, after all, you will not be alone. By golly, where is Zoltan?" All of a sudden he remembered that his brother had his own grief.

The two men were discussing what might be the best route to get them to their destination when Zoltan entered. He seemed calmer. He must have had the opportunity to sort out some of his feelings, Kata thought, as she looked at him with sympathy.

Baumgarten tried to explain his leaving. Someone, for whom life and death were still options, was waiting for him. He could not let him down.

If Zoltan had calmed down during his walk, he had reason to look tense now, though he assured Laszlo that there would be no problem. Baumgarten sensed his disappointment and feared the anger that would probably go with it.

"I must leave now, Zoltan, but I hope to be back tomorrow," he tried to reassure him.

"Yes, Laszlo, just go!"

Kata, too, had pulled herself together and told the minister: "Don't worry. I realize the old gentleman's hopes are in your coming. We'll see you tomorrow."

Baumgarten placed a light fatherly kiss on her forehead and reminded her she was not alone. "You remember, not a sparrow, not even a sparrow—" He did not complete the well-known sentence.

Maybe not sparrows, but Jews, yes, she thought angrily, as Baumgarten and Szantos were closing the door behind them.

She went to the kitchen to finish up the dishwashing.

When she returned to the dining room, Zoltan was sitting in the corner armchair with a book in his hand. Kata had never seen him read—not beyond the daily papers—and was curious what might have produced this change. With somewhat forced gaity, he started to explain.

"I just picked up this Petofi. It is amazing to see his love for girls and the fatherland. Well, the first I can understand. The latter—it cost him his life. The same that happened to my friend. I think he would have done better to stick with the former devotion," and he looked at Kata.

"Well, maybe yes," she found herself stammering. "Had he, he would not have been the man he was, I guess."

Kata recalled the poetry of Petofi and its ardent nationalism rising even above the love of women.

"Maybe not," Zoltan replied. "But, he might have been a happier man and lived longer, too," he said wistfully. His eyes stared into the distance as though searching the secrets of a far-away grave.

"Who knows? A lot of speculation, isn't it? I guess I'm too weary for that now, Zoltan. I think I'm going to bed early tonight." And she walked toward her room.

The young man's distant gaze returned. He looked at her as if wanting to say something. But he just rose for a moment in mock courtesy and uttered a curt "good night."

* * *

Kata could not sleep for a long time. She was frightened. What if Mr. Baumgarten did not return shortly? How could she manage without him? Of course, Zoltan was there. But the Russians might arrive sooner than expected, or the Germans might decide to concentrate their forces near, or in that very village. What then? Even if she were sure that Baumgarten would be back tomorrow, even tomorrow was far away.

She closed her eyes. She tried to concentrate on some pleasant thoughts. As if by magic, Istvan appeared. She did not want to dwell long on the sweet memories, though. The thought of Istvan, the reliving of his kisses and embraces, was too tantalizing even for dreams. But the remembrance of that last night before his departure did not leave her so easily. Was it the news of a young man dead and an old man dying, with the threat of new separations and unknown dangers, that brought to her memories of the heartbreaking mixture of tenderness and mourning? That, too, was a night when sleep eluded them, when life's treachery was a matter of tomorrow, though in those very moments, he and she were still lying in bed together, still holding firmly to each other. She could still cling to him and dream as though the morrow would be the same, that Istvan would continue to share her bed, and that they would spend the weeks and months to come together. Yet, she had known, even then, that this was but a dream.

But, what made it so hard to yield to sleep now? What was there to fear? In all likelihood her host and protector would return tomorrow.

As she struggled with thoughts and tossed on her pillow fighting both fatigue and the inability to relax, she somehow felt that it was not tomorrow that kept her awake. Things might be resolved by tomorrow.

She turned on the light and saw by her wrist watch that it was only eleven-thirty. She turned to her right once more and tried to sleep.

She might have dozed because she seemed to have wakened to some noise outside. She sat up with a start, holding her breath, to understand whether what she heard was imagination or some actual sound. Yes, there were steps, the door of the kitchen closing and those steps going through the dining room on to the master bedroom. She even seemed to hear the squeak of the bed in the other room and for a moment she thought with relief that Baumgarten might have come. But it was really too early for that. No, such an occurrence did not seem likely, unless he had changed his plan. And even if by some miracle he had arrived, the house sounded unusually quiet for this. It would have been strange for him to return without a word, without an explanation at least to Zoltan.

All was quiet now. She put her head back on the pillow. Then again she heard light steps from the bedroom, crossing the dining room. Steps nearing her door. She pulled herself up once more to be able to listen more intently.

The door opened slowly. She stiffened.

Could it be a stranger, a prowler? Was it perhaps Baumgarten? She seized the thought. Maybe it was Baumgarten after all, wanting to be sure she was all right. But it would be very odd for the minister to enter her room in the middle of the night without first knocking.

The tall figure in the dark doorway stopped for a few seconds as if waiting for some response. When none came forth, a quiet "Hi" reassured Kata as to his identity. It was Zoltan.

What does he want? She thought perplexed. She uttered a venturesome "Yes?"

Zoltan repeated the "Hi" in a muffled voice and moved toward her bed.

"Yes?" She asked again, her tone demanding clarification.

"Kata," Zoltan spoke to her in a strained, not at all hostile manner. "Kata, I was thinking. I couldn't sleep and I was thinking of the craziness of this war, of the life or rather the death of my friend, of the lives of you and me.

"Everything, everything is on the roulette table. I wish I had a conviction that some God is throwing the dice, but maybe a righteous and awful God is not interested in dice and maybe this is why He left us to the mercy of the Red and White."

"But Zoltan, it's hardly the time now," she protested.

"It is time to take life into our hands," and he reached out for the half-lying, half-sitting figure whom he could but vaguely see by the intruding moonlight, but whose breathing and pulse he could sense.

"Kata, Kata," he whispered huskily. "This is the only worthwhile thing to do while waiting for death," and with awkward fumbling, with inexperienced eagerness, he tried to pull her close. The girl held her arms firmly. The heat of the night, the memories of the past, the presence of this young man—this innocent, unsophisticated, demnanding country fellow—these all pulled her toward him, except—

"Zoltan, please! Please, stop!" Her voice was now both pleading and commanding.

"I couldn't, you must not!"

Zoltan edged nearer.

"Don't be silly, don't be foolish!" He muttered with fervor. "We're young, this is our chance. We mustn't let it go!" He fervently begged. His mouth was seeking hers as if he had never kissed a girl before.

No, he never has, she thought.

She felt a sweet longing, a magnanimous desire to be his first, to yield and forget the suffering, the danger, all the cruelties of life and death.

The memory of Istvan's love came to her again and for a moment it served to reinforce the desire, then, gave her the will to defend herself.

"No, no!" She felt the strength to fight the enchanting and enticing nearness. "No," she said resolutely. "I'd rather die!"

Zoltan shrank back for a moment, as though he was not sure he had heard her well. And Kata did not give him a chance to talk or move; she continued with manic fervor: "I'm at your mercy in this house, Zoltan, but I can't. I can't. Please understand! I would have to cry out for help. I don't know who would hear me, maybe nobody," she concluded in despair. "Maybe nobody," and her voice broke. "But if they did hear me and came to my rescue, it might mean death in some other way. Please, Zoltan, don't! Please, please, don't!"

The young man loosened his grip, hesitated for a second and then let her go altogether.

He rose and his voice carried both anger and embarrassment. "If you think I want your destruction, you're mistaken. I want you to know, though," he raised his voice bitterly, "that you and my brother—yes, the two of you—live in a dream world, a world of fantasy. Neither of you is facing reality. You came here to save your life in the same household with two men, and thought that no feelings would be aroused? How could you?" he challenged angrily.

Kata was struck by his words. Zoltan had touched a sensitive spot. For her, it was a matter of survival. For him the issue was of being a man: conquering, yet maintaining a sense of integrity at the same time.

"I'm sorry," Kata responded in a hardly audible whisper.

Zoltan was out of the room now.

Kata was shaken, depleted. She rose, tiptoed to the door and turned the key.

* * *

Baumgarten returned the next afternoon. The man whom he went to visit had died on the operating table. However, he was still alert when the minister had arrived and Baumgarten felt his was a necessary and important journey.

That evening Zoltan did not get home until late. Kata went to her room as soon as he arrived.

There was an embarrassed uneasiness in the air during the days that followed. Zoltan returned late every night and for several days gave little opportunity for the talk his brother offered to have with him. He seemed to avoid not only Kata but Laszlo as well. Baumgarten had a puzzled look about him. One night, however, Kata heard them talking late into the night. She felt somewhat relieved. The incident the other night had left her with guilt and fear that if the young man was so hurt, he might turn against her. Kata was sure that Baumgarten would have a soothing effect on him.

A week after the minister's night journey, he suggested to Kata that they go for a walk. By now she had ventured out with Baumgarten in the evening on a few occasions. Lights were dim in the deserted neighborhood and Laszlo Baumgarten's apparent confidence and courage touched her and imbued her with strength. In any case, they chose back roads and it was most unlikely they would meet anyone.

It was a brisk evening and she appreciated the opportunity to exercise.

After a lengthy silence interrupted only by some comments about the crisp air and the beauty of the night, Baumgarten started:

"Kata, Zoltan is a confused young man. I had a good talk with him yesterday. He seemed to have said that there was something with which he offended you; did he?"

"Well, there was something, yes."

They walked on. There was a long pause, then she said:

"I feel badly that my presence here has upset your lives so much. It was to be expected I guess. But your house meant such a refuge when I was so desperate."

"It is all right, Kata. There is really nothing to be sorry about—not as far as we here are concerned. You understand, and Zoltan must too, that the first order of living now is simply to stay alive. For the young, this is often not enough. Zoltan is young, naive, vulnerable, you know.

"Yes, I know, which is why I am sorry."

"All right then. I'm afraid he will not be able to stay out of active duty now. I'm sure it would make him feel good to know that you understand."

"Of course," Kata looked at Baumgarten with relief. It was good to feel that he was not so vulnerable. But he was quiet, as if trying to decide what more to say.

After a few minutes of silence he suddenly stopped in the moonlit frosty night, turning toward her and said:

"Kata, you say you understand. I wonder. Maybe you are too young, too, to grasp all the ramifications. But all this is not important now. The task is to stay alive!"

He moved on, Kata walking along without a word. Then, Baumgarten abruptly said: "It's time to go back."

* * *

"I have a surprise for you, Kata," Laszlo Baumgarten called in to the kitchen from the entrance hall. It was startling to see an unknown woman at his side—tall, simply clad, with interested look and a warm smile.

"This is Ilona Tothazy, a good friend of ours and my youngest daughter's godmother. Of course, this is Kata," he explained with a gesture toward her, "of whom I have spoken to you."

"You must be wondering about my sudden appearance," the woman seemed to sense her unspoken question.

"Let me explain," Baumgarten said. "Ilona is a nurse. She left Tokaj—where I used to serve, too, and we all met—as the Russians were approaching. She wants to move on to the West but first had to look up a sick aunt in the hospital in Pest who begged her to stay. So, I invited her here. Ilona needs shelter, you need company. I hope you don't mind."

"Of course, not." Kata was wondering how much Ilona knew. But she trusted Baumgarten's judgment.

"Three weeks ago my life was rather uneventful back at home," Ilona said later at the dinner table. "But it seems since I decided to leave I embarked on adventures: the travel on crowded trains, apprehension, an emotional encounter with an old woman whom I haven't seen for years, and now being involved in my meeting you, Kata, in your predicament."

"She was scared stiff but then I convinced her of the value of all kinds of experiences," Baumgarten said with a twinkle in his eyes. "Seriously, she wanted to come."

"I'll be visiting my aunt every day—the doctors say she's going downhill—but I'm looking forward to talks with you in the evenings."

So by the time Zoltan was to leave for the military, Ilona was settled, at least temporarily, in the Baumgarten home.

"Zoltan, I wish you well," Kata said as they shook hands. "I know your patriotic feelings, don't be reckless. I hope you'll have a long life before you, full of opportunities."

"Thanks. Thank you for your patience, too. And, I honestly wish you the best.

Kata nodded.

"Good-bye." She reached up and gave him a light kiss on the cheek.

"I'm ready, Laszlo," Zoltan told Baumgarten as he came in with his coat on.

They picked up his belongings, moved toward the door and, before it was opened, Zoltan freed his right hand and waved to Kata once more.

"Pull through! I hope that you and the child—and your husband—will soon be reunited."

"God bless you, Zoltan."

In a minute the two men were out of her sight.

* * *

It was good to have Ilona around. For Kata, it was a chance to talk with a woman again, even about such everyday things as setting one's hair or getting a pair of stockings, though Ilona wore her hair straight and believed in simplicity. Indeed, Ilona was different from her in many ways—serious, single-mindedly devout and somewhat reserved. Yet, she seemed to enjoy her conversations with Kata and to have a glimpse into her world. The two also exchanged gruesome stories—Ilona relating first-hand rumors from those who escaped the Russians, Kata telling about the three days before Baumgarten brought her to his home. In some ways they became quite close. But Kata was cautious about probing into her personal life. Ilona obviously was not married and there were no indications of men in her life.

"Really, it was not difficult for me to leave," she admitted. "My parents died when I was young and I used to be quite lonely. Ties with the Baumgarten family meant a great deal. Then they left, too. But I like my work and try to serve God as best I can."

Before Ilona's arrival, in spite of the men's company in the evening,

Kata had begun to feel quite isolated from the outside world. Of course, there was the radio and the news brought home from the city by Baumgarten. The minister also regularly visited her father in the hospital and saw her mother there as well. In the beginning Mrs. Vaghelyi even sent some clothing with Baumgarten. But it had been six weeks now since she had seen her parents and she often daydreamed of visiting them. But that would be foolish. If only she had some acceptable identification papers!

Ilona heard the conversation, as the topic came up between Kata and Baumgarten. In her quiet way she did not say much. After supper she excused herself and went to the bedroom where she rummaged through her valise. She returned triumphant.

"Look what I found!" She had a piece of paper in her hand.

"A birth certificate!" Kata exclaimed. "Whose is it?"

"It belonged to a cousin of mine, Katalin Tamassy, born in Brasso in 1917. Same first name as yours. She became orphaned and my mother took her in. It is the sheerest coincidence that I had the paper, mixed in with old photographs. I noted it yesterday when I took some snapshots for my aunt to see."

"And what do you want to do with it now?" There was hopeful curiosity in Kata's voice.

"Don't you know? It's for you! You can go to the city with it!"

"Oh, Ilona! But won't it be dangerous—for you, I mean."

"Don't worry. Katalin died of polio at the age of 12. Since her birthplace is Romania now, nobody would connect the name with me in any way. Nobody who does not know the family thoroughly."

Kata hugged her strongly. "It's great! I'd never have thought—"

"I'm glad I can do something at last."

And so Kata, with the help of Baumgarten, of course, went for a quick jaunt to Pest to see her father.

"I told your mother not to be there," Baumgarten warned Kata. "A visit to a hospital may be innocuous. But for three people—I mean both your parents and you—to control their emotions in public, is too much to expect. Your mother immediately agreed. She said she was fine and sick people needed visitors more."

"It's like my mother, I must say," she said with a smile. "Always deferring to Father. But you're probably right."

She put on a turban, wore dark glasses, sat primly in the train, reading. When they got off the tram, near the hospital, she and Baumgarten spent some time in the dark anonymity of a "Newsreels" moviehouse until the start of visiting hours so as to avoid needless loitering on the streets.

"Kata, I'd like to remind you," Baumgarten said as they approached the hospital, "we cannot stay long and you must be general in your statements. I warned your father about that last week. It's best for you not to get involved with others in the ward."

"I know," Kata replied. She needed great willpower to suppress her excitement and follow the minister as he led the way to her father's bed. Her father's eyes were flooded with joy. After Baumgarten's handshake, Kata bent down to kiss him. "I was afraid I'd never see you again," her father whispered.

"But I'm here!"

The visit was over in about ten minutes.

"Give my love to Anyuka," she whispered as she kissed him good-bye. "Perhaps next time!"

The next Saturday afternoon while Kata did the ironing and was waiting for her friends to return, an exhilarated Mr. Baumgarten, arriving alone, greeted her in the door while struggling with the wet galoshes before entering the parlor.

"My, you look happy!" Kata commented. "Did I miss some important news?"

"Listen Kata," Mr. Baumgarten finally came into the room. "Listen girl, last night—this part is sad news—all the Jews were taken from the so-called Jewish Houses to the ghetto. When I first heard of it, I was very concerned, wondering what had happened to your mother. I passed by the house and everything seemed to look the same as before. Then I went to visit your father in the hospital and your mother was there. She says some policemen came, looked at her documents, gave her a fright, but then, seeing the letter of exemption issued to your father by the church, they left. Can you imagine, all the other people living down the street—all those counting as Jews, that is—were taken to the ghetto, but your mother was spared!"

Kata felt a second of panic at the news of the ghetto transfer, the frightening image of friends and family probably within its walls, but

then she quickly focused on her mother's good fortune. She was free!
Her mother was free!

She repeated her exclamation of joy and finally placed a big kiss on
Mr. Baumgarten's jovial face. It was not only a kiss. She took his arm
and turned the man around and around, mimicking a dance.

"Mother is free, Mother is safe. Thank you for this wonderful message, thank you!"

Mr. Baumgarten was startled. He certainly could understand Kata's
joy and he himself felt elated. "Kata," he finally turned toward her,
freeing himself from the young woman's jubilance. "Kata, I understand
how you feel. I rejoice with you. I want you to know, though, that if
the Lord wants to save your mother, He can do it, whether in the ghetto
or otherwise."

Kata stood quietly for a moment but her buoyancy returned. "I know,
Mr. Baumgarten, I know, really. But isn't it much better that Mother
stayed in the building and that the Lord does not have to rescue her
against all sorts of odds? Isn't that simpler?"

"If the Lord wants to save Mrs. Vaghelyi, He will," Mr. Baumgarten
repeated his point.

Kata accepted the statement in the knowledge and relief that the poor
Lord would not have to carry out a very difficult task now. After all, her
mother was safe in her own apartment.

And so they rejoiced at supper time. Yet, stubborn little Mr. Baumgarten kept repeating, even in front of Ilona later: "It is up to the Lord
to save Mrs. Vaghelyi."

CHAPTER 10
MOTHER

DECEMBER 1944

I t was the eighteenth of December, and rumors of the Russians' nearing Budapest grew. The Hungarian news broadcast still boasted of German victories; it attempted to boost the spirit of its audience with the invigorating tune of "Marlene." But the careful listener could detect a slightly forced euphoria in the tone of the newscaster, a somewhat louder and quicker beat of the song to compensate for weakness in the content of the news.

Whatever the political implications of an imminent Russian advance, the collecting and hoarding of food became indispensible as an immediate measure of action. But the inhabitants of the ghetto had more basic worries.

No new developments had been heard about the people collected there and this Kata took as a good sign, trying for optimism. The Nazis might have priorities other than the deportation of another quarter million Jews. Trains were needed for more vital purposes, she speculated, for transporting and evacuating industries that still remained, and assisting the large group of Hungarians who had decided to move West, to Germany, if need be.

One has to wait and pray for them, she thought. She hardly noticed that the words were for "them" as if she and her nearest ones were not included in the predicament. But of course she could not avoid the issue, and she went over and over the potential dangers when she awoke one morning.

Ilona's rising diverted her thoughts. It reminded her of Baumgarten's plan that he and Ilona, in the course of their trip to the city, would try to pick up additional supplies of potatoes, in view of the potential Russian entry.

"We could carry ten pounds each on our way home, Ilona. I'll help you, don't worry," Baumgarten had suggested the previous evening. "It's expensive on the black market but without potatoes? No Hungarian could survive that!" Ilona was already dressed but she encouraged Kata to stay in bed and catch up on sleep. Kata did not need much coaxing. She did not really have much to do and getting up early in the morning only tended to make the day longer.

She turned off the bedside lamp, pulled up the blanket and listened for the slam of the door to be sure Ilona and Baumgarten had left before she could relax and abandon herself to the luxury of returning sleep.

The door did bang but she could not hear their departing footsteps.

The snow fallen during the night must have covered up the passage again, she thought. They must be gone. Yet, Kata had the feeling that instead of their leaving, somebody had come in. She sat up quietly and listened. It was always frightening to hear something unexpected.

She heard Mr. Baumgarten's voice without any doubt. Then there was Ilona also uttering just a few "Ohs" and "Ahs." Wasn't there a third voice, though? She tried to decipher its source and resolve quickly what to do with herself. But the voice seemed to be feeble, suffering.

Who could it be?

She listened more intently.

It was the muffled crying of a woman she heard, along with Baumgarten's sympathetic response. The minister's voice did not sound alarmed. Rather, it seemed to carry a good portion of incredulous compassion.

I must find out what is going on!

She rose, put on her robe and was nearing the door when she heard Baumgarten's calling her: "Kata, come out, see who's here!"

Kata first opened the door into the living room a small crack. Through the opening she could see Baumgarten and Ilona hovering over somebody and uttering words of comfort. She could not understand any of those words, but the posture and the tone were obvious. She was sure there was no threat here.

She entered the room. The two turned, stepped aside and said: "Look!"

Kata stood as if petrified. In the chair opposite her was the bent figure of her mother. Mrs. Vaghelyi's head was resting in her two hands covering her eyes. Her moist and tousled hair suggested a prolonged exposure to snow. Over her black dress she had on a wine-colored sweater.

Even the sweater was wet, Kata noted. She'd never seen her mother so dishevelled! And dirty!

She dashed over to the sitting figure, gave her a passionate embrace, and, erecting herself as if to be able to see once more for sure whom she was addressing, she asked with a disbelieving exclamation: "Mother, what are you doing here? How on earth did you get here?"

Kata's startled question was met with her mother's continued sobbing. Then, with a weak voice she muttered painfully: "They killed them all, they killed them all!"

Kata stood there, stunned, waiting for more. She was thinking of her father. There were recurring rumors about the raiding of the seemingly safest places. She had tried not to believe them. But now she had to face up to it. Could he—? Her mental question had to be voiced.

In a hardly audible voice she asked: "Father?"

Her mother's response was an unalterable: "They killed them all, they killed them all."

It was as if she had not even heard the question, as if she had been compelled to repeat the tragic news that somehow accounted for her presence here.

"They killed them all, they killed them all!" she continued unchecked.

"Mother, dear, hush. You're here with me now. It's all right!" Kata gently clasped her arms around the weeping figure. She tried to comfort her as if she were a child. But Kata herself was overwhelmed. She put her head against her mother's and her own tears intermingled with those of the elderly lady.

"Tell me, when did it happen?" She tried to impose some calm on her voice, but had to ask: "When did you see Father last?"

"I went there last Friday," Mrs. Vaghelyi finally heard her daughter. "I went to tell him the police were after me; they would not accept the paper."

"Paper?"

"Yes, the statement from the church justifying our exemption." Her hands jabbed at the air. "It was no good, they kept probing, asking for some other document. I didn't know what to do." The sobbing continued.

"Then? What happened then?"

"Your father said he'd try to talk to Dr. Garay, who was supposed to visit him that afternoon. I was to come back next day to find out what happened. But next day was too late. They took me and I couldn't get back. They killed them all, Kata, they killed them all." She looked at her hands and began to cry with renewed force. "Look, I have blood on my hands, I have blood on my hands," she wailed, as if in agony.

Baumgarten and Ilona first watched without a word. Then, beginning to gain some insight into the tragedy which must have preceded the coming of their unexpected visitor, they tried to offer some simple means of comfort.

Why don't you help your mother into something more comfortable, Kata?" Baumgarten suggested. "The best would be a nightgown. She should try to rest."

Mrs. Vaghelyi feebly protested. She wanted to remain awake, to savor the safety of this home and the nearness of her daughter. Besides, she was too keyed up to fall asleep now, she said.

"You must have some rest, Mrs. Vaghelyi," Baumgarten gently gave his order. "Take this," and he handed her a sedative that Ilona had taken out of her purse. The nurse had carried these pills with her ever since she left her home.

In spite of her protestation, Mrs. Vaghelyi obediently took the glass and the pill. As if in approval, Kata sank her cheeks again into the messy hair of her mother who seemed to be quieting a little.

"Come, come, Mother dear, you need some rest," she crooned as she led her to the bedroom.

Kata helped her mother out of the dress, slipped a nightgown on the limp, exhausted body, gently helped her into the bed that she herself had just left and, sitting on the edge of it for a few minutes, held her mother's head in her arms in silence. Only the tender touch of her lips upon the weary head spoke of the love that she felt.

Mrs. Vaghelyi's tears began to dry. She was clutching Kata's fingers, but her eyes were closed.

"Sleep now, Anyukam. We'll talk later," Kata whispered. A drowsy nod of the head accepted the suggestion.

Kata returned to the living room. The whole story was still an enigma.

"What happened?" Kata asked them in silent awe after she closed the door behind her mother on whom the sedative was taking effect.

"I'm not sure," Baumgarten said. "She didn't tell us more either. She must have seen some mass killings, Kata, but thank God it did not involve your father. At least, this is not what she is talking about. Let her sleep, and when she awakens maybe she will have a more coherent story to tell."

"I don't know what to say. This is just so incomprehensible. What shall I do now?" she asked, like a child who encountered a situation for which she had not been prepared.

"Do? Nothing. Rejoice!" Baumgarten said with a half-smile. "I know it is incredible," he continued. "I wish we could stay with you now. But we really ought to go to Pest. We'll need food now more than ever. Will you be all right, though?" Baumgarten seemed worried. "Would you rather have us around?" he asked with some uneasiness.

Kata shook her head. "You'd better go. You have to. Maybe you can come back a little earlier."

"I'll certainly do that. I guess your mother will be asleep for a while. Then you may want to be alone with her for some time anyhow."

Kata nodded.

"I'll leave the hospital earlier, too," Ilona offered. "I can meet you," she turned to Baumgarten, "and we can go and pick up the potatoes."

"We won't be long," Ilona tried to assure Kata as she kissed her good-bye.

Kata looked out the window in a confused and puzzled state as the two friends disappeared from her sight. It was entirely bewildering to think that Mother, whom she had thought safe, had gone through some unknown drama and that now she was here in this house, in the refuge of that good man.

"Oh, Lord, bless Mr. Baumgarten!" she said aloud.

This was all she could think of for now. In her thoughts she tried to unravel her mother's mystery but every idea was too painful to consider—a futile exercise—since her speculation might not be close to the truth.

Her mother would tell it herself.

She tiptoed into the bedroom and lay on the bed of Ilona and looked long at her mother in the other bed. She had not seen her since October and felt a flush of warmth come over her when looking at the curved figure under the blanket. The room was dark with the shades still drawn. After a while, Kata's eyelids began to close. She felt sleep coming over her. She tried to fight it at first, thinking of the need to be alert and active. Then she reassured herself that she needed to do nothing. It was all right to rest. Indeed, the presence of her mother with all the mystery that enveloped her arrival, filled the room with a feeling of security that she had not experienced since she had left home.

Mother and I together; we are safe. She felt comforted by the thought as sleep took over.

She slept and dreamed of the dawn of a new day when the snow would melt and the spring sunshine would bring new vigor to an exhausted world.

* * *

It was about one o'clock in the afternoon when Mrs. Vaghelyi began to stir. Kata, who had been awake for some time, thought her mother might find herself disoriented in her new surroundings upon awakening. So, she immediately spoke to her to convey her own presence in the room.

"Mother dear, you slept a little. How good! How do you feel?" And she bent down with a kiss, to accompany the words with the seal of love between them.

"Now I'm well, oh, how well! Rested." She confirmed as she held her daughter for a while as if to assure herself that Kata was indeed there. There was a sigh: "I can't believe it. I can't believe I'm here. I can't believe I'm alive."

Kata was aware of the trembling shoulder.

"Anyukam, why don't you slip into this robe of Ilona's? I'm sure she won't mind. Let's go into the living room. I want to hear your story," and she held the robe while she waited patiently for her mother to sit up, rise and slip into it.

"Thanks, my dear."

"The story?" She repeated as they were proceeding to the living room arm in arm. "It is a terrible story, Kata. I don't want to think of it," she said curtly.

"Of course, Anyukam. Relax. Put your legs on this stool here. I'll go and heat up some coffee."

She returned with a steaming cup and some butter—a treasure carefully rationed and consumed as special treat. What could be more special than this occasion, she rationalized as she dipped into the jar containing their savings for Christmas.

But Mrs. Vaghelyi would hardly eat anything. She slowly turned the bite of bread in her mouth without swallowing.

"I can't," she finally declared. "I can't eat now. But I will have some coffee." And she slowly sipped the Ersatz. For a while, she said nothing and Kata became concerned about the distant look in her mother's eyes as she emptied the cup. From time to time Kata's hands gently stroked her mother's sticky hair, which seemed in great need of a wash. She must have lain in dirty places to have her hair in knots like that. The touch of the stiffly distorted curls brought her in contact with whatever happenings her mother had lived through. It gave Kata a chill. She got up, paced the room a few times, then pulled the easy chair opposite to Mrs. Vaghelyi, sat down and quietly waited.

"I'll try now," her mother started.

"You know, they left me in my apartment at the time all Jews were taken to the ghetto. Not that they were unaware of my existence," she added with a sad little smile. "They did ask for documents, read them over, asked for more, looked at papers from our church and at notes of acknowledgment your father got from friends, and decided that I could stay where I was. What shall I tell you? It was a tremendous weight off my mind. We had hoped I would be exempted, but you know how these things work. One day they say you're all right, the next they put you on the list of the condemned. So after they came, the danger seemed to have passed. I thought once they sent all those people to the ghetto and once they left me in our apartment, I thought it was decided. But it wasn't that way." She paused and sighed.

"Maybe it's too soon for you to go over this," Kata said. "I shouldn't have pressed you."

"No, no. I want to tell you. I must!"

Indeed her mother, having started, appeared to have a need to spill it all out. She went on, talking rapidly.

"The next week they came again, different people, of course, and asked to see the document once more. They objected to its date, its stamp, and who knows what else? They wanted me to get the signature of the Bishop to validate it. At first it didn't seem impossible, except that I didn't want to spend more time on the street than I absolutely had to. Also, you know I'm not so familiar with official procedures and how to get into high offices. It would have taken too much explanation anyhow to get through to the Bishop and one never knows about secretaries and subordinate officials. So, I thought I better have Dr. Garay handle it. He's a good friend of ours, he's on a first-name basis with the Bishop and he could get the signature if it could be gotten at all. They told me I had time, until December 21st. So on Friday I visited your father and told him about the situation. He was expecting Dr. Garay later that day or the next and would take the matter up with him. If Garay could handle the matter, I would only have to wait for the return of the paper. If for some reason he couldn't, or wouldn't, I still had almost a week to try myself."

She stopped, her eyes staring ahead of her. Kata tenderly bent over her mother's hand.

"Oh, my dear," she whispered, "what terrible agonies you must have endured. Trying the impossible."

Mrs. Vaghelyhi's face produced a twisted smile.

"Agonies, yes! Much more came later, too." She nodded, confirming her recollection of the events of the last ten days. Her pressed lips seemed to be rearranging the words. She seemed struggling for a way to express the pain that she was now reliving.

After a deep sigh she continued.

"Friday night I went home. As I was sitting at my lonely supper thinking through my conversation with your father and our planning, impatient rings of the bell hurried me to the door. I looked out the peephole and saw the concierge with three uniformed Nyilas. I wanted to run away, to disappear. But where and how? It was impossible. I had the craziest ideas—to jump out the window, to hide under the bed. It was foolish, of course. I knew there was no escape. The bell rang again. I opened the door.

"Mr. Kocsis, the concierge, stood there helplessly as the three soldiers ordered me to show them my exemption. This time they just threw a quick glance at it and nodded me to follow them. I told them about the date when the signature was required, reminding them that there were still eight days left to get it.

"'Get going!' they ordered. They allowed me to step into the bath-room and put on a sweater and my coat. I tried to catch the eye of Mr. Kocsis, but he wouldn't look at me. I said something silly to him about watching out that no burglar enter the apartment, and followed the soldiers."

Kata listened, barely breathing.

"Their car was waiting downstairs. They motioned me in without a word. We drove toward Andrassy Avenue. Of course, it isn't far from the apartment and soon the car pulled up at Number Sixty.

"We entered.

"After the lieutenant glanced quickly at my paper, he impatiently shoved it to the side and ordered: 'Take her!'

"'Sir, I must get the signature,' I frantically tried to convince him. 'I was to get it on Monday and the date it was to be presented wasn't until the following Friday.' I continued with the fantasy that these were normal people who would be interested in and would listen to logical explanations.

"He didn't even answer, but, pointing his finger to the next room, he waved to the guard and then continued the dirty Jew joke he was telling his friend at the moment we arrived. 'So they decided to be smart and fool the Army and Itzig said . . . ' The door behind us cut short the sentence.

"We went through a narrow and dark corridor. There was a door and steps were leading down to the cellar. I could hardly see. I suppose the place was dark, but coming in from the brightly lit ground-floor room

I found it even harder to see. My escort pushed me through another door. I almost fell. By the time I straightened up, the door had closed behind me and the key had turned."

Mrs. Vaghelyi buried her face in her hands as if to shield off the next chapter.

"You want to stop, Anyukam? It might be too much for you to tell it all at once!" Kata encouraged her to rest.

Mrs. Vaghelyi shook her head. "I can't rest until you know it all," she whispered. She beckoned to Kata to come nearer. Kata pulled her chair close beside her mother's. Mrs. Vaghelyi wound her arm around Kata's shoulder and holding her tight, kissed the flushed cheeks.

"I can't believe I am here with you," she said, looking at her daughter, a crippled smile coming forth through the tears. "Only yesterday— But let me continue where I left off. Better to tell you all."

She sat back in the chair, arms folded as if bracing herself for the reliving of the experience.

"Where did I leave off? Oh, yes, going down to the cellar. I was terrified. At first everything seemed completely black. Then my eyes got used to the darkness. In a few seconds I was able to see figures. There were several men and women in the room. They sat on benches, or were spread out on the floor. I felt they were wondering about me—the newcomer.

"'Good evening,' I greeted them quietly, waiting for them to explain why we were all there. 'Welcome,' somebody responded sarcastically. 'Welcome to this Nyilas paradise,' and he swept a semicircle with his arm as if to point to the dark soiled spots on the far wall lit up by a kerosene lamp.

"I won't describe this in every detail, Kata, I can't." Mrs. Vaghelyi disrupted her story. "No, I can't. I must tell you this, though. There was no food. We had access to the water tap, that was all. There were no toilet facilities. At first I struggled with my needs. My companions said the guard would let us go into the lavatory before night time. We had several more hours to go. I became aware of a stench in the air. Those who were unable to wait for the guard had to invent make-shift arrangements. One of the corners served as the spot for public defecation. When the Nyilas finally came in about ten at night, they were furious at this. The man who had used the place as an emergency toilet had to clean it up—with his bare hands! We all turned away in disgust, feeling nauseous.

"We spent the night huddled together. Some of the younger ones whispered of escape. The rest predicted inevitable tragedy. We slept on and off and could hardly wait til morning. Though we had no inkling about the purpose and length of our stay, it seemed somehow that daylight would bring some measure of safety compared to the secrets of the night.

"The morning came. There was no breakfast. The guard referred us to the water tap.

"At about ten, some new people came. There were two men and a woman. The guard gave a special introduction to the woman.

"'Here is a loyal wife who has received her reward,' he announced. A middle-aged man slowly arose from the bench where he had sat for hours despondently. He stared at the woman coming toward him. She put her arms around her husband, fondly, gently, then passionately kissed his face, his head, his lips. 'At last!' she said as she pulled him to the bench. He was trembling. We later learned the woman was the Aryan wife of this Jewish man. She came to the place asking about her husband and insisted that she wanted him back. She was his legal wife and she had a right to be with him. They gave her the alternative of leaving, or joining her husband. She chose the latter. Poor Mr. Roth kept muttering: 'You shouldn't have, you shouldn't. What a wonderful woman you are! How lucky a man I am, but you shouldn't have, you shouldn't.' Magdolna sat beside her husband with spent tears, patting his shoulders, caressing his cheeks and rocking him, gently. She kept saying: 'I love you, David!' She sat there, leaning against the wall, erect, carrying herself proudly—a true aristocrat. But in the movement of her arms there was no pride. She embraced him as—not even a wife, as a mother, coming at all cost to the rescue of her child."

"How horrible! Or maybe I mean how great," Kata could not help commenting.

"The horrors are yet to come," Mrs. Vaghelyi sighed deeply. "Did I speak of rescue? If this is what she had in mind, it was wrong. Around noon, when our second tour to the lavatories was accomplished, the lieutenant who did the screening upstairs came down. He briskly patted his boots with the cane in his hand while scanning the victims. He pointed to David Roth and another woman, older than I.

"'You two, come!'

"Mr. Roth looked up with frowning eyebrows. Magdolna stiffened and firmly kept her arms over her husband's shoulder.

"'What are you waiting for, you bastard?' the lieutenant started toward him in anger. 'I said you come here!'

"There was no doubt that he wanted the man there.

"'You wanted to be with your lovey-dovey husband' he chuckled contentedly addressing Mrs. Roth. 'You will see now what a lover he is!'

"As Mr. Roth and the old lady, Mrs. Grunbaum, came forward, the lieutenant ordered them to the floor. 'You take off her skirt,' he ordered Roth. He turned in disbelief. 'But, but—,' he muttered. The stick came down upon his shoulders. 'No, no!' Magdolna dashed forward, ready to smash her hand into the Nyilas's face. 'Don't you dare, you bitch,' and his hand swung with a big blow to her cheek. 'You wanted to be with your husband, honey, you have it now. You can enjoy his presence and his activities. Down to the floor' he repeated the command. 'I said you take off her skirt!' Magdolna stood back in horror.

"'Now you make love to her. Off with your pants,' and he poked the slacks and shorts with his stick helping the man to nakedness. By now, David Roth hardly knew what he was doing. He acted as if hypnotized. He followed the instructions of the lieutenant, getting off Mrs. Grunbaum's skirt and bulky panties. 'One, two, one, two,' the Nyilas excitedly commanded. 'Look, the poor fool, he is impotent.' Come on, my boy, come on, shall I help you?' and he slid the stick along his genitals to arouse him. Roth was in a trance. He grabbed old Mrs. Grunbaum, he moved forward and backward, and was groaning like an animal expecting that the end was near.

"I held Magdolna's hand and squeezed until it hurt her. As she felt my touch I think it took her mind from the filthy scene for a moment. I helped her to sit down again. She leaned her head against the wall and sat there for a few minutes with closed eyes, motionless. Her cheek had reddened from the Nyilas' blow.

"'It's enough now, you lover.' The lieutenant apparently had had his thrill. He was all smiles and satisfaction as the door closed after him with a bang.

"David Roth straightened himself with difficulty. He was not really sure what had happened to him or to that old lady still on the ground. He helped her up. He seemed such a nice man, such a polite man, Kata. And the old woman was sobbing as she picked up the poor underwear. She staggered to the corner and lowered herself to the floor in disgust and shame.

"Time has stopped. The people in the cellar were silent. The water dripping from the faucet, the muffled sobs of Mrs. Grunbaum and the desperate lullaby of Mrs. Roth created a strange and frightening mixture of sounds. It is in my ears still . . .

"We thought we had seen the worst. But more was to come."

Kata quietly squeezed her mother's hand. She did not want to interrupt any more. But she had to make her mother know that she was no longer alone. But Mrs. Vaghelyi, if she took note of the gesture of her daughter, did not acknowledge it this time. She was apparently back in the cellar, reliving those shattering hours, and she continued as if driven to come to the ending of the story—the ending which would make her escape real.

"Our little group in the cellar was so exhausted," she went on, "that we hardly noticed supper time had passed. A full twenty-four hours, without any food for us then.

"Next day, there was little strength left in us as we were herded to the toilet. We all sat silently after we were escorted back. I began counting our numbers numbly. There were seven men and eight women. It seemed to me we were more yesterday but it was really too difficult to keep track or to think any more. We continued to sit in a stupor.

"In a while, the door swung open and the Nyilas shoved a young figure down the steps.

"'You bastard, you sneaky coward, you tried to escape!' He kept slapping young Isidore Cohen, a rabbinical student who had spoken of escape the day before.

"'I'll show you what your kind gets! Look!' He pushed Isidor toward the wall. There was a whip in his hand and it lashed down on the young man. We heard the groans and pleading: 'No, please no!'

"'You dirty bastard' the Nyilas continued, 'you smart alec who wanted to outwit us! What do you think, are we so dumb as to be deceived by a worm like you?' And his whip saw to it that Isidore Cohen's tall body slowly shriveled to the form of a worm. His shirt sweated blood. The soldier now went at him with his bare hands and knocked his head against the wall several times. Cohen stopped groaning. And the rest of us just sat there.

"'You will have to be punished for this,' he turned to us as if trying to rationalize his beastly outburst a minute before. He pointed to me, Magdolna and Mrs. Grunbaum. 'You come with me!'

"We proceeded to the yard. 'There, you pile up that wood; you're lucky to escape with that.' There we were, three feeble oldish women piling up twenty-five quintals of wood on an empty stomach. But the activity in a way felt good. At least we felt alive. Work seemed normal. We reminded ourselves that logwood has to be piled up when strewn, doesn't it? There was purpose in what we were doing.

"We returned to the cellar at night and slumped on the floor. I don't recall what else happened. The next I knew was that we were awakened. It must have been the middle of the night. 'All right, you beautiful ones,' the lieutenant's screaming voice expunged any sleepiness. 'All this will soon be over. Cars are waiting. On to the ghetto!'

"Kata, there were cars waiting outside. We weren't allowed to take our winter coats. 'You won't need them there.' Who cared? The ghetto seemed a safe place to us by now. I thought of Aunt Ferike and Uncle Tamas. At least I would be with people I knew, I thought. I was sure anything was better than the days of nightmare in that cellar."

She shifted her posture, and touched Kata for a moment as if drawing strength from her nearness. Yet, the gesture was instinctive. Though her eyes rested on Kata's face for a second, she continued absorbed in thought, and seemed detached from her surroundings.

"There were three cars outside," she related. "My place was in the third with Mrs. Grunbaum.

"We rode in silence. The night was dark and frightening. There were hardly any lights on the street. Curfew was at eight. The cars slowly rolled along Andrassy Avenue, then turned left on Terez Boulevard and right on Kiraly Street. Yes, we were going toward the ghetto. But wait, what is this? I thought in confusion. Here we were moving on on Rakoczy Avenue now on Kossuth Lajos Street and here is Erzsebet Bridge! We had passed the ghetto! I remember I looked at Mrs. Grunbaum to check my observation but she sat there with closed eyes. She did not seem alert and I did not dare to utter a word.

"The cars rolled on.

"As we crossed the Danube, in Buda we turned left, descending on the road along the quay.

"Suddenly, after about a hundred yards, the cars stopped. I saw the other passengers escorted out of their cars and disappear. Then our turn came.

"'Get out,' the Nyilas said and motioned us down the steps. All this happened suddenly and there was no time to think. 'Get down.' He ordered us to the pavement, covered with snow, where the rest of our group lay. I heard him say, 'Put your heads down'—and I was afraid not to.

"There were seconds of shuffled footsteps; I knew somebody stood over me and was now bent. I felt something cold on my neck for a moment and heard a click, but felt nothing.

"Then the man moved on. I didn't dare to stir.

"For a few minutes the three soldiers were still around—I heard them laughing and kidding with each other. It seemed they were bending down again but I did not feel their touch. I then heard one of them saying,'I think we can go, it's done,' and their quiet steps in the snow faded soon.

"I didn't move for quite a while. I wasn't sure whether any of the soldiers stayed and it seemed it was safest not to move. After a while it felt very cold, though. I knew I had to move soon or freeze there."

Mrs. Vaghelyi grabbed Kata's hand and held onto it, squeezing it. Her forceful grasp conveyed the emotions which accompanied the final part of her travail.

"I turned my head cautiously to the right," she continued, "where old Mrs. Grunbaum was lying sprawled out. Just a while ago I had heard her rattling breath. But now she was silent. I cautiously touched her. There was no response. By now it was really cold. I just had to do something, I decided. Again, I lifted my head just a little bit. Apparently everybody was gone, because there was no noise. As my head rose further, I saw red spots coloring the snow-covered ground. I touched Mrs. Grunbaum, but she didn't move. I sat up, looking around. There were no soldiers. Then I dared to look at my left. There were the sprawled-out figures of my companions, their blood trickling on the snow. I realized what had happened. I suddenly became aware that out of the fifteen of us two days ago, only I was alive at that point! I stood up, looking around. There was no soul to be seen. Before I left, I touched every one of them to see whether there was a response. No one stirred. I moved further down those steps, now quite near to the water. I must say, Kata, it invited me. I felt I could end it there, quickly, and the ordeal would be over. But then I thought of you, of your father, of Jancsi and my incomprehensible escape. I decided I must try further. If somehow I was left behind by some miraculous design, I could not give up the fight.

"So I went along the quay at the edge of the river. Here the snow was thin, the water biting into it from time to time. The pebbles made a little noise under my feet and I was scared somebody might hear me. I decided to turn toward the bridge and get up on the regular road. Carefully I climbed those stairs. Nobody was in sight as I crossed the street and was under the shadow of the big citadel. The Gellert Hotel—you know it's headquarters of German officers now—it was dimly lit. I couldn't hear the pacing of the guard, but I saw him. I decided to go the other way. So I quietly walked along the foot of the hill. The snow at that time helped me. It was not so deep that it hindered my steps. In fact, it must have fallen just some hours before. But it absorbed the noise of my steps. Soon, I was far enough from the hotel, the possible gathering place of my persecutors.

"'What shall I do now?' I wondered. 'Where can I go?' And then the crazy idea came to me to come here. It seemed an almost impossible plan. But any plan was impossible. To cross the bridge would have been out of question—the guards would surely have stopped me there. And where would I go, even if I did cross? I couldn't possibly go back to my apartment. They must have taken it by now, thinking that I would never return. I could go to the ghetto, maybe, but why should I? What was waiting for me there? It might be the same horrible experience all over again. No, if I had to take a risk—and there was no other way out but through risking—I'd better try to get to you, I thought.

"And here I am!"

Mrs. Vaghelyi looked at her daughter. Her eyes seemed to reflect a strange calmness, like the sea after a violent storm.

Kata looked at her in awe. Incredible! So these things do happen and they are true, after all. She could not understand how her mother had escaped, but the story was so potent that explanations could not be asked—at least not yet. Was it faith? The power of God unquestioned? She had no answer at present.

"Mother, but how did you get here?" she asked. "It's a long way from the Citadel to the streetcar stop and then to this place. How did you get here?"

"Kata, I think this is an even more unbelievable story, though it's not as dramatic. I decided to walk to the Szena Square. Of course, it is a very long walk. But I was so tense, in such suspense, so much in motion to do something and get away, that the excitement moved me along. I must have walked at least an hour but I did get to the end station. Then, there was the problem of money. They had taken away our purses before we left, supposedly for the ghetto. But the previous day, when the horror of the beating of that young man took place, I decided that our situation was beyond any reason and I must take irrational steps. So I took two one hundred pengo bills from my purse and tucked them into my stocking while in the lavatory. I knew this was a dangerous maneuver should they detect me, but then, everything was dangerous. So, before I got to the streetcar in a dark spot I took out the money and in the tram presented it to the conductor. This was his first run—five o'clock in the morning. He looked at me incredulously. 'You don't imagine I have change at this hour?' he asked and there was a touch of suspicion in his voice as he saw me undoubtedly ruffled and without a coat. I quickly got off. By the time the second car pulled in I smoothed my hair and tried again. By now there were a few passengers who probably were heading toward an early job in the suburbs. Again the conductor had no change. But now one of the passengers, a better dressed man—I wondered what his business was on the street so early in the morning—tenderly touched my arm saying, 'Allow me to treat you, my dear, you won't be able to get change at this hour.' I uttered a quick 'thank you' and sat quickly in the back seat, looking intently out of the window so as to avoid any questions. I did not have to fear. My benefactor discreetly took a seat in the front row.

"The streetcar rolled on. Finally, we arrived at the end stop.

"Of course, I didn't know exactly where this house was, but I recalled the address. Mr. Baumgarten told it to your father who had then told it to me. At the streetcar station a couple of sleepy Nyilas were doing their routine walks up and down. I passed them but they didn't notice me. I couldn't ask directions from anybody just then, lest they notice me. I just followed the widest road. As I marched on, a few early commuters passed me but said nothing. After four long blocks I decided to turn left, it seemed this was how the directions read. I moved along another three blocks and tried to make out the numbers. Some of the gardens were fenced, though, and the houses seemed to be far back. But I just couldn't find number twenty. I became nervous. It didn't seem wise to go back to the center and face the soldiers there who might question me. A man walked toward me and I decided to ask. He hurriedly showed me the side entrance to the house which was just two lots away. I found the long passageway leading up to the cottage and rang the bell. You know the rest. Baumgarten and your friend, I don't really know her, were about ready to leave. But he escorted me in and made me comfortable. And then you appeared."

Kata was speechless. She kept stroking her mother's hand which rested on the armchair. They sat there for quite a while. Then, finally, Kata said, "It sounds like a miracle, it really does."

"It was a miracle," Mrs. Vaghelyi quietly but resolutely stated. "Yes, it was nothing else but a miracle," she repeated.

* * *

It was slowly getting dark. "I'll set the table for supper," Kata said, returning to the reality of the place and hour. "Take some soup now, Mother. The warm liquid will be good after you haven't eaten for days!"

With the story told, Mrs. Vaghelyi seemed less burdened. She was able to sip the vegetable soup Kata had brought her before she set the table for the family. Fortunately they had some leftovers from the previous day which only needed heating up. Today, Kata could not have handled cooking.

Mr. Baumgarten and Ilona arrived at six. They quietly inquired about Mrs. Vaghelyi and asked no questions.

Actually, Mrs. Vaghelyi talked very little now. Kata later told the story in condensed form. She could not go through all the horrifying details now, she said; neither could her mother. Baumgarten understood.

"Rest, Mrs. Vaghelyi, rest, you dear soul. I'll tell you one bit of news though. I did visit Dr. Vaghelyi, I had to tell him the news. He was radiant, though he said he knew."

"He knew?" The two women looked at Baumgarten baffled.

"It seems Dr. Garay went to look up your mother, Kata, after she did not show up in the hospital on Saturday as she had promised. At the house they told him that your mother was taken to Andrassy-Avenue Sixty." He addressed himself to Kata, feeling that Mrs. Vaghelyi was still too weak to get involved in regular conversation. "He proceeded then to Nyilas headquarters. They chased him away. First he tried to insist that he speak with your mother. The soldier told Dr. Garay that he could do that if he wanted to, he could go in where Mrs. Vaghelyi was, but that they could not guarantee he could get out. Well, Garay felt that he might be more useful on the outside than if thrown into captivity, so he departed trying to think of some higher authority who might open the door for your mother. Before doing anything else, though, he went back to your father.

"'Erno, let's pray.' he said solemnly. Your father immediately knew something terrible had happened.

"After a while Dr. Garay told him as much as he knew and said he would go now and try to do something for his friend's wife. He left.

"Your father says that the first few minutes were heavy with doom. He had all sorts of wild ideas of getting up, rushing to Andrassy Avenue, calling up whomever he knew. But he realized this was all impossible, not only because of the political situation, but because he could not even move. His ribs were still bandaged and he was not allowed out of bed alone. So he remained lying there and kept thinking.

"Then he began to pray. He recalls that he prayed a while, then must have dozed off. At one o'clock he awoke as if in a start. Terrible fear came over him as he thought of his wife. A sense of helpless rage filled his mind. The frustration of inactivity seemed intolerable. But he was so limited. There was nothing he could do. Then again he decided to do the only thing available to him: he prayed. After a long while, he felt he could not go on any more. His strength seemed to have left him. There were no more words in him, no more thoughts. But somehow he felt a peculiar peace. Once more he sought God's help for his beloved. Then he felt the point had come when he would have to leave her in the Lord's hands. 'You know what you have destined for us and you will carry it out,' he concluded his one-sided dialogue with God. He looked at his watch. It was three in the morning. He felt depleted, exhausted but strangely at peace. He went to sleep."

"Three o'clock in the morning?" Kata asked in unbelief. "But Mother says that was the time her companions were all shot. She says she knows because once she got up she looked at her watch which was also hidden in a pocket and it showed three-thirty."

"Is that so?" Baumgarten quietly said. "Is that so?" he repeated. "I did not know this, but I told your father that your mother was safe. Of course, he was beside himself with joy and said he somehow knew that the Lord would take care of her."

Silence filled the room. The horror of the last seventy-two hours, the thought of the fifteen who died, the inscrutable ways of God, the unrelenting prayer of a man of faith and the choice of Sarolta Vaghelyi for life—all these were incomprehensible. But that evening the joy of the miraculous survival blotted out their questions.

Mr. Baumgarten looked at his watch. "Perhaps we shouldn't stay up late tonight," he said. He rose, crossed to the corner table and returned with the large family Bible. "Let me read before she goes to bed."

He opened to the Psalms.

"'He who dwells in the shelter of the most High, who abides in the shadow of the Almighty, will say to the Lord, My refuge and my fortress, my God in whom I trust.' " Mrs.Vaghelyi silently repeated the words. " 'For He will deliver you from the snare of the fowler and from the deadly pestilence,' " Baumgarten read it to her alone.

Kata's thoughts wandered. She recalled the joy she had felt when mother was left in her apartment, while the rest of the Jews down the block were taken away. "And I thought she was safe!" She felt so ashamed. "I was a fool!"

O Lord, forgive my unbelief! Kata offered her own personal penitence in silence. Then she listened again:

"'Because you have made the Lord your refuge, the Most High your habitation, no evil shall befall you, no scourge come next your tent,' " Mr. Baumgarten read on victoriously.

"I have mercy on whom I have mercy and I have compassion on whom I have compassion," Kata remembered in awe the verses she had repeatedly turned to in these last months. "Therefore, it is not his who wills it nor his who runs, but of God who shows mercy."

Baumgarten continued: " 'Because he cleaves to me in love, I deliver him; I will protect him . . . and show him my salvation.'

"And here endeth the lesson for tonight," the minister formally concluded.

CHAPTER 11
THE RUSSIANS

DECEMBER 1944-
JANUARY 1945

Kata spent less time listening to the radio after Mrs. Vaghelyi's arrival, satisfied with second-hand news brought from the city by Mr. Baumgarten.

She relished sharing each moment with her mother. She wanted to return, as it were, to her childhood when the world was safe and no harm came to her as long as Mother was there.

During the day the household chores and their very chit-chat made them suppress the immediacy of the evolving drama. But at night when the far-off city sounds subsided, the distant rumble of cannon reached them at the supper table. And if they ventured out for a short stroll protected by the darkness, the red coloring of the horizon, the darting bronze-hued lightning brought home to them that battles were now being fought in their vicinity. Kata found her fists tighten, her heartbeat race. She did not want to think of what tomorrow would bring.

In a sense they all tried to avoid painful issues. Mr. Baumgarten too—his separation from his family; how they were faring in his parents' home; what would happen when the military operations reached them? Indeed, what would his own encounter with the Russians mean?

They hardly noticed when Christmas Eve arrived, though they had a quiet celebration. Ilona brought home a small tree. They put on no ornaments. But they lit a few candles just to symbolize the hope for better days, a hope for the peace that had been heralded to mankind in Bethlehem two thousand years before. And, as they softly sang "Silent Night," it seemed to them the noise of guns came nearer.

* * *

Next morning, when Kata was heading toward the kitchen, she stopped at the living room window for a moment. The room itself was chilly and she hoped Mr. Baumgarten would soon be up from the cellar with their meager coal supply to provide some coziness on this cold Christmas morning. The smell of the small fir tree affirmed the season and while the day had started so differently from many former holidays when the "Merry Christmas" greeting of Father or Istvan would announce the morning, she felt comforted by the familiar sight of the snow-covered garden.

At least it is a white Christmas, she thought.

She rested her eyes on the whiteness spreading before her. Kata was pleased with the silence and the view. Red berries on nearby barberry bushes spotted the white monotony. At the far end of the garden, a fence served as footboard against the white down of snow with its grey bedposts of stone—the pillars of the garden gate.

All was peaceful. Nothing stirred.

As she stood there for a few minutes in quiet enjoyment, she became aware of some grey balls sitting on the stone ledge of the fence. It seemed to her she had never noticed them before.

I should know this place by now, she chided herself for inattention.

But as she kept viewing this hitherto unnoticed feature of the garden wall, she became more perplexed. Those balls seemed to be moving!

I must be dreaming, she thought, and she turned toward the room in the hope that she could check her impressions with somebody. But the room was still empty and Kata returned her gaze to the window. She pressed her forehead to the glass panes and with bated breath tested her senses.

All of a sudden she saw the balls moving to the right, then, forming a straight line, entering the long garden path. Now she understood.

She tore to the door and cried out for Baumgarten:

"Come, come, they're here!" Back at the window she saw the fur hats approaching.

Not only the minister but the rest of the family charged breathlessly into the room to check the happenings. Indeed, the Russian soldiers became visible one by one. They were nearing, cautiously moving up toward the house.

"My God!" Mrs. Vaghelyi muttered.

"Yes, they're here," Kata whispered. "They're here at last!"

Ilona just stood in stunned silence.

"Kata, go and hide! All of you, go, disappear!" Baumgarten burst out in a frenzy. "Don't you just stand there, please!"

And he gave a slight push to Kata to stir her to action. But nobody moved. It was a history-making moment. And Kata was not sure she wanted to avoid the experience. Indeed, for her and her mother, this was liberation.

But whether the women stayed by their own volition or were immobilized by panic, there was really no time to hide. The front door was thrust open and the powerful figures of four Russians towered above the family. The redness of their chill-bitten faces underscored the frustrated passion of the conqueror suspecting a trap in every corner.

"Quiet! Don't move!" A bulky lieutenant roared his command pointing the gun at them.

"Zdrastvitsy—Good Day!" Katalin said meekly.

After a second of silence, a disgruntled answer followed.

The man seemed to hesitate for a moment as if trying to decide whether the gun or his words should dominate the situation. He vaguely decided on the latter.

"Food!" he demanded in Russian, but nobody understood him. "Speak German?" and he asked for it in the idiom with which he obviously was only slightly familiar.

"Ja, ja " Baumgarten beamed and he pointed to the officer's right.

The lieutenant sized up his hostages and waved them to the kitchen. "Go, in there!"

Baumgarten stayed near the door waiting for the next command while the women quietly retreated from the sight of the uniforms.

The soldiers went to search the rooms, the lieutenant staying in the hallway from where he could keep an eye both on his own men and on the Hungarians.

The soldiers opened the bedroom door. Baumgarten's eyes narrowed uncomfortably at the sight of the unmade bed staring at him from across the living room. But the inspection there lasted only a minute. The men proceeded to the second bedroom, then to the lavatory. They returned to report to the officer. Baumgarten moved out of their sight.

A short period of questions and answers among the soldiers was followed by the bang of the front door. But if Baumgarten was prepared for a sigh of relief, it was too early to rejoice. Only three of the Russians left. The fourth, the lieutenant, was glancing at him with renewed intensity.

"Food," he snapped, repeating his earlier demand as he moved toward the kitchen.

Baumgarten solicitously pointed to the table. It displayed the treasures of the household hoarded for Christmas. Mrs. Vaghelyi and Ilona had gone to the kitchen in the morning to get breakfast together. And now, the smell of substitute coffee hit the nostrils of the soldier as he entered.

"Here, *harashow*," Baumgarten offered, and he proceeded to open the lid of the jam container.

The Russian glanced at the table's supply, picked up the loaf of bread, broke off the heel and greedily bit into it. He munched it with satisfaction for a few seconds.

"Take, sweet," the minister insisted.

The Russian eyed the blond apricot preserve with some suspicion but dipped his bread into it, then picked up the jar and cleaned out its inside by wiping it with the diminishing piece of bread in his hand.

A trace of contentment found its way into his tense features. He looked around.

The freshly washed curtains let through the sparkling white of the garden snow. The colorful print of the kitchen wall stood out in sharp contrast—a strangely cheerful background for the events of the day! The stove in the corner radiated heat. And the Russian noticed the women of the household scurrying around it.

"Coffee?" The minister intercepted his glance. And he was already at the stove filling a mug and returning with it. The soldier took it and gulped with gusto.

With his immediate hunger and thirst satisfied, his eyes now continued their wanderings. They went again toward the women. One of them was busy at the serving board of the old-fashioned cupboard adjacent to the stove. To the left of the furniture there was a door, slightly ajar. The Russian noticed this now. He frowned. With heavy steps he moved up to it, stuck his rifle into the wedge, then cautiously put his head into the opening.

There was not much to see.

The pantry was empty except for a bag of flour in one of the corners, a cut of fatback hanging from a peg on the ceiling and two or three jars with their unrecognized content behind the enamel finish. As he reached for the fatback, his boots caught in some metal.

"What the hell is this?" he blasted, angered by the unexpected obstacle, and kept attacking the handle of the trap door with his bulky boots.

"Cellar, shelter," the explanation came with unnatural lightness as Baumgarten lifted the rectangular metal to show. "Bomb," he said, pointing to the ceiling and swinging his right arm from its upward position towards the opening. A mimicked sound of "zoom" accompanied the word.

The Russian watched him intently, then peered into the gaping darkness.

He looked back at Baumgarten for a second, trying to size up the importance of his discovery. Then, as if deciding against further exploration, he began to turn back to the kichen.

As Baumgarten cleared out of his way, the Russian took a better look at the women and his eyes rested on the youngest. Kata had the kettle in her hand, the flame of the stove reflected in her cheeks.

He looked once again at the man of the house, then at the girl.

"Down!" He motioned Kata to the trap door with determination. Seeing her hesitation, he moved up behind her.

Kata stole a glance at Baumgarten but the impatient push of the gun stock made her move on. There was no time for consultation.

At the top of the cellar steps she tried the electric switch. It brought no results. She remembered that earlier in the morning the light had not worked but only now did she realize that it must have been cut off by the entering Russians. She reached for matches and the candle in a holder on the shelf.

"Go! Go ahead!" the Russian impatiently repeated.

They began descending into the dark.

At the bottom of the few steps, she struck the match and held it to the wick.

The soldier took the flickering light from her hand and cautiously proceeded. He lifted it to light nooks and corners. No peril lurked there. He turned back.

Kata took this as a signal that the search was over. She started up the stairs but the soldier ordered her to stop. He deposited the candlestick on a small table and with his long uniformed arm pointed to the sofa in the middle of the cellar. It has been left there by Baumgarten to serve as accommodation in case of bombing, though they all knew that a small house like theirs could not resist a direct hit. Yet, the shelter could protect them from debris and it was only sensible to be prepared.

The soldier, apparently relieved at the thought of finding no enemy hidden in the basement—and he must have felt safe enough about the one man upstairs as long as this younger woman of the household was his hostage—settled himself on the couch, with his gun leaning against it to his right, and with an immense yawn, stretched his arms upward. He spread his legs apart, unfastened the buttons of his overcoat and now, beginning to relax, eyed Kata with interest. He motioned her to be seated.

Kata sat gingerly on the edge of the sofa. She could not understand the words addressed to her in Russian, though she realized it would be important to try to talk. She said a few words in German; she had heard him ask for food in that language. She was lucky. The soldier seemd to have some knowledge of German—not a large vocabulary, just a smattering. The familiar words bolstered her confidence.

Kata made her decision: She must not panic. She must talk her way out of any potential difficulty.

She showed herself quite busy in trying to decipher the soldier's German. She gathered he was a teacher and she expressed some tribute to his vocation.

"What grade do you teach?" she asked, hoping to continue communicating.

He understood her carefully enunciated German but found it hard to reply in that language. Instead, he indicated with his hand raised, the height of a ten-year old. Kata nodded her understanding.

"What's your name?" It was the soldier's turn now.

When she replied, he offered his: "Vasilij."

They continued with their broken conversation, searching for words, putting effort into deciphering answers. Kata was glad to gain time. Yet, it was eerie to sit alone with the soldier under the feeble light of a candle in the musty cellar, isolated from the rest of the household. She kept up with the conversation while thinking of ways to leave.

"*Ich bin kalt*," she said in German, rubbing her arm vigorously.

"Never mind," he waved.

Kata pulled her sweater together.

The natural chill of the place was augmented by her fear. She sensed the increasing pressure of the situation. She knew she had to continue, though. Talking, prolonging was her only chance.

"You fought Germans on the front?" she ventured.

Her question was received with suspicion.

"I hate the Germans! They took my husband away," she explained. "*Die Deutschen nimm meinen Mann . . .*" She felt it was important to let him know. Or was it? And for a moment her idea of having the Russian know that the man above was not her husband did not seem to have been a wise decision at all. Well, she had said it.

Then, as if searching for a safer topic, she continued. "I have a son, too—look!" And the picture of Jancsi left her skirt pocket to bring a faint smile to the face of the soldier.

"*Harashow, harashow, wie seine Mutter.*"

Kata was not too happy with the comparison.

She tried to pursue the talk about the child. "I must go to see him soon—in the country."

The Russian nodded. For a while, he kept listening to her words, a mixture of Hungarian, Russian and German—perhaps incomprehensible but having something to do with a sweet little baby. Kata sensed the man's mellowed mood. He was looking at her with alarming eagerness. She felt uncomfortable. A strange memory came to her. It was a movie seen years ago, Russian soldiers in it courting a barmaid. In her adolescence the scene had seemed so colorful and adventurous. How different was real life! But she must struggle through, to survive.

Vasilij was moving nearer, his arm on the back of the sofa, encircling her in a tentative embrace. Kata stiffened.

She managed to move away, mimicked shivering and repeated: "*Ich bin wirklich kalt*"—really cold.

At this moment, Baumgarten appeared, muttering something in Hungarian.

"What the hell does he want?" The Russian's mood hardened. He grabbed his gun.

"Go, get out!" he shouted.

"Fire is upstairs, he says," Kata explained.

"*Feuer. Feuer oben*," the minister confirmed.

"It's really freezing here," she insisted.

He looked at her, muttered something and then resolutely stated: "*Genug warm*"—warm enough.

"Go!" He waved to Baumgarten with the gun. "Go back!"

The minister seemed undecided, but the soldier raised the rifle toward him with both hands, forcing him to retreat.

As Baumgarten disappeared, the Russian put the gun down again, but he continued fuming about the interruption. Then he turned to Kata, more forcefully now, ready to seize her hand. But he found her rubbing one hand against the other. He reached out anyhow and, as he touched her, she insisted: "*Ich bin sehr kalt*." Her hands were indeed cold!

Vasilij frowned. The thought of a cozy room upstairs was probably appealing.

"*Feuer oben?*" He turned Baumgarten's earlier comment into a question now. Kata eagerly nodded.

He thought for a moment, then relented.

"All right, let's go." He rose.

As they crossed the kitchen, Kata halted for a second. Her eyes met those of Baumgarten. She did not dare to look at her mother for fear Mrs. Vaghelyi might make some commment, arousing the wrath of the Russian. Her lingering, though, was an attempt to test the patience of the soldier. But he was no fool. With new authority assumed in front of these members of the household—the household of the enemy—he propelled Kata with his palm on her back into the room across the foyer.

"Get in there," he ordered her firmly. Then he followed on her heels into the bedroom and closed the door.

The room smelled fresh—and the bed was made. Her mother must have attended to this while they were in the basement, Kata gratefully noted.

The smell of the Christmas tree in the living room accompanied them through the crack of the door. Kata lowered herself on a chair beside the small round table in front of the window.

Vasilij pulled his chair near and took her hand.

"*Harashow*—pretty girl," he said, leaning forward and drawing Kata to him.

The need for action, for the use of some further delaying tactic, overwhelmed her. It was hard now to think of new topics, topics amenable to conversation in scanty German. She was frantically searching for possibilities. She managed to slip out of the arms of the soldier and as she turned she found her new topic.

"Look!" She pointed to the big black book on the night table.

"What? What is it now?"

"The Bible." She knew she was taking a chance.

"The Bible? What the hell do you want with it now?"

"The Bible is against adultery. I have a husband, you know."

In spite of her words, uttered in a seemingly matter of fact way, it seemed utterly preposterous even to herself to have referred to religion. Yet, she had to say something. To keep talking, gain time—this was her only chance.

After a second of perplexed watching, the Russian laughed somewhat uneasily.

"What rubbish is this, your Bible? There's no God. *Gibt nicht Gott!*" He almost shouted.

"I trust there is," Kata said with a low but firm voice, and some courage returned into her eyes as she viewed the man in the other chair. "I trust there is," she repeated.

"Fool, what a fool!" It was not clear whether his words referred to Kata or to his own willingness to prolong the scene.

"Fool!" Now he said it in anger and he grabbed her with a deliberate effort to act. He pulled her up as he rose from the chair and seized her wildly. He took her face into both his hands and his mouth pressed violently on her lips.

Kata fought and again got away. Without thinking, she wiped off the trace of the Russian's kiss on her mouth.

"No!" She said fiercely. "No!"

The Russian was in rage. He grabbed his gun, raised it angrily, and with fingers on the trigger poured a flood of curses upon the girl.

Kata knew the talk was over. "Please, don't," she begged. "Please," and she stretched out her arm towards the soldier. "I'm sorry." Tears were escaping from under her eyelashes as she held on to the chair and closed her eyes.

Everything was so unreal now—the long-awaited and prayed-for liberation now meant death or surrender. She had a flash of long-forgotten kisses—Istvan's kisses. For a second it stirred her to renewed resistance. But only for a second. Another image, that of Jancsi, demanded caution.

I must live, whatever the cost, she decided. She looked up at the soldier.

A minute of pause and watching. The tense coated arm slowly lowered the rifle and set it against the chair. The man moved forward and grabbed her shoulders.

Hungry lips pressing, pressing, pressing against her, his clumsy fingers now fumbling with her skirt.

Images, pictures, longings, wells of hatred mingled. Kata Vaghelyi Fogaras, eyes closed, was now in another world. She recalled once more the movie scene from the distant past. She was the barmaid now, the poor victim of ageless wars and numberless men.

Time stopped. And as she almost collapsed from fear, submission and despair, suddenly the eager hands loosened their hold on her waist.

The man stepped back.

Voices reached her numb ears from the other room—the Russian speech of one or two, mixed with excited Hungarian replies. In a second, the door pushed ajar and there stood the major and his adjutant taking in the scene and greedily inspecting the comfortable bed, the now warm room, thinking of nothing else but sleep under warm covers.

Vasilij stood at attention. His loosened belt hanging improperly on the side of the uniform. The major did not reproach him for it, perhaps he felt sorry for the young man whom he had evidently interrupted in an awkward moment. But his own need for rest was overwhelming and the order came with a shrill voice:

"The room must be ready for occupancy in five minutes."

Vasilij's hands dropped from his fur hat. His face showed frustrated anger. He bit his lips for a moment pondering whether to go against the order. But the girl was already in the far corner.

Vasilij grabbed his belt, adjusted the buckle and picked up the glove he had dropped earlier.

As he walked out of the room passing Kata, he threw a last glance at her. The major's arrival had changed her panic into humble gratefulnesss. She knew she was safe, at least from this danger, and she looked at Vasilij now with a friendly smile as if thanking him for the patience he had demonstrated.

And Vasilij, with apparently mixed emotions of frustration, anger and tenderness, muttered under his breath, moving his finger in front of the girl as if expressing admonition.

"*Lese Biblia, Katalin und sei gutes Madchen*," he told her in broken German. "Read the Bible, Katalin, and be a good girl!"

With this, he slipped out of the room.

Kata stood there for a moment with unbelief. He was gone! Then she rushed toward her mother in the living room. "Mother, another miracle, another miracle. This time it happened to me!"

* * *

On the day that Kata escaped the advances of Vasilij, and escaped them with a sense of providential guidance, the family began to experience other aspects of life in a village occupied by the Red Army. The major who sequestered living quarters in their house must have guessed Kata's earlier short-lived trial and decided to play the refined cavalier to the Baumgarten household. He invited the family to join his dinner table, which he shared with a captain. The captain himself proved to be a friendly Jewish chemist from Kiev. He knew Yiddish, and hence, understood German. He and the members of the household were able to communicate with one another.

The major presided over the table with self-conscious dignity and said little. But the captain listened with interest to Kata's story about her husband who had been deported by the Germans. He himself had lost his family in the Ukraine. When Mrs. Vaghelyi told him about her own ordeal under the Nazis just two weeks before, Captain Ilievitch gave her a warm embrace, expressing his sympathy for the sufferings of this elderly woman.

This was but the first of similar gestures experienced from time to time when Russian soldiers approached Mamuska. It did not require an educated officer to show respect for age. Some days later when Mrs. Vaghelyi washed a shirt for a young corporal, he paid her generously, as though she had had any choice in the matter.

Then again, there were wild groups of young Russians barging into the house from time to time. By now, the women knew they had better hide, at least until more was known of the particular men who happened to enter the house. If a group held wild celebrations in the living room, Baumgarten himself represented the family. Once they had searched the house and felt relatively safe in the strange surroundings, the Russians were in fact quite respectful of the families with whom they lived. Soldiers quartered in a house offered protection against outsiders. Only when they were under the influence of alcohol did one have to be careful. Baumgarten endured some trying hours of one evening's revelry when one of the soldiers goaded the others by teasing that he would throw a hand grenade into their midst.

"It was terrible," Baumgarten told the women later. "If he'd thrown the grenade, it might have killed not only those in the room, but you in the cellar as well!"

After two weeks of occupation the first group of soldiers moved on. The Baumgarten house was empty of the military for a while. That is, there were no troops stationed in the house itself. However, they never knew who might appear during the day or night for food, for room, or just companionship.

The women never undressed at night. They changed only in the morning, while one member of the household was watching the garden and the street beyond it so as to be able to announce the possible arrival of any soldiers. The women took their turn washing up, quickly and furtively.

The siege of Pest raged. A group of soldiers knocked at the door one night. The three women were sleeping in the bedroom and Baumgarten rose from his bed to open the door. Of course, the women awoke, holding their breath as the bedroom door was pushed open. Flashlights blinded them for a moment.

"Get up, get up!" The soldiers snapped.

As it turned out, this was a friendly group who wanted some company—nothing else. A young officer among them, Fedor, took a liking to Kata. He was respectful and gentle. He looked at the family pictures produced in an effort to provide a peaceful atmosphere and showed his family—mother, father and sisters—in return. Though he understood that Kata was married, he returned to visit her several nights in a row. He inquired from night to night how the family was; he made some vague half-joking hints of marrying Kata should her husband not return and after two weeks he disappeared with the rest of the group— probably to join the combat forces participating in the siege of Pest.

* * *

Pest fell on January 18 and there was at least some hope now for reunion with Father.

CHAPTER 12
BACK TO PEST

FEBRUARY 1945

Kata was on her way to the county hall to find out about a pass.

"Let me try to see, Anyuka, if we couldn't get back to Pest soon," she had explained as she was getting into her boots that morning. The county hall was on the far edge of the village, serving two adjacent communities—about an hour's distance with a comfortable walk.

The snow-covered village seemed to be coming alive after lengthy hibernation. Hibernation? The word struck her as strange. But in a way it was true—the village was merely surviving from one extreme to the other. Five weeks ago, Hungarian Nyilas had been surveying the lonely streets. Now, Russian soldiers were busily moving here and there.

They were not quite as ominous looking on the streets as they'd been in the beginning. They were almost "old friends," Kata thought wryly. The Russians now had an air of settledness about them. They were not the front-line combat troops who had been moved to Pest and would be moving on from there—Pest had expelled the Germans! And the Jews were free, Kata thought jubilantly. They had already heard rumors of the survival of the Pest ghetto and its population.

The Russians, the soldiers, were dangerous. The country's future was uncertain. Communism loomed in the doorway. But it would affect everybody, not just her, not just her family and her people.

"At least, the Russians are not my personal enemy!"

But it was not just a change in the Russian occupants that gave the village a more vital and less fearful appearance. A number of civilians were in sight, swinging open iron garden gates and moving in the same direction as Kata. Though the village at this morning hour did not seem lively and populated, the pre-siege gloom was now replaced by pur- poseful activities of men and women here and there. The time had come to think of food tickets and travel permits, the latter issued on a very limited basis. The main object of travel passes was to try the newly constructed makeshift bridge to Pest where many of the little town's inhabitants had families and a majority of them gained their livelihoods. At least one could find out who was alive and which building had survived the bombings and shellings.

The path she took was a country road with long stretches flanked by farmlands resting under the snow. The air was crisp, the winter sun shone brightly and life seemed almost joyful after the weeks of self- imposed incarceration.

Kata began to feel good. It was wonderful to be out, to move freely, to be able to think of the future once more. The strange thing was that her anticipation did not encompass important events and significant reunions. Her thoughts were rather prosaic—eating a fresh roll softened by two layers of butter embracing several slices of spiced Hungarian salami, followed by a cup of hot chocolate with whipped cream. What a combination! How earthly her wishes had become! But to think of people, the return of Istvan—oh, no, she'd better stay with non-essen- tials.

She stopped on the road to take in a wider sweep of the landscape. On this stretch there were no houses for a distance of about three hundred meters and the view on the left was clear and unshadowed by clouds or creatures. The earth was welcoming the touch of the sun above her head.

She took a deep breath, wanting to confirm with every sense the long-missed goodness and wholeness of life. A peculiar sweetness hit her nostrils. She turned to her right. Another field stretched its snow cover far to the horizon. But the white in front of her was marred by a dark blemish some hundred yards away, breaking its innocent virginity. Kata eyed the spot but could not really make it out. She was puzzled and aroused, even annoyed, at such interference with her carefree daydreaming. She wanted to see this sore on the earth, the dirt on the gleaming white. She walked toward it dipping her boots into the snow of the field. All of a sudden her feet became rooted. There was the body of a German soldier frozen in a snowy cradle. From the road only the dark shoulder of the uniform and the rim of the tilted cap had shown an undefined heap. But now, nearer and from another angle, the gaping mouth of the soldier, the jellied eyes staring at Kata, the bayonet lying beside the body brought home to her the reality not only of her own life but that of all people. She shivered.

I'm dreaming of food and he's dead forever, she thought. I was not even thinking of my family, or their survival, only of my satisfaction, and this man is dead. He will never eat, never sleep, never see his family.

The soldier looked to be in his late twenties.

He might be married. Maybe he has children. Maybe his wife is telling them that the war will soon be over and father will be back!

I am crazy, Kata thought. The Germans are not waiting for the end of the war, they are not yearning for peace. They want to kill and conquer. They want to exterminate all the Jews. One less German brings the day of peace nearer. Yet, the thought of two little children persisted.

Maybe they've just got the telegram about "faithful and loyal service to the Fuehrer and country." Two little children, now fatherless, Kata continued in her imagination. Maybe Jancsi is fatherless. Who knows, if Jancsi is even alive?

She turned and with much slower steps, as if burdened by a weeping heart, continued her journey for the pass.

* * *

A week later, her heart pounding, her legs ready to sprint, her brain mindful of the need for caution and alertness, Kata was getting her belongings together and calming her mother. They were leaving. The events of the last four months zig-zagged in their consciousness—flashes of terror, human compassion, divine rescue, priceless friendship and a haven of safety and comfort. And today, on February 16th, mother and daughter would once again risk the odds, but now with reasonable confidence that they would see better days. Going home! Going home! Yet she had no idea what they would find there.

"Mr. Baumgarten, how can we thank you?" Kata muttered with her coat on and her knapsack tied. "There are no words, really no words," she repeated.

"Thank you," Mrs. Vaghelyi said with voice cracking, throwing her arms around the man. "What a gift of God! First my rescue, then your home! I can't thank you and Him enough."

"All right, all right," the minister rushed them with some embarrassment. "It's important that you be off early. It will take a long walk."

Mother and daughter slipped into their coats, Kata adjusted her knapsack and helped her mother's nervous fingers tie the scarf on her head. There was a quick exchange of kisses all around.

"Ilona, you were magnificent, too. That birth certificate!" Kata hugged her fondly. Ilona smiled with uneasy disbelief remembering her contribution to the rescue operations.

Mrs. Vaghelyi and Kata walked for at least two hours before they reached the Danube. The flow of people increased, converging from various localities of the Buda shore, and they found a crowd near the entry of the bridge, the only means of crossing this section of the river. The narrow bridge could not accommodate two-way traffic. The military monitored the movement alternating toward and from Buda and the long lines brought frustration, tiredness and mishaps of varying kinds to those waiting on the shores. The wait seemed endless.

Finally, they were on the pontoon. The crowd pushed and pulled. "Let's stay in the middle, Anyu," Kata warned. "It's easy to be swept off." Mrs. Vaghelyi looked at the ice crust below and huddled closer to Kata as they moved along with the throng.

They reached the shore of Pest around three in the afternoon, later than they had anticipated.

As they walked from the Danube toward Kata's old apartment, beyond Varosliget, the skeletons of bombed buildings stared through their broken walls at them. Here and there on the way, dead horses littered the avenues and filled the air with the sweetish smell of their carcasses. On the main thoroughfare, where their route led them, human bodies had been removed earlier but the turn for clearing the street of dead animals had not come yet.

During the final hour of their journey, Kata and her mother walked without words through the dusk. The nearer they came to the house, the more their anxiety mounted.

And now they were on the block.

Mother and daughter embraced each other wordlessly. Then they moved briskly toward Kata's house.

Their first glance seemed to indicate that the building—the front of it at least—was intact. Of course, everything was dark.

"Shall we see the rest?" Kata asked with hesitation. "I dread going into the apartment, Anyu. Particularly at this hour, with no light—who knows who or what is within. I'm scared." She glanced across the street. "Let's see if we can find Irene first. I see some light flickering through the window." Her mother nodded.

The two women crossed the street and moved to the gate of the two-family home of the Banats.

Their fumbling with the latch, as they tried to open the garden gate must have alerted some people within. An inquiring face appeared behind a candle light. The flame wavered; the hand holding it was losing control. Then, in the swiftness of a second there was an exhilarated exclamation announcing their arrival to those inside, rushing steps, and before they knew it, two strong arms held them firmly.

"Papa, Papa!" Kata turned to her father-in-law. "You're here, you're well! And the others?" came the trembling question. "Who else is here?"

"All is well, Kata, welcome Sari, welcome, my dear," he turned now to Mrs. Vaghelyi. "All is pretty well." He would not amplify until they got into the apartment where her mother-in-law and Irene appeared and Kata and her mother were firmly clutched in their arms.

"Erno is well; he is in a deaconess convalescent home but sent word two days ago that he can leave any time you arrive. And—did Papa tell you?—we got word from Mrs. Kovacs, too."

"You did? What? Jancsi?" And her sister-in-law's smiling face conveyed the wonderful news more eloquently than her words.

"He's fine, he's grown. They say he even speaks Russian; can you imagine?"

"Jancsi can talk, and even speaks another language!" Grandmother exclaimed. "So the two—Jancsi and Erno—are alive and well. God, O God, how can I thank you!" Her hitherto repressed sobs burst out with full force now.

"Anything about Istvan?" Kata hesitantly asked.

"No, nothing—we couldn't really expect that. Nobody has heard anything."

Of course, Irene had not heard of her husband either. Imre Banat had been inducted into a labor group under the military at the end of the summer. But they all knew that at least in the past a number of labor units had returned and their members survived. It might be safer even now.

The women sighed. "No news is good news," Kata tried to tell herself. "How insatiable one becomes. Two wonderful pieces of news must be enough for tonight!"

"There is so much to ask, so much to hear, I don't really know where to start," Mrs. Vaghelyi turned to her in-law.

"We'll warm up some soup first of all. You know, our supplies are very meager," Mrs. Kalmar said as she moved toward the kitchen.

"Maybe, maybe we can settle down in our own place soon. Can we? How is my apartment?" Kata asked. "I didn't dare go in."

"The back part of the building has had some shelling damage, Kata. Most of your furniture is intact, but I'm afraid the closets are empty. I checked."

"But can we sleep there?"

"No! The windows are mostly gone. It's terribly cold, particularly without firewood. But look," Irene continued, "your parents' old apartment seems to be intact. There are some people living in it—in two of the rooms—the rest is yours. Mr. Szakacs, the concierge, looked us up last week. He brought the news of your father and said you can all use the place there."

"Hm. Maybe this is what we should do, Anyuka. At least for now."

"But, listen, this is no time for planning," Mrs. Kalmar interrupted. "You can certainly stay here for the night. You need the rest and we can continue talking. Then tomorrow—tomorrow you can decide on the next step."

They washed up, were warmed by the soup, and for a long while listened.

It was the story of the Pest ghetto, where the Jews of the city had awaited their destiny for about six weeks, hearing continuously changing rumors of coming deportation and executions. Some of the men were indeed picked up from the ghetto apartments, never to return.

Others disappeared from the street when they went out for the food ration during the appointed hour. But the ghetto as a whole remained intact and with few shell marks at that. There were wild guesses going around as to the reason for its relatively unharmed survival. The Germans, overtaken suddenly by a many-pronged attack, apparently had had no time to do anything about the ghetto. As for allied bombs and other attacks, some said they had not been directed at that segment of the city because the Russian commander leading the siege had had a family member there.

"And here we are, the two of us, too," Kata added her mother and herself to the number of those who had survived.

"But tell us about you, Sari!" Mrs. Kalmar asked. "We heard that you had escaped when we learned of Erno's survival. But we don't really know how it all happened. How was it?"

"It's a long story—a miracle!"

"Why don't we all get ready for bed," Irene suggested. "As you can see, we all live in this one room, the rest of the apartment has been occupied in our absence. But we do have an extra mattress. I'm afraid that the two of you will have to share it."

"At least we can keep each other warm!"

Soon the five stretched out on three mattresses. One candle spread its feeble light. Then the family heard the details of Mrs. Vaghelyi's miraculous escape and a lingering chill filled the air.

Kata and her mother in turn asked about other members of the family and friends. Some had escaped, others had died, and not all by Nazi actions—Mrs. Kalmar's sister had died three days after leaving the ghetto.

But in spite of the tragic stories, they could see that a surprising number of people among the Jewish population of Budapest had emerged from one place or the other.

"Why me? Why us?" they asked, and silently remembered all the others taken from ghettos all through the country. It was impossible to understand why some had perished and others been saved.

"I have mercy on whom I have mercy," the words came to Kata again. "It seems it is not up to us," she said with awe. The others quietly nodded.

* * *

"Dr. Vaghelyi? Room 214," the front office told her. "This is his daughter," the receptionist explained to the white-coated figure coming into her cubicle in search of an address.

"Oh, yes, he's been waiting for you for the last several days," the man nodded to Kata. "I'm on my way to the second floor; I'll take you there if you wait." He jotted down the information he needed and waved toward the stairs for Kata to join him. She could hardly control her excitement.

"I am so happy my father was brought here; is he well?"

"Yes. Rather frail but basically healed. He needs a lot of rest still. He—in a way all of us—went through trying times. There were decisions to be made, difficult ones—he will tell you about it. Why don't you just go in, over there?" He stopped at the second floor landing. "I'll be back a little later."

Her father lay in bed, napping. She stood at the bedside a few moments choking as the tears welled up unrestrained. He was alive! "Oh, God . . . " Her gasp aroused the white-haired sleeper. It took but a second for him to awake, to grab her hand, to clutch her shoulders bending over him. Sobs burst from him.

"And your mother?" A momentary shadow crossed his forehead.

"Oh, she's fine, Apu, she's fine, she can hardly wait for your return. I persuaded her not to come, we were on the road yesterday for eight hours. It was a difficult trip in many ways. We'll tell you about it later."

Her father nodded. "You and she," he gazed at her with the gentlest fondness, "yes, particularly she, I guess, has gone through terrible events. But God brought us through, in miraculous ways. Even I, you know, I too, was in a most precarious situation, a very frightening one until the last minute."

"I'm so glad they brought you here."

He nodded, closed his eyes as if to rest for a moment. But tears still escaped from beneath the shut eyelids.

"Oh, Garay was wonderful," he continued, looking at her once more. "But then the director—a fine Christian in a way, but I don't think he really understood the implications. He was, of course, ordered to report on the true identity of each patient, and he knew. He took pains to talk to me about it several times. He seemed undecided as to what to do—the lives of other patients would be at stake. Then, 'Let what you say be simply "yes" or "no." Give Ceasar what is Ceasar's.' It was—he was to submit my name the next day. Then the Russians arrived. He was absolutely happy, relieved, the decision had been taken out of his hands."

"Apu, apu!" Kata bent down again to hold him in her arms.

"Here he is," her father whispered as the director entered the room. "Dr. Balogh, meet my daughter."

"I already did," the man who had escorted Kata upstairs put out his hand. "At last your father can join his family. How he has been longing for the day!"

"I want to thank you," Kata tentatively started. The man had wavered, Father said, but then— "I'm just realizing how precarious the situation was, even here."

"Everywhere. You may not have heard it, in some hospitals they rounded up all the patients—down to the cellar and then the firing squad. I just was told about the Maros street Jewish Hospital in Buda— over 100 people. But let's talk of your going home," he addressed Dr. Vaghelyi. "Do you have a place?"

"Oh, yes, my parents' old apartment—a part's available," Kata answered, then turning to her father said, "in fact, Mother is waiting for you even now. When can I take him, Dr. Balogh?"

"Well, any time, really. I guess you need some transportation. Why don't you come to the office a little later? I'll be down in ten minutes. We can discuss details then," and Balogh left.

Her father was stroking her hand, his moist eyes fixed on her joyous face. For a while he said nothing, then added: "Unimaginable ranges of human behavior: fear, ambivalence, courage and faith."

She kissed him again and held his head in her arms for quite a while.

"Let me go to see what arrangements are possible, Apu," she finally said, dabbing the tears off her cheek. "I'll be back soon."

She found the doctor. "Could you—would you like to—take him today? The driver has to pick up some patients at the Magdolna Hospital and could pass by your address. Are you prepared?"

She shrugged her shoulders, laughing. "Prepared? No. What do we need? Unless, could he perhaps have a meal here before we leave? I don't know how much we can get organized this afternoon, but we'll be settled somehow by tomorrow."

"Surely. He may have dinner; the driver won't leave for another hour."

So father was coming home! Or at least the couple of rooms they could still claim as home.

They got him into the ambulance, and the driver and his assistant carried him up the one flight once they arrived. Father could walk on flat ground, though with utmost care, holding on to someone or using his cane. But it was obvious he would have to be stronger before he could try a staircase.

While the attendants were helping her father in, Kata went ahead to tell her mother.

A shriek of joy—a dash towards the door. "Erno, Erno, my dear," she cried.

"Wait, Anyu, wait!" Kata sprang to her side, grabbing her by the arm, until the men seated their ward.

"Now he's yours!" She let go.

A delirious cacophany: outbursts of unintelligible sounds, threads of endearment—arms entwined.

Once the outside door was locked after the attendants, who were eager to leave, Kata wandered aimlessly into the kitchen. No one else was there so that she sat down in her mother's domain—that's what it used to be when she was a child, then growing up, ages, ages ago. She kept sitting there, just looking into the air.

So the three of them were reunited.

The next step was Jancsi. It would take some time, but as soon as she could she would have to bring him home. And Istvan? It was out of her hands. There was nothing she could do about him. She would just have to wait.

"Lord, help him, please, bring him home, too!"

CHAPTER 13

THE CHILD

FEBRUARY-APRIL 1945

A struggle started, very different from that of the previous year. They had to find ways to live in a starving city.

The food package handed over to Kata by Baumgarten just before she closed her knapsack lasted three days; it gave her a little leeway to get organized. It was obvious she would have to reach out in all directions. Stores were still closed and people lived on supplies they had been able to hide earlier. But where were the Vaghelyis to find provisions?

The capital's food supply had been extremely low even before the siege. The stringency of a world war rationing beginning in 1940 had, in retrospect, been "good times." If imported goods, such as coffee, tea and cocoa, were available only at increasing prices in the beginning, and if later meat was rationed in the city, on the whole, nourishment had still been plentiful. Even with the advance of the war, supplies were limited but not unattainable. And the population had begun to store and budget, pay black market prices and hide purchases, preparing for bleaker days to come. Then, during the three or four weeks when the bombs and guns were at their peak, the city's first effort was to survive

167

the ordeal. No lines of communication with the agricultural section of
the country were open then, and the population had to rely on ac-
cumulated provisions. Some had enough to last them through the siege;
others, a little more than that. But their carefully guarded supplies often
went into raiding Russian hands, while the stores were empty and, in
any case, still closed.

But even if some people possessed staples, the Jews found nothing
upon their return to their homes. Their struggle for survival continued;
this time the enemy's name was hunger.

Hurriedly resuscitated Jewish organizations, municipal kitchens and
some church groups distributed daily bowls of soup to the city's hungry, and at times corn bread was doled out as a treat. And one either
lived on the minimum portion of charity, and people often collected
their due from public kitchens so as to amplify whatever else they might
have been able to procure, or else, tried to get items on the open market.
But at what cost! Money, if one had it from before, went like nothing.
The only way to survive on one's own was to have a supply of dollars
or gold, a venture beyond city limits to gain access to products of the
agricultural countryside, and then barter.

Dollars and gold—they were of premium value. But who had them?
The possession of the former had always been prohibited in this country
of soft currency. And gold? Those who were well-to-do, perhaps. But
the Jews had been ordered to surrender jewels and other valuables. Of
course, everybody had tried to hide something. So had Kata, to a very
limited degree—she had kept Istvan's fine Swiss gold watch. But when
her mother had arrived in Magasmezo in December, she had no cash.
Kata felt she could not expect Baumgarten to provide for every small
need of theirs. Her mother and she just had to have some money right
then. So just before Christmas, she'd decided to sell the watch. Baumgarten found a buyer who paid a respectable amount. Most of it was
still unspent and available.

And now, when Kata made her black market contact and asked the
prices, she could hardly believe her ears. She counted the money. It
would pay only for fifteen pounds of either oil or sugar.

"Fifteen pounds of sugar or oil?" she asked incredulously. It was hard
to believe—in a country where food at least used to be plentiful and
relatively cheap when compared to industrial products and such luxuries

as a genuine Swiss import. But what was there to do? She bought some of each.

Once they were in their apartment, friends came to welcome them back, bringing small gifts of food items.

Old Mrs. Gondos appeared with a piece of bacon. "So happy to see you, Dr. Vaghelyi. I was so worried about Mrs. Vaghelyi and your daughter. I'm afraid the lard is a little stale, but it's all I have left."

"Thank you so much. What a treat to add to our legumes!" Mrs. Vaghelyi exclaimed. "It will last a while."

Those legumes! They were their menu day in and day out. Everybody had his fill of beans and lentils. Only the fortunate ones were able to complement them with treats as lard, perhaps a bit of sausage, an occasional egg, a portion of farmer cheese. Not that the riches of the agricultural hinterland, depleted as they were by Russian foragers, were within normal reach. Travel conditions were nearly impossible, and of course, only to the eastern part of the country at that. And yet, Kata knew that she had to make a trip—for food and to find Jancsi. Fortunately, both goals were in the same direction.

It took a few weeks to organize herself, to get the household going with minimal supplies, to find two suitcases given for safekeeping to a neighbor and duly returned so that they had now at least three changes of underwear and one extra garment each. Her mother exchanged the additional dress for a sheet and two towels. One sheet only, just for emergency. Otherwise, they slept on the bare mattress. It was fortunate they found two blankets, and their winter coats did extra duty at night. So she had to make the trip. But how? When? Rumors about travel were less than encouraging.

* * *

"Kata, a man was here this morning," her parents greeted her excitedly as she returned from an errand three weeks after their return. "He brought news of Jancsi—he's well!"

Her father and mother beamed with joy. Father was growing stronger, Kata noted with delight. He walked more and more on his cane, first in the apartment, then even around the corridor outside.

"The man will come back tomorrow or the day after to tell you more."

"Oh, God! Our first direct news of the child! Maybe, maybe I can

really make plans now." And before her mother had a chance to protest—the trip was a risky one though hundreds were venturing into the
farmlands in spite of the Russians, the impossible travel conditions and
the lingering chills of the winter—she wanted to hear more about the
message bearer.

"He knows Mrs. Kovacs and apparently has seen Jancsi, too," her
father explained. "He says he is going back in a few days."

The man came next day. He bragged that the little boy from Budapest not only talked, but spoke Russian well!

"Russian?" the family echoed in amazement.

"I must hear that!" Kata added with a grin. "Anyhow, it's time to see
the child. I can't wait!"

The man was agreeable to escorting the lady to Kunhegyes. He
would be returning Sunday.

* * *

The platform at the suburban railroad station was full. Resolute
Hungarians in their late thirties and older—the young ones were still
in the Army or preferred to remain unnoticed by Russian eyes—
anxiously watched for the arrival of the one train heading toward the
capital. Plain-looking women wrapped in worn winter coats stood in the
shadow of their men making themselves inconspicuous. Their ker-
chiefed heads purposely created nunlike contours of make-up free faces.
The less desirable they looked, the better: they were venturing on a trip
in Russian-infested territory.

They had been pacing up and down since two o'clock. The train, on
its way to the city, was to stop at suburban Kobanya at three, reach the
Nyugati Station at Budapest within half an hour and return to the Great
Plains East of the Tisza river at six the same evening.

It was now four and there was still no engine in sight.

Kata was nervously stamping her feet to combat the chill of the early
March wind. Her guide, Molnar, was constantly on the alert to learn the
latest developments. There was not much conversation between them.
He had the abrupt shyness of the peasant whose deference toward the
educated makes him short of words, particularly in the presence of a
lady. Still, he was familiar with the route and Kata was glad to follow
his clues.

Uncle Jozsi, a bachelor cousin of her mother-in-law, had volunteered to make the trip with them. He had been an early admirer of Jancsi but it was not clear whether interest in his great nephew or a longing for more palatable food than that available in the city stirred him to undertake the journey. In any case, he proclaimed himself Kata's protector should that country clod desert her on the way.

Though they had well passed the scheduled arrival time of the train, the crowd was still growing; it semed people had expected a delay. Here and there a person extracted a sandwich from his knapsack and munched it. It made Kata's mouth water. Her only meal of the day had been in the morning. She had only a piece of bread and a sliver of bacon, the remnant of Mrs. Nagy's donation, and she did not want to touch them yet. This had to hold her until they arrived in Szolnok, their point of transfer, where she had heard that vendors at the station offered immediate relief to starving city dwellers.

At four-thirty an excited voice from the far right proclaimed, "Here it is, here it is! Forward!"

Whatever was meant by this last comment, the mob responded to it by pushing toward the train which was still in motion. Fists banged at the car doors. Plaintive cries burst forth from women, protesting injuries to their feet and backs as they ferociously and unsuccessfully tried to turn the train doors' handles. Angry voices put neighbors in their places, or pushed them toward the back. No one really got beyond the platform, even when the train had been at a standstill for five minutes.

Kata was careful not to become interlocked with the crowd but how much time was left? The engine might start any moment. She kept her eyes on Molnar. All of a sudden she noted his movement towards the window of a car and managed to keep at his side. In a second the window, raised slightly to provide those inside with some air, was pushed further up by her escort; Molnar linked his hands for her to step on, pushed her through and in no time climbed in after her. They were still trying to gain a foothold in the packed compartment when another man appeared in the window, squeezed his way through—and the train was already on its way. Angry protests and curses came from the crowd left on the platform.

It was six-thirty by the time they reached Nyugati station. It was diffcult to know what had delayed the train, but it did not really matter any more. The important thing was that she was finally on the train which was to unload its passengers in Pest and take the new group of food-seekers from the capital to their destination in the country.

We may be a little late in starting tonight, Kata thought, but by boarding at Kobanya, we avoided the impossible struggle that will take place in a minute when not fifty but at least three hundred people will try their luck.

Indeed, the mob was pouring in.

* * *

At ten in the evening the train still stood in the station. Though a good share of its original load of passengers had fought their way out of the cars, pushing back those who were simultaneously trying to force their way in, the car was now filled to the limit. Kata had a seat near the window, but standing figures filled every passageway.

No one could leave his place. Those who tried for the toilet at the rear went through an ordeal. Kata attempted it once or twice, then gave up. She would just have to last until the morning. The train ride to Szolnok normally would take three hours. If all went well, they could still get there by next morning. They had better get there! Otherwise, they would miss their connection.

The train was still at the station at midnight, though it had moved a few hundred meters through the yards. The lights were turned off. A sliver of moonlight coming through the window mitigated the darkness inside.

She dozed off for a while, then opened her eyes to the quietness of the sleepy train. She could hear the mystical noises of the night—some carousing soldiers' singing at a distance, a faint thread of official conversation from some point of the station, a whispered and at times more impatient protest of a fellow passenger who could not move or was pushed to awakening. The dark-blue silhouette of apartment houses flanking the tracks towered over the train. A feeble light appeared in one of the windows on the far right. It spurred her fantasy. Did the candle behind the shades betray demands of bodily urges, sickness or love? She thought about the hundreds of people living so near, their lives unknown.

Kata had always liked to speculate about people around her. Even as a child when she and her parents would go on a Sunday afternoon outing and settle for a light supper in the kiosk on the top of Gellert Hill, it was her favorite occupation to look around at the couples relaxing at various tables and let her fantasy roam about the lives these people led. Some seemed happy, others sad, and here and there she had noticed the glances of a man and woman exchanged under the soft music of the gypsy's bow. As she was reaching her teens, such scenes had become even more fascinating. She would dare to watch but for seconds. Then, guided by propriety and her parents' watchful presence, she would turn her head away. "There is only one girl in this whole world . . . " the gypsy used to sing at some table nearby. She would look at her plate and think of the day when someone would have it played and sung for her. She was fourteen then.

Kata stirred herself into the present. The light in the window opposite her faded and she dozed off again.

* * *

At eight in the morning the train still stood at the Pest station. In some way the bodies in the compartment seemed to have consolidated and she could now see Molnar at the other end of the car, drowsing under his cap. But where was Uncle Jozsi? She suddenly recalled that in fact the last she had seen him was on the platform.

"My God! I hope he got on!" She could not help smiling. Uncle Jozsi had come to be her protector! Well, at least Molnar, who knew the countryside, was visible.

Some people near the door stepped out onto the platform to stretch their legs. This provided a little additional space inside.

Kata finally could make her way to the lavatory, and the physical relief made her feel more confident in spite of the uncertainty of the coming hours.

At ten, rumors spread that the train was waiting for the arrival of clearance from the Russians. Why it had taken hours was unclear but it was some information for the weary passengers to chew on. At eleven another rumor spread—the Russians had taken the engine away to bring in a military train which had broken down in the vicinity. Their train's departure time had become completely uncertain.

She felt wretched. Now that the reunion with Jancsi was more than just a possibility, every delay produced painful frustrations. There were practical reasons for worry, too. She had no more food with her. If they started soon, there would be no problem. But if they were delayed beyond noon?

Her fellow passengers had similar concerns. Some contemplated aloud if it might be wiser to leave and try again the next day. Kata was reluctant to do that. She thought with dread of the ordeal it had been to board this train. She might not be as lucky another time. Besides, Molnar might be determined to stay on. She'd better wait and see what he would decide.

She retreated into daydreaming. What would Jancsi be doing now, she wondered. She spent some time in evoking the picture of the little blond head, the dark brown eyes and smiling lips. She, too, was smiling.

Her reverie was interrupted by the comment of her neighbor that he would take a short leave. He lived in one of those buildings along the tracks—might as well warn his family of the delay. He would be back within the hour. He felt certain the train would be standing there for a long time yet.

The car seat designed for five people seemed quite comfortable now that the sixth passenger had relinquished his place. Kata leaned back to continue her daydreaming. But in a minute the shrill tooting of the engine brought her and her fellow passengers to attention.

Two or three quick whistles, some scuffling of hurried footsteps, and the train jolted. Another jolt and they were slowly moving.

"Incredible, wonderful, hurray!" The group cheered.

"We are going, we are going," somebody put into words the long-awaited event and one man feebly began singing the well-known song:

"The train is going, the train is going to Kanizsa . . . " Though the group happily watched the soloist, they were too weary to join in.

* * *

It took a while for the passengers to descend from their jubilation into a more settled state. It was really a misnomer to call it settled. The conductor's whistle brought a quick return of those who had earlier stepped out to the platform, and the car was again jammed. Yet, Kata had the sensation of being somewhat more comfortable than earlier. As she turned around to assess the situation, she suddenly realized that her neighbor who had wanted to alert his family of the delayed departure was not there. Of course, he might well have got on the train at the other end. The time between his leaving and the train's moving was really quite short.

While contemplating his fate Kata suddenly threw a glance at the little brown bag crumpled at her side, a grease spot indicating its contents. For a moment she was ready to believe that the stranger, by miraculous circumstances, was having lunch with his wife and children and would never reclaim such a meager allotment as was possibly hiding inside the brown paper.

But the thought seemed silly. Or was it? And after all, what if the stranger did not get back on the train? It was an exciting possibility! Indeed such a thought made for two uncomfortable hours during which conscience battled the instinct for survival, which hoped that the man would never return from his self-imposed holiday.

Finally it was four in the afternoon. She was really hungry. Soon it would be 24 hours since she had eaten. Some others near her took out a piece of corn bread or even a hard-boiled egg. Someone shyly asked whether she had anything, but did not offer to share his supplies though he looked sympathetic. Then he spotted the brown bag.

"Whose is it?" he inquired with forced naivety.

It was quickly established that the bag had belonged to the man who had left.

"Now it's yours!" The man of good will and healthy self-interest offered the prize to Kata.

She refused at first. The rightful owner of the bag might still find his way to his seat, she said.

The issue became quite a matter of conversation among her fellow-travelers, who wanted to mitigate their consciences by seeing that the young woman had something to eat. They insisted that the owner of the bag could not possibly get back. If he had ever gotten on the train, by now he would have fought his way to their compartment. And if he had decided not to do that, even if on the train, he must have given up recapturing his belonging.

"Yes, you must take it," munching co-passengers coaxed Kata.

Finally she gave in. The luxurious taste of lard and onion softened by the matter-of-fact dryness of two-day old bread made her ready and fit for another night. The train was moving ever so slowly. But the beat helped her to a new drowsiness.

With constant stops, standing and then moving at times at walking speed, they did not arrive at Szolnok until late Tuesday morning. A distance of less than a hundred miles! Incredible! Of course they had missed the connecting train running every other day. Well, tomorrow.

In the meantime, peasant women offered boiled eggs, butter and bread at the station. The price charged the inflated city purses was high, but much more reasonable than the products of the black market in Budapest. Kata relished the newly acquired riches of the Hungarian farmland and by the afternoon she strolled about to become acquainted with the town. But she dared not go too far and even then only in company with others.

As darkness set in, Kata settled down with her fellow passengers on the floor of the station's waiting room. They used their knapsacks as pillows. The number of people huddled together reduced the chill and they were able to relax, even sleep a little, in preparation for another full day.

At daybreak, Wednesday, Kata and Molnar went to look for their train. Of course, others were doing the same. And with time the group expanded. Travelers were coming from all directions. The number of those waiting spurred her alarm. How could she get on?

At last the train was identified—it had been standing in front of them for quite a while without a sign or a word from any official to reveal its secret. But now its doors opened. The crowd pushed, trampled, squeezed, filled every possible opening. The crush was frightening and Kata held back. She tried to discover some possible wedge of entry into the train. But not only were the doors and windows blocked by the mob but men and women were pushing to reach the roof of the train by the iron ladder attached to the end of each car. They must have something to hold onto, Kata speculated, as she tried to muster courage to follow suit. But she did not dare. She'd never expected to board a train by way of a window, but climbing on top was too frightening. It would be too easy to lose her balance. She shuddered.

Molnar was heading toward the ladder. He shouted to her his determination to leave with the train. "Try the top," he called. But apparently seeing Kata's hesitation, he waved and called down from the roof. "I'll look for you at the next stop."

She checked her tears. Her second escort had abandoned her!

She had to get on, somehow. It would be a very short trip, but there was no other way to cross the river.

Maybe if she could find the conductor—

She walked toward the front of the train with quick steps, looking for some solution. None of the compartments offered any. Her panic rose. Soldiers were dashing back and forth with increasing rapidity. It looked as if the train would leave soon. A friendly looking Russian was coming her way. She reached for the ever-present snapshot of Jancsi in her inside pocket. *"Harashow?* Baby, my son! Must go to see him!" Her fingers pointed to the train and its blocked entries. "Please!"

The soldier looked at the picture and then at her. Then he took her by the arm and ushered her to the box car next to the engine. He opened the sliding door, let Kata in and immediately closed the door behind her, and the train was in motion.

"Oh God!" she gasped.

She could not see anything, though, and wondered where she really was. But her pupils soon became used to the darkness; she was the only passenger in the car filled with hundreds of bundles of envelopes. It was the mail car! She laughed.

The crossing of the Tisza river did not take long and in less than an hour the train stopped. Even before she had a chance to think of how to get out, the door opened, the Russian helped her out and was already moving ahead to signal departure.

Not many people got off at the town of Fegyvernek. Kata scouted those scrambling out of cars and from the roofs. There was Molnar!

"So you got here!" He beamed at her with some embarrassment. "We'd better eat something first, Madam, before starting the journey by foot."

He led the way to a nearby cottage where the women of the house had hot soup ready for a modest price.

The big bowl of vegetable soup and two slices of home-made bread appeased their hunger and warmed them up as well. They needed both; the weather was menacingly gloomy and heralded snow. Kata worried a little at such a possibility but Molnar brushed off her concern and said that they had to take a chance.

* * *

After they had walked an hour, the blizzard started. The strong March wind cut into Kata's cheeks. She pulled down the woolen shawl to shield her face from the icy white particles. In spite of her heavy coat, she could feel in her body the effects of winter's last struggle. At first the briskness of her movements generated body heat. But it was difficult to continue moving at the initial pace. To cut the distance shorter, they were trying to follow the route of the railroad's branch line to Kunhegyes, out of operation since the occupation. Here the pathway between the rails was relatively clear either of snow or rubble, but the wind was powerful, untamed by intervening trees or homes that would normally block its path had the track not been on elevated ground.

Plodding along was enormously trying. It was not the cold alone. Kata could make that more bearable if she pulled the shawl across her face. But, then, her view was blocked and she feared losing track of Molnar, who was forging his way ahead with hurrying steps. And if she pushed back the wool knit to orient herself better, the bitter-cold wind pierced her cheeks with an almost intolerable ache. Her eyes became sore and she began to feel it impossible to go on. She made a concentrated effort to catch up to Molnar and pleaded with him to stop, but the man was unshakable. He was determined to move on. He spoke of the possible alternatives, his voice muffled by his scarf. But, in truth, there were none. One or two isolated ranches were spotted on the horizon. They seemed far and it looked as if reaching them was beyond her strength. And even if they got there, Molnar was not willing to go in with her. Those ranches almost certainly quartered Russian soldiers, and if Kata was not afraid, he, Molnar, was. He had no intentions of going to labor camp.

Finally, Molnar was willing to stop for a few minutes in an abandoned station house—it was not even a house, just the wooden shed of a flag-stop to protect waiting passengers from rain and wind. But even in normal times when the line of the railroad had been in operation, few people used the stop; they had preferred to get off and on at a regular station and would either walk from there or be picked up by horse-drawn carriages. Though the shed allowed for a few minutes of respite from the cold, it could not offer any real protection for a longer time. Besides, Molnar was on edge to continue while there was at least daylight.

Years later Kata physically shivered as she recalled the terrifying and everlasting two hours they fought the blizzard on their way to Kunhegyes. Besides the experience when she was hiding in the church communion closet at the time the Szalasi regime came to power in Budapest, this was the one other occasion when she felt near to death.

In fact, the walk in the blizzard was almost more of a trial. During that night in the church, she had been able to do nothing. The danger had been great but she had only to lie quietly in the hope that there would be no search of the building and no one would find her hiding place. Now, she could not afford to be passive. Her fate was in her own hands, or, rather, in her legs.

She pulled all her strength together as she thrust on, indulging, too, in wild daydreaming about her son. It seemed a fantasy that she might see him soon—only a dream in face of the hurdles she had to conquer first. Yet, the dream gave her strength, propelling her feet and giving them speed as she was tracing behind Molnar.

Once or twice Molnar turned back as he heard her pleading voice only to shrug his shoulders and wave her to continue. Not that he was insensitive. In fact, he himself might have had some doubts about their trip at this point. But there was truly nothing else to do but to go on and, with his determination to get home that night, he shared some willpower with Kata, even as she kept begging him to slow down.

After nightmarish hours the wind abated. And soon after they reached a village with houses where a shelter could be found. The sinking sun escaped from under the clouds and in its gentle slope toward the horizon it spread a glow of encouragement over the white cover of houses, the patchy blue of the sky. There seemed to be no sense of lingering now. After resting a few minutes, she continued in Molnar's company toward the country town where her child had spent the second year of his life.

She occupied her mind with questions. What would Jancsi be like now? At the age when an infant becomes a child, every month, every week, even every day has its significant moments in the growing process. Those few words of "mommy" and "daddy" expand to "dog-gie," "baby," "granny," "apple," and before you know it, sentences are formed and enchanting connections uttered, at times to the amusement of parents and grandparents. There is the increasing activity, a change from running into mother's arms to running from door to door or across the yard or cautiously trying to venture beyond; the gradually achieved ease in walking beside mother and father on a Sunday stroll—what peacetime images!—digging in the sand along the river, or the artificial beach around a swimming pool, where he might be taken by the family;

the growing and increasing ability to listen to a story and grasp part of it, all this could happen from day to day with amazing rapidity at times hard to believe.

But she had not seen her child for almost a year, and it was hard to anticipate what he would be like, what his accomplishments would be. Would he know who she was? What if he was frightened, what if he cried? There were brief images of recoiling weepiness, hiding in a corner, running to the old woman who had taken her place for such a long time—had it been irrevocably long?

But these apprehensions were nonsense, Kata reassured herself. A child knows his mother instinctively.

It was a simple conclusion, but it helped her to return to the immediate present. She walked on in the reddish-hued aftermath of the sunken sun. She carefully followed Molnar on the road illuminated only by sparse kerosene lights beckoning from some country cottage window and then by the emerging stars and a thin strip of moon venturing on the sky.

She was weary to her bones when at last they reached Kunhegyes at eight. The town seemed asleep. Many of the houses were dark by now. It was not a large community but still, one would have to make some inquiries to find the address. It would have been difficult without Molnar, particularly at that time of the night, but with him she headed straight toward the little cottage similar to many others in the town.

A knock, verbal self-identification and a suprisingly quick response in opening the door allowed them an immediate view into the big kitchen. There, around the brick stove, the sleepy flames languidly licking its iron door, and surrounded by the warm glow of two kerosene lamps, was a little boy on the lap of a man—Uncle Jozsi of all people!—playing horse. Her heart pounded. Her son! A baby a little less than a year ago and now a sturdy little boy! "My, how he has grown!"

In the meanwhile, the man roguishly continued the horsie-horsie game. Only after an indignant reminder from Mrs. Kovacs did Uncle Jozsi release his ward and begin to coax the boy to see who was there, to go and greet Mommy. Jancsi looked at his newly found friend askance, then toward the door, and stood still with some uncertainty.

Kata moved toward him. It needed much self-discipline to restrain her steps. But she did not want to frighten the child. Their glances met.

Then her trembling hands barely touched the silky head. A quiet "Hi" was to acquaint the boy with this long-forgotten stranger who, however, did not seem at all forbidding, not really frightening to him. There was this lady with whom he seemed to be vaguely familiar, who may have even held him long ago—so long ago that a little boy could not recall. He could only sense there was some safety with this visitor.

He looked at her with growing interest and response. Kata lifted him up and her kisses fell softly and tenderly on his face, his hair, his pudgy little hands, his legs which she sought out from under the long pants, his lovely little nose and now those closed dark eyes.

"Sweetheart, sweetheart, sweetheart," she whispered, walking around with him as if dazed.

Jancsi calmly rested his head on her shoulder. Only when he felt the moisture of her tears did he pull away his head and look at the woman who declared she was his mother.

By now, Uncle Jozsi, whose acquaintance he had made earlier, and Mrs. Kovacs, whom he was used to all these months, reaffirmed the notion that "there is your mother, dear, kiss her: she loves you, yes, she came to see you."

But this was too much for Jancsi. His earlier spontaneity began to give way to the reality of strangeness all around and the small face puckered itself in preparation for a cry.

"Maybe you'd better take him now, Mrs. Kovacs," Kata said as she handed Jancsi to the woman. The matron took loving hold of the child.

With one arm embracing Mrs. Kovacs, the other hand reaching out to fill her palm with the boy's hair, Kata stood quiet, her throat becoming tight.

"Thank you, Mrs. Kovacs, thank you." She gave the woman a brief strong hug then let her go. "Take him. You take him to bed."

"Oh, Mrs. Kovacs, how can I ever thank you enough," she muttered as she followed the pair with moist eyes on their way to the child's room.

She sat down in the wooden armchair in front of the stove, to rest her exhausted body, to gather her thoughts under the glowing greetings of the flames licking the iron stove's door. Her thoughts hopped from here to there, from the moment of reunion, to the earlier desperate hours of walk in the snow, the unbelievable odds of the journey. She heard fragments of Uncle Joe's explanations—a Russian soldier had given him a lift through the bridge, he was old enough not to worry being taken for forced labor. She nodded with a bemused smile at the foxy bachelor's maneuvers and thought again of the little boy and the tomorrow and tomorrows and tomorrows . . .

Mrs. Kovacs was back. She insisted on giving Kata warm soup and poured the contents of the big kettle on the stove into a tin tub for a quick cleaning up. Finally Kata stole into the room where Jancsi was in bed and where the woman had prepared a cot for his mother.

She went to the crib. The kerosene lamp on the corner table threw a soft light on the child. "Good night, sweetheart!" she whispered as her hands touched the silky blondness once more.

* * *

Next morning, as she opened her eyes and for a moment tried to orient herself as to where she was, a little boy standing in his crib was eyeing the stranger and soon addressed her with a babble of questions forming themselves into more understandable words of greeting: "Hi! Hi!"

Her muscles ached yet she jumped out of the bed, noting the crescendo of the greetings and the shaking of the crib's wooden bars as a musical accompaniment and ended the action by a swift lifting of the child and pushing him up and up and up and up with intermittent kisses—up and up and up toward the ceiling. Jancsi giggled; turned cautious, then giggled again. And as the play continued, his giggle grew into loud spurts of laughter, an exhilarated scream evaporating into a playful giggle again.

"It's Mommy, Mommy," she laughingly exclaimed. "Your Mommy!"

Jancsi, having exhausted himself in the play, listened, looked at her with a touch of suspicion and echoed the words: "Mom—, Mom—, Mommy!"

A barrage of kisses on the rosy cheeks.

The door opened. Mrs. Kovacs gathered from the noise that no one was asleep there any more.

"I brought Jancsi clean corduroys for the day—it is a special day after all." And she placed the pants and the underwear on the nearby table, reaching out for the boy. Jancsi was watching them both.

"Mrs. Kovacs, could I bathe him today?" Kata asked with a touch on the woman's arm. "It's time to start being a mother again with everyday chores!"

"You're not taking him yet," the matron grumbled. "Here!" She sought out a fresh towel. "I'll carry him to the kitchen," she said gathering the child under her arm. "The water is heating there."

Preliminaries done, Kata carefully placed her child into the tub. She splashed the water over the round shoulders and teasingly pinched the navel to elicit a protest and then laughter. Istvan had never liked her to do that. He had some faint memory of pinching from his own childhood and at this point he had always rescued the boy from his mother's hand. Rescued? How much he had loved to bathe and take care of him! Kata used to be grateful for his helping her out. It is true, at times she had been a little jealous. Jancsi, even as a baby, had loved to be with his father. He had responded thoroughly to his patience and strongly safe arm; his words, meaningless then to the boy, had been just another lullaby stronger than Mommy's but just as pleasant and so secure. And they had laughed with joy as one of them would turn the baby on the palm on his belly and playfully spank the round buttocks and then smooth them with the balm of the water.

It was not so easy to turn Jancsi now, she thought. The little rascal was more independent and stronger, and as familiarity with Mother increased, he put up a mock fight. No, he did not want to turn, and he grabbed Kata's arm with quite some strength to resist her maneuvers while he protested with only half-intelligible words.

Kata offered a truce by bending to kiss his head.

"Honey, you'll like this, you can swim!" Swimming meant nothing to Jancsi but the new word disarmed his resistance for a moment. There was something reassuring in Mother's voice, too, and he did allow himself to be turned so that she could wash his back.

He was quite heavy now, Kata thought, as she lifted him up and wrapped him in the towel. The motion was familiar, of course. Yet, it had changed tempo and pace.

She used to talk to her baby in those first few months of his life, back home in Budapest. She would tell him all her loving thoughts, all the hopeful dreams for the future. Of course, in those times Jancsi had not understood that Mother was talking to him, that she wanted to explain something. But now he listened with more comprehension and after he was dried and Kata began to dress him, he did ask clearly what it meant to swim. Kata made the motion and promised real swimming when the weather would be warm and they could go to some big water in the summer. Jancsi had many more questions, but the smell of heated milk and freshly baked bread hit his nostrils, and he was quite willing to have breakfast.

Mrs. Kovacs emerged again and eagerly volunteered to feed the boy; Mrs. Fogaras and her uncle should have breakfast, too. She herself was in the habit of eating as soon as she started the morning, very early.

There was fresh bread, long-forgotten butter, and apricot jam on the table. And a lively, sunny child's face across. What a beautiful, wonderful morning!

Mrs. Kovacs asked many questions and wanted to hear more about the trip and then of the besieged city. While listening, she eagerly handed the cup to Jancsi. Kata thanked her for her help. It would not be easy for the woman to relinquish Jancsi, she knew. The boy accepted the cup from Aunt Maria's hands while watching whether Mommy saw. She did, and commented on his deftness in handling the mug.

When they had finished eating, Jancsi took out his building blocks and asked Mommy to sit down with him. The red and blue blocks soon shot up into a tower, and Jancsi duly admired, then demolished the creation. He started the venture all over again, inducing her to make it higher and adding his own blocks until it all crumbled. It was laughter and fun, kisses and serious work: building.

Later they took a walk. She admired the garden and let Jancsi point to the sled which must have been Gyuri's, an older orphan in Mrs. Kovacs's care. "This is nice, Jancsi! And where do you play?"

The little fingers pointed to the far end of the garden and, hand in hand, they moved down the path.

"Let's run," Kata invited him to a race. She allowed him to outrun her, and when Jancsi anxiously turned to see where she was, her outstretched arms offered him a sure haven as he returned to the figure—so big, tall and safe: Mommy.

The game was repeated several times. On every occasion there was some anxiety as Jancsi lost sight of his companion. Every time he turned there was increasing certainty that those arms were waiting for him. And as he ran into them, he responded more and more to the joyful welcome. As if in reward he kept repeating: "Mom, Mom, Mom," relishing the words, playfully seeking the effect—the more words, the more hugs and kisses.

"I love you, sweetheart. Mommy loves you, my darling." Jancsi looked at his mother and his lips opened into a broad smile. Then he hugged her and whispered mischievously as if in some joke: "Love Mommy, I love Mommy . . . Mommy,. Mommy, Mom, Mom . . . '

Then he gave her many short kisses.

It was time to go in, to return to the warmth of the big stove.

* * *

Mrs. Kovacs had made arrangements for Kata to purchase a goose. This would be her main booty as she returned to Budapest. She could also get a cut of lard and eggs through her hostess. But for sunflower oil and flour Mrs. Fogaras had better go to the village grocery, Mrs. Kovacs advised, since neither she nor her neighbors had a supply to spare. She explained where the store was and Kata decided to walk there alone. She could examine the village on her own a bit now that she was walking in daylight. She could also relive the emotional experiences of the last twenty-four hours.

The neat country town seemed an entity in itself with its own limited shopping center hosting one grocery, a pub and a general store. The latter seemed to be closed for a midday break but the grocery window suggested to Kata that she could get what she needed there. A solitary man was reading a newspaper. Though yesterday's, it still attracted his attention. At the squeak of the door and its announcing bell he looked up, almost as if in surprise. Kata felt awkward in the empty place. She stated her needs and the man weighed the flour and poured the oil into a tin container, making a special effort to seal it well after Kata explained she wanted to take it back to Budapest.

As she watched the man carry out his task, she noted the relative sparseness of his merchandise. The empty shelves did not befit the storekeeper's apparent expertness. How could a person make a living with such low supplies and meet his responsibility for a family as well? She was in the mood to explore a little, to find out more about the store, the man, the village.

She commented about the weather and how nice it was to take a walk. The man seeming to assume she was tired, offered a seat in front of the counter, almost as if pleading for company.

Yes, she was from Budapest. Her son had been staying in the village during the siege and she had come to visit, she said. She would be going back tomorrow with some foodstuffs and then would come again to pick up the boy, perhaps within a month or two. She began relating her experience with the blizzard and particularly the climax when she had found the boy and embraced him. She was aware that perhaps she was too carried away in the presence of this stranger, but somehow, now that the actual experience could be viewed with the perspective gained during her morning walk, she felt almost compelled to speak about her joy and share her happy thoughts with someone.

"I am Samu Katz," the man introduced himself.

Kata murmured her name in exchange.

"Forgive me if I intrude on you a little, Madam, but it was good and at the same time heartbreaking to hear your story. I wish I could be reunited with my children, but it will never be. I know they and my wife are dead.

"You know it?" Kata asked, startled.

Katz nodded. "Random shooting just before boarding those trains. A villager witnessed it all and told me about it as I arrived back from the Russian front. I survived labor camp and was so hopeful. But it's all over now!" he said with a tremendous sigh.

"Forgive me for telling you my gruesome story," he said and picked up a newspaper from under the counter to wrap the can of oil. "I wish you the best!"

Another customer entered. Katz returned to business, and Kata quietly slipped out of the store.

* * *

That night Kata found it hard to sleep. Just one day ago, totally exhausted by her perilous journey, she had been lulled to rest by the sight of her child, the warmth of the cottage and the filling of her stomach. But now, in the darkness of the room, remembering Samu Katz, she was hit by the thought never fully faced before, that Jancsi, too, might not have survived. She began to sob.

But Jancsi must not be awakened!

She listened. She could hear his even breathing, like spring rain drops kissing the soul's parched terrain. She swallowed hard and found the sobs turning into silent laughter. She had her child! Her lovely son!

She thought back of that wonderful Sunday with Istvan when their abandon abolished all barriers, when they both dared to be creators and risk the unknown doomsday. Istvan and she had dared!

She had wanted a child of Istvan's flesh and blood, and she hoped of his insight, his creativity, his gentleness. And when she had first held Jancsi in her arms, she had felt a conqueror, a queen, But that state of joy had not lasted, not even for a year.

Jancsi had left and Istvan was gone, too. She had had to survive. Indeed, one of the most terrible thoughts allowed into her consciousness had been the fear that even if Jancsi was well, his parents might not be there at the end. But she was here now!

A flowery meadow appeared. Spread on the grass a wool blanket, on it a child. She was running toward him with open arms and he, too, reaching to receive his mother. In the far distance the vague figure of a man—he should hurry, we should hug the child together! But that vague figure of a man was not approaching and she could not wait any longer. She clutched her child.

And the meadow was filled with red poppies.

In her dream, she closed her arms tighter around the baby. Yes, she had her child! She had her child!

* * *

Sunday morning the sun embraced the town and the fields. It was harder than she'd imagined to leave Jancsi, once having found him and become reacquainted. But, how could she take him while traveling was so impossible?

She walked alone, laden with a packed knapsack, on the long, long trek to the train. Uncle Jozsi had decided to stay for a few more days. The countryside showed a very different face from the one huddling under the sweep of the blizzard only four days earlier. The air was crisp but its smell, flavored by the sunshine, spoke of spring.

The vast stretches of land, with their motley tapestry of earth-brown checkered by the remaining snow, sparkled against the sun's rays. It was beautiful and comforting— the promising caressing of nature.

She walked for over an hour before she saw a soul. But she was not frightened. She stopped to revel in the radiance of God's Universe. In her elation, as in a joyful dance, she whirled around where she stood.

With the movement she caught sight of the mounted figure of a Russian soldier some four hundred meters away. Her heart jumped. But the horse and its master continued their way in the opposite direction. She resumed her walk.

CHAPTER 14
ISTVAN

MAY 1945-
AUGUST 1946

Two months later, Jancsi was back in Budapest.

By summer, Kata had begun to work. Businesses were not truly functioning as yet. But her friend Zsuzsa, who had survived with many adventures during her hiding, knew of a two-man operation where someone was needed to mind the phone and meet customers. It was not the kind of work Kata would want for any length of time but it brought a little money and allowed time for further planning.

After three months, her previous employer offered her a job in a newly started venture, a retail store of medical supplies in Buda. The former owners found nothing upon their return from the ghetto—the supplies had been first expropriated by the Nazis and then looted by the Russians—and they were too feeble and old to initiate a new business on their own. Kata's employer, in deference to earlier business contacts with the couple, offered to take the business over, pay them a minimal monthly sum in return for the premises and the good name of the store and for the couple's token involvement in it.

So Kata had a job and was paid every other week. It was a farce.

Though salaries provided for the minimal food rations sold in food

189

stores at regular prices, there was little else she could purchase from a fixed income. Oh yes, she could obtain a set of tramway tickets to last between pay periods, and if one were lucky—at least at her level of pay—a pair of stockings on payday. But, if she missed her chance!

"Anyu, imagine, I got out late yesterday so I thought one day wouldn't make much difference. But this is impossible! The stockings in the store window for 5 forints yesterday sold for 10 today. And I didn't have much money left! Now, I'll have to darn what I have, and be smarter on the 15th."

"I'd better begin to contribute to household expenses," her father commented. "I feel much stronger now!"

"But Erno," Mrs. Vaghelyi fussed, "at your age and with the accident—

"Apu, you can get a small pension and if I'm careful, we may manage," Kata said.

"That's nonsense," her father emphatically retorted. "First of all, we couldn't manage. But even more importantly, you don't want me to stay idle! That's like death!"

His doctor agreed; it would be better for Dr. Vaghelyi to keep busy. So he happily set up his old desk in the middle room of the three which became available to the family by the summer—the whole apartment would be theirs in only another year—and accepted cases for advice and consultation and eventual legal representation.

"It's true, people have little cash," her father said after the first few client contacts. "But I was offered flour and oil instead. It will have to do!"

Have to do? It was a blessing! Now, with Dr. Vaghelyi's compensation and Kata's salary, they could manage. It was difficult, but they did not starve, and as the months passed by, the meals became somewhat more varied, too. Even then, meat was on the table no more than once a month for quite a while until parcels from abroad changed the picture. It was in October that Kata triumphantly brought home the first Red Cross gift package from Scotland, containing Spam and tea.

Not until the following spring could she improve her material circumstances in a more steady way. It was then she obtained a job as secretary-interpreter at a foreign church welfare unit, and from then on more American goods reached the Vaghelyi home.

As less energy was needed in the struggle for everyday existence, her suppressed feelings of deep anxiety about Istvan's absence forced themselves into her thoughts, and they brought a new kind of misery during the months of uncertainty and anxious waiting.

With the surrender of Germany, some of their friends, few in number, had begun to return from concentration camps by the summer of 1945. This started a period of prayerful, hopeful and finally, doubtful waiting for Kata, as well as for the other thousands of women in Budapest who themselves had been fortunate enough to survive the Holocaust and now had to face the future.

It was said that out of Hungary's 600,000 Jewish population, 400,000 had perished. From Budapest alone, a city of good fortune when compared with the countryside, 150,000 out of a quarter of a million were not as yet accounted for. But here and there some of the missing still reappeared.

Every week Kata would walk down to Red Cross Headquarters where the diminishing list of newly located persons was posted. The coveted name of Istvan Fogaras was not to be found! And after a while she dreaded the Wednesdays when her ever reconstituted hope, that this week would be different, was demolished.

Leaving the Red Cross building, she would go for a walk alone, roaming the damaged city, aimlessly turning from one corner to the other, mechanically crossing thoroughfares, spending her energy in order to leave herself no strength to devote to the emotional burden these Wednesday visits placed upon her.

Sometimes the day ended in peaceful storytelling, in a joyful encounter between mother and child. She would be able to push the questions and gnawing apprehensions from her consciousness and dedicate the evening hours to Jancsi. She would tend to his physical needs before bedtime, tuck him in, spring to his bedside if he needed her during the night. She was thrilled by his joyous response. He was a wonderful boy!

At other times, she could not be so easily appeased and even the child could not redirect her thoughts of Istvan. On the contrary, her joy in Jancsi would be mixed with bitterness and guilt. How could she enjoy fulfillment, she thought, when her partner in creation was absent and his fate uncertain? By what right had she been allowed to survive the last years and arrive at night at a home where love presided, where three people whose blood she shared were living in relative comfort, looking forward to better days to come, three people who could have hopes for the future, and the fourth, the child, himself the future. Why had she been spared? How could she have this joy, when Jancsi's father had been deprived of loving human closeness for so long?

The loneliest time for her was at night. In her bed, she would lie with wide-awake eyes, and long for the warmth of Istvan, his nearness, his touch, his caresses.

Some Wednesday evenings Kata would take out her husband's writings, some unfinished sketches and outlines, and a few completed ones. The sight of the well-known handwriting first brought her a sensation of cherished familiarity. Where the manuscript had been left unfinished, the joy of recognition would soon be followed by her apprehension about the ending. Of course, it was not the plot's culmination that invaded the evening with torturing questions. She would not care, she was sure, how the stories would develop, whether she liked them or not, whether they portrayed happiness or gloom. Only, if only the writer could have a chance to pick up his pen again and conclude, in whatever way he saw fit, what he had started.

No, the content would make no difference. Yet, curiously enough, the material at hand did make her think of Istvan not only in terms of nostalgic reminiscences and powerful hopes and fears. The thoughts of her man contained a philosophy, a message which she sought over and over to rediscover and test out against the bleak realities of the present.

When at first she reviewed the writing in this light, she thought that her effort was absurd. None of Istvan's stories described anything like the years past with their vicious massacres and demonic destruction.

So far his writings had spoken of human situations—love and jealousies, missteps and pardons, domestic idylls and turmoils, longings and short fulfillments, romantic encounters and, at times, crude awakenings. Yet, was not this an oversimplification of Istvan's work and thinking? Kata wondered as she settled into bed. She was looking now at the "Souvenir."

And as she reread the familiar pages she realized once again that they contained much more than the travail of a foolish pretty woman and her simple-hearted, all-forgiving husband. Of course, this was just the moral: heroes at the soup bowl. The setting was in the then present—

the years before World-War II—in the tepidly comfortable surroundings of a storm-free world. Yet, a tempest was germinating even in this setting, catching its victims unaware, a conflict of love and hate, condemnation and forgiveness, the violence of suffering and shame.

She had thought when she had first read it that the story might have a Christian slant. Istvan did not claim this. But his idea of forgiveness was still something to explore in the light of the day's aftermath of horrors. How would Istvan feel today having experienced the depth of cruelty by man to his fellowmen?

She remembered how sensitive Istvan had been about the passivity of Hungarian Jewry, their willingness—whether from ignorance, fear or a dreamy wishfulness for something better than the reality—to submit to fate. Was it the circumstances, the lack of opportunities, the overall psychology and concrete reality surrounding them all that had made him one of the millions who went unresisting to the guillotine of the twentieth century, the labor forces, concentration camps, the gas chambers?

Oh, no, Lord, don't let me even think of such a possibility, she moaned. No, I will only think of the good, the hopeful, the magnanimous and forgiving human being who, before the full-time terror, could at least in the lesser transgressions of his characters resolve conflicts through his awareness of human weakness and belief in the power of understanding and forgiveness.

* * *

At the end of August 1946 a strange message reached her. Mrs. Szakacs, the wife of the concierge of their former apartment, brought a hand-scribbled note. The woman had found it among a batch of bills which her husband must have picked from the mailbox and put aside on the kitchen shelf for the first-of-the month disbursements.

Kata picked up the piece of paper. First, she looked at the signature. She was puzzled by the name of Father Barat. Then, moving to the window to be better able to decipher the penciled words which had lost their sharpness by the mixture of smoke and grease descending upon them on that kitchen shelf for at least a couple of weeks, she suddenly became aware of a pang in her chest.

"Dear Mrs. Fogaras," it started. "I hope this note will reach you and that I will find you in person while in Budapest. I knew your husband

Istvan well. We spent two months together in a concentration camp, before he moved on. I am sure you will want to hear about him. Please call. I discovered you don't live here any more. I found no one to give me your address; otherwise, I would have looked you up right away."

Kata read and reread the message. She felt a tremendous pressure of competing feelings accompanied by a racing succession of thoughts. At first, there was the rise of indescribable hope that there was word of Istvan. For a second or two, with the rapidity of thinking which is possible in dreams and surpasses the pace of waking moments—was she awake now, or perhaps in a dream world though with open eyes?—she could visualize the homecoming, she could feel the triumphant embrace and believe in the ending of torturing questions and fears. She swiftly changed this soothing fantasy and tried to postpone thinking of an actual reunion, deliberately bringing to mind the post-war inefficiency of travel even now, more than a year after V-Day. She became aware of sweat beads forming on her forehead. She knew her face must be flushed and burning. At the same time a numbing cold crept over her arms and legs. She thought she might faint.

Why didn't he tell me Istvan was well? The obvious question came to her mind. If he's alive, wouldn't he have started the note with such good news? She felt a faint shiver—as if touched off by a passing icy wind.

She kept rereading the note. Now her eyes were fixed on the words "before he moved on," and this statement revived her hopefulness.

Of course, the man may not know exactly where Istvan is now, but he seems to know he moved on from the concentration camp. This information will surely give us directions for further search.

Having dismissed Mrs. Szakacs—she did not want at this point to discuss the issue with her parents and hoped the woman would leave before her mother came home—she dialed the number given in the message. A woman answered. Apparently this was the home of Father Barat's parents. Older Mr. Barat was not at home but his sister, to whom the name Fogaras apparently meant nothing, was willing to give out their address. She was expecting her brother home in the afternoon. Mrs. Fogaras might want to call then.

Kata paced the living room, trying to think how to proceed. In a way she welcomed the opportunity of being alone at home. She did need to think through, on her own, what to do, what to expect. No, she quickly corrected, no, she must not think of what to expect. It was enough to figure out what the next step would be.

Mother might be home with Jancsi around two. Father was expected at four. It had been fortunate that Mrs. Szakacs found her in this morning. Kata had an appointment with the optometrist at eleven-thirty, the reason she had not gone to work at her usual hour. She decided to keep her appointment, call in to the office that she would be out for the day, and visit the Barat family as soon as she could get there.

It's too trying, too frightening to wait until I get him on the phone, she decided.

She went into the bedroom. Going through her limited wardrobe, she picked out the little navy blue dress with the white collar that Istvan had liked so much. The dress somehow had survived. Survived! What a stupid word to use for lifeless belongings!

"Anyhow, Istvan used to like this dress, I did find it upon my return, and I want to look good today. I want Istvan to be proud of me as I'm going to greet his friend," she retorted to her questioning self.

She put on her makeup carefully. She wondered if Istvan had spoken about her to Barat—what had he said? Istvan used to be so generous with his compliments. "Oh, my dear, what lovely things you used to tell me! I want to hear you again my darling, say it, come—," she ventured again in hope-filled dreamland. Her eyes filled with tears as she thought back to the caresses, and the praising words she had not heard for years.

"Why am I crying now, why?" and she broke into uncontrollable sobbing before thinking of the answer.

Then, as the tears exhausted themselves for the while, she returned to the bathroom, washed up again with cold water, put on her makeup, now taking little notice of her red nose and swollen eyes, and concentrated on getting to the optometrist on time.

The practical tasks of the day having been accomplished and the prescription of new reading glasses taken care of, Kata took the tramway to Ujpest. It was a long way from Pest and after they rode through the populated areas, the tram moved toward the smaller houses of the industrial suburban complex. She was not familiar with the neighborhood and had to watch the streetcar stops closely so as not to go beyond her destination.

She felt rather businesslike as she finally stepped down and picked up the telephone in the corner coffee house. The voice that she had heard that morning answered again. Yes, her brother was at home now, she would call him.

"Never mind, just tell him I'm coming over, I'm already on your block," Kata quickly replied and put down the receiver. She wanted to forestall any possible delay Mr. Barat might suggest for her coming.

But obviously Mr. Barat had no intentions of canceling the visit. He was a man in his mid-sixties who shook Kata's hand with a warm welcome and put his arms around her in a fatherly way as he escorted her into the living room. He pointed Kata to one of the armchairs and lowered himself into another.

"It's good to see you, my dear, I've heard much about you," and the man looked at the young woman tenderly and sadly. He could not suppress a sigh. "He loved you a great deal, he truly did."

There was no time to wonder about the meaning of the past tense and the way Mr. Barat approached her. She did not even absorb well what he said. So she asked him, as if indeed she had not heard a word: "I came because of the note I got from a Father Barat who knew my husband. Is he here?"

The older man forced a polite smile. "No, my dear, he's my son but he left the city a week ago. He hoped to talk to you, but he had to return to his post. School will start soon. He teaches in a high school. But I knew your husband, too!"

Why does he speak in the past tense? Kata realized that the pattern of communication repeated itself. Why doesn't he go on with the story? Why doesn't he tell where Istvan is now?

"Mr. Barat, you must realize I'm impatient to hear about my husband's whereabouts. Do you know where he is now? Do you know when I may expect him back?"

A few moments of hesitation, a short preparation for the answer, the clearing of his throat.

"I see, you don't know anything then. I see. I'll tell you the facts first and then you can ask whatever you want.

"Both my son and I were in Auschwitz. My son really should not have been there, since he's a Catholic priest. But you know how these things were, they didn't observe their own rules. Anyhow, this is not important now, we were in Auschwitz—so was Istvan. My son and he became friends. But I myself had the chance of talking to him at times.

"He was a great person, my dear, who loved you very much," Mr. Barat continued. "He spoke to us all the time about his wife and his little son. How is the boy? I trust he's safe and well." Mr. Barat hesitated.

"Yes, Jancsi is fine, thank God. Tell me, what about after Auschwitz? Is there an after Auschwitz?" The panicky words were finally uttered.

"Forgive my garrulousness. Yes, I should go on. Oh yes, he was moved out from the camp. He did spend three months in Auschwitz, but during that time—and you ought to feel good about this—he worked in the kitchen. No, no tragedy befell him in Auschwitz. But then, he grew physically weak. He knew he was losing strength quickly. We were all aware, too, that even with extraordinary luck, one could not afford to be sick in Auschwitz. Any medication prescribed would be terminal. So he volunteered for railroad work near Dachau. In fact, my son and I were shipped to the same place, too, only a month later."

Hope was returning again. Kata was even able to smile. "So he went to work, did he, in Austria you said? Were you, was he," she asked with some hesitation, "liberated there? When?"

It seemed an eternity before Mr. Barat replied.

"My son and I, yes, we were liberated there over a year ago."

Kata moved forward, gripping the chair arm. "And Istvan, what about Istvan?"

"He worked for about four weeks, then came the pneumonia. They took him to the barracks hospital. I am sorry to be the one to tell you; I understand he died there at the end of December, 1944. We saw him enter the hospital, but not after. I'm truly sorry. We liked him very much, he was a great person."

The old man bent his head in reminiscing, or perhaps trying to avoid the perplexed and tortured features of his young visitor frozen in the opposite chair.

Her painful numbness lasted a few moments, then gave way to shaking tears.

The hopes, the dreams were over. She could not take it in. Istvan was dead. No!

It took her a while to realize that Mr. Barat was speaking again. She wiped off her tears and looked at him.

"I'm sorry," she whispered, shaking her head.

"Sorry? It's good you can cry. What else is there to do when learning of such a loss? But look here, my dear," and Mr. Barat pulled a chair nearer to Kata so as to somehow convey with his physical nearness some of the sympathy, some of the wish to soften the grief of this young woman. "Look here, my dear, he died in bed. Little consolation perhaps, and yet—"

"I know. Yes, if it had to be, at least he died in a bed.

"You know," she continued, "here at home we tried so long not to believe in the existence of the gas chambers. But then, people came back and we couldn't fool ourselves any longer. And yet, I could never face thinking of it, never—that he might have been gassed. Never. In truth, I never could face thinking—that he really might be dead." She buried her head in her hands and her shoulders shook again.

They sat there for a while, dusk descending on the room.

The chimes of a clock in the hallway were heard.

"It's getting late, I have to go," Kata finally dried her eyes. "But maybe you can talk about him a little more." She did not move from the chair.

Barat turned on a light.

"Yes, I knew him, though my son had more contact with Istvan. I'm really sorry you could not talk to my son. But he told me to let you know, he had many talks with Istvan, not only about wife and family."

"Yes?" Kata tried to help the man go on with the story.

"Well, you know we were all in constant danger of death. Istvan and my son spoke at length about faith and Christ. My son told me to let you know, Istvan was searching, seeking and hopeful. I will not express myself in Catholic terms. No, he did not have the extreme unction, but after all, I understand he was Protestant, wasn't he?" Kata silently nodded. "But even my son was touched by the sincere questionings of a man preparing for death. 'De profundis—'Some people became bitter and defiant, hateful and looking for vengeance. Istvan was preparing to meet the Maker whom he did not quite comprehend but to whose mercy he commended his future and that of his loved ones. 'Seek and you will find.' You know the quotation, don't you?

"No, we were not at his bedside at the time of his death. But we saw him being taken in on the stretcher. Some people did leave the hospital alive. You ought not be concerned on that account. It's tragic that he had to die, but he did die in a bed, I'm sure, and we believe he died in peace."

It was a while before Kata temporarily exhausted her tears. It was a while until she could rise and accept Mr. Barat's offer to use the washbasin in the bathroom.

The cold water felt refreshing. She looked at herself in the mirror above the sink. She noted her pale face. How befitting, she thought, Mr. Barat is not to be impressed now with Istvan Fogaras' wife. It is his widow whom he met.

"Thank you," she managed to say though her heart was shattered. "I'm glad you saw him and at least I know how he died. Of course, if your son comes to the capital, I would like to talk to him, too."

"It's quite uncertain when he'll be back; don't count on it," Mr. Barat said. "But I'll tell him, anyhow."

She felt numb as the tramway rolled along slowly toward the city. But the long ride brought her back to the present. With the stops here and there, the conductor's request for tickets, people moving from one seat to the other, she was spared the opportunity of quiet reminiscing. Everyday life with everyday tasks was all around her. From time to time the sickening reality of the news she had just received came to her and the question repeatedly arose: what now, what would happen with her child, and what would be with the rest of her life? But then, a jolt of the car, the pressure of an elbow, an announcement of the next stop— She could not find answers now, not on the tramway.

BOOK THREE

QUEST

CHAPTER 15

WHERE NOW?

OCTOBER 1946

K ata, come with me today," her mother said, "I'm going to visit the Kalloses."

Kata had not seen much of the Kallos family, her mother's second cousins, but even loose family bonds these days offered some stability. They embraced each other warmly.

"So you got word about your husband?" Mr. Kallos commiserated with Kata. "What can you expect? Those still absent can surely be called dead," he said with resignation. He had his own pain.

"You haven't heard from your son, have you?" Kata recalled the younger Kallos' early absorption into labor camp.

The wave of the mother's hand expressed her despair. "He, and then Karoly—"

"Karoly?"

"Marica's fiance," Mrs. Vaghelyi nodded toward her cousin's twenty-year old daughter.

"A bullet spree along the Danube," the girl explained with controlled calm.

"Hangmen! Miserable murderers!" Mrs. Kallos spilled out her bitterness.

"Words, words!" Her husband muttered angrily.

"Papa's right. No use wailing and talking," Marica said.

Kata sighed. "And you? How're you doing?"

The girl shrugged her shoulders. "Life goes on, I guess. People started to marry and remarry even right out of concentration camp. But I, I'm more interested in politics now."

"I see."

"She's had some proposals and I'd like to see her settled," Mrs. Kallos added.

"Don't rush her," her husband protested. "As things are developing now, there'll be all sorts of opportunities."

Marica smiled enigmatically. She suddenly looked at her watch. "Oh, my, it's six! I have an invitation."

"Why don't you go with her?" Mrs. Kallos prodded Kata.

"Would you like to?" Marica asked on her way to her room. "It's an informal gathering at my girlfriend's. She usually collects an older crowd."

"You can go," Mrs. Vaghelyi encouraged her daughter. "I'll get Jancsi from Irene and put him to bed when I go home." She turned to her cousin, boasting: "He's a treasure; very bright, too."

Marica was ready purse in hand. "Have you decided? It's really the group of my girlfriend's brother. I find them exciting."

Kata hesitated for a second.

"Why not! I won't be late though," she told her mother as she was taking leave.

The two women decided to walk to the Voros apartment.

"I brought a guest along, a cousin of sorts," Marica announced when the hostess welcomed them.

Young men and women were clustered in groups of three or four, involved in heated discussions.

"They're bastards!" Kata heard a bitter young man exclaim.

"Who's that?" Marica asked one guest.

"David Engel, a first-timer. Want to meet him?"

They were introduced and Marica said, "Don't let us interrupt."

He nodded. "Where was I?"

"Back in Tolna," someone helped along.

"Oh, yes. I got back from labor camp—Dachau—only to learn the family was gone." He drew a deep breath, then continued.

"Well, I went home, not expecting a miracle, but just to see what was left, the house, belongings . . .

"I'm walking slowly with trepidation to face the emptiness. And I see Kapas, a former gendarme, coming toward me. As he's getting closer he looks at me, then stares as if he were facing a ghost.

"I mumble something about being back. Silence. Then he clears his mouth, spitting his tobacco onto the dirt road. He's clearly amazed to see me and his astonishment soon turns into insolent rhetoric as he reviews the happenings of the war, the ravages of the Russians, and then weeps about the lost virginity of his eighteen-year-old daughter. Lost virginity! Innocence!"

He stopped, his features taut.

"They all claim innocence," someone burst in. "They even turn the cards around."

"True," David nodded. "When I mentioned the silverware my parents gave him for safekeeping, you know what he said? He spoke of the greed of some who should be weeping over lost lives rather than thinking of reclaiming belongings! Practically lecturing me!"

"Why are you surprised? Isn't an attack the best defense?"

David continued. "He managed to make me feel like a vulture, as I was trying to gather my family's property. As if losing my parents and six of my brothers and sisters was not enough, he kept lamenting about the village's misfortune of Russian lootings which, as far as I could see, had left his family intact, at least in terms of survival."

He stopped for a minute, rethinking his statement.

"Did I say, he made me feel like a vulture? That was my first reaction. Then, his words evoked violence in me. I wanted to do something, to pick him up, ring his neck, to kill him.

"His glorious daughter was touched by dirty Russian hands—but she was alive!"

"Callous beasts," Dora burst out.

"So this was last year." It was Robert, a young man from the Upper Country. "And now? What are you doing about it?"

"What can I do?" David snapped back in despair. "I can't bring back the family!"

"No, not the families. But remember, the system has been rotten right from the beginning. Kings, capitalism, the Admiral on his White Horse—it has to change, it *has* to! It's obvious!"

The room became quiet. Robert continued: "I gave up on the old order long ago. And now, with all that's happened, the road is clear: To change the quotation a bit, 'Downtrodden of the World, unite!' " His voice rang with conviction. "Yes, unite!"

Dora shrugged her shoulders. "Some see the solution in Palestine," she said with a skeptical voice. "My brother went to Palestine in 1942, with the last *aliya*. I got a note from him the other day. He wants me to join him. There are ways to get in, he says. But, who knows when things will get settled there? Besides, I don't want to be identified as a Jew again."

"Why do you need to leave?" The host, who had been going from group to group and was now back with them, turned to the girl. "You heard what Robert said. Just wait a few more months and we'll overtake the Kisgazda Party," he said as an afterthought.

"The Smallholders? Didn't they have sixty percent of the votes last time?" the girl naively asked.

"So what?" Misi looked at her impatiently.

Kata, who was only listening up to now, mustered courage: "And the Social Democrats? I know they didn't gain many votes, but Szakasits is still Vice President."

She got no immediate response and made another effort: "Do you really think Hungarians are inclined to vote Communist?"

"Who the hell cares about votes?" Misi snapped. "They deserve bullets!"

"You're right, the answer is in the Party," David said. The group buzzed in unison. Engel turned to Kata. "And you? Where do you stand?"

"You're all so sure, so determined, no questions at all," she said.

Misi pricked up his ears. "Aren't *you*? Aren't we here all?" he looked at her intensely. "Maybe you were untouched. No losses?"

"Why, of course . . . " Kata stammered. "I lost my husband."

The young man sized her up with disdain. "Well then? How can you have any questions what the future should be? Don't you have a sense of loyalty, a need for revenge?"

Kata felt a wave of heat reddening her cheeks.

"Take it easy, Misi," David relented somewhat apparently seeing her discomfort. "Don't overdo it!"

An announcement of refreshments by the hostess: "Hot *chai* and corn squares," stopped the interchange. They drifted toward the table.

Kata moved around with her cup of tea to hear what others had to say. Their comments were basically the same: despair, bitterness, thirst for retribution. And loyalty to the Party.

The emotionally charged atmosphere was exhausting. And it was late, too.

She went over to Marica. "I think I'd better go home. I like to put Jancsi to bed whenever I can."

Her cousin looked at her skeptically. Did she suspect how often Kata let her mother take over?

* * *

It was nine-thirty by the time she reached home. She found Jancsi in bed after all. Naturally, at that hour.

Kata took a long time changing into a robe, putting away this and that, making sure that the boy was asleep. It had been a trying evening: memories, relived trauma, brewing violence, endlessly.

Her own life—hardships, years of mortal danger, one unbearable tragedy. And yet, how did this compare with the experiences of people who had lost everyone? What did David Engel say? Mother, father and six siblings?

Incomprehensible!

It was a miracle that there were some who could go on living.

She stretched out on the sofa bed, thinking.

"A year has passed," that young man Robert said, "and what are you going to do now?"

What are they all going to do now? This matter of "now" was truly devastating because the now, in response to the "then," contained the very hate which had been the enemy's weapon.

Anxiety gripped her. What was *she* going to do ? Where now?

Restlessly she rose. She paced back and forth in the room. Then, she drifted toward the kitchen. She needed some physical comfort at least—a snack, a cup of hot milk?

When she was through and crossing the office on her way back to her room, her father appeared in the doorway.

"Oh, you're here?" He closed the door behind him. "I thought I heard some movement. Mother told me you went with Marica."

He did not press further. But his face revealed his question: "How was it?"

"It was disturbing in many ways, Apu, raising a lot of questions. But, I don't think I want to go over it again, not tonight."

"Of course, we'd both better go to sleep. Just one thing, I thought you'd want to know: Baumgarten was here for a visit."

"Really? I'm sorry I missed him!"

"Well, he will be in town a few days, may drop in tomorrow again. Will you be here?"

"Yes. How is he?" She moved a little nearer, interested in the news.

"He looks fine. He and his family are settled in Gyor—he likes it there. You know, it was so uplifting to talk to him," her father went on. "It's not that we discussed anything important. But just to think that some men followed their consciences! To know that in the midst of destruction and despair, there is hope when individuals dare and care."

Kata thought about the statement. Was he right? Were the deeds of a few decent souls—? What did they add up to in the face of the deaths of millions?

"You know, it's not only that without him both you and probably your mother would not be alive," her father continued. "No words can express how very grateful I am. But beyond my personal gratitude to him, it means everything to know that there were a few true Christians. Baumgarten's behavior toward us was more than exemplary. But there were others, at times blind, at other times meeting the challenge. If it were not for them, I, too, would give up on mankind. Well, it's late, let's go," and he approached the lamp on the desk.

Kata went to him and gave him a loving hug. "We ought to talk about this some more, Apukam. Some other time."

She was on her way now to bed, ready to sleep. With Father around, life had always been easier to bear.

She had her father. She had her family. But the others? Many had nobody. No one!

* * *

"Mr. Baumgarten!" Kata cried with joy as she opened the door. "Jancsi!" she called into the other room, "Come and meet a very good friend."

"Oh my, what a handsome fellow!" Baumgarten exclaimed.

"And from what I heard from your father, he's smart, too."

Jancsi eyed the stranger curiously and cautiously allowed himself to be picked up for a minute, then happily returned to his building blocks.

"How is your new parish?" Kata asked.

"I'm content. People are hungry for God—I find this particularly true now. For me this is, of course, a challenge, though I feel our work will be curtailed soon. God is too big a competitor for the Communists. But look, how about you? I was sorry to hear about Istvan. Of course, after such a long silence you'd suspected the news, hadn't you?"

She nodded. "Still, it hit me hard. Little things, opening up a drawer with some shirts of his, finding something in his handwriting." She shook her head.

"At times it's hard to understand God's ways," the minister admitted.

"I'm trying, Mr. Baumgarten. But when I think of the horrors, how could it be? There are so many questions unanswered."

"Some may never be answered here on earth."

"But then, how can one go on? There are some, even Communist adherents, so certain of their convictions."

"So you have questions of your convictions?"

"Well, you know me," she muttered a little embarrassed. "I'm not so unequivocal as some Christians, or even Communists."

"One can't be sure of everything Kata, even those who claim they are, have doubts. The important thing is to build on our convictions rather than to be deterred by our doubts."

* * *

Some two weeks later, Kata was thinking of Baumgarten's visit as she was standing on the corner of Rakoczy Avenue, waiting for the street-car. A girl in the office had invited her for supper and now she was on her way home. But the Number 19 did not come, nor did any other streetcar. The few would-be passengers craned their necks to catch a sight of the yellow vehicle. It had started to rain.

A supervising conductor appeared. He announced a delay. Kata was annoyed. It seemed the expected half-hour tram ride to her home would now be extended.

As she was waiting for the light to change, someone called out: "Do you want a ride?"

At first, she paid no attention. Few people owned cars in the city and she could think of no one she knew. But the voice repeated the offer, this time calling her by name.

She turned. It was David Engel. "Oh, it's you!"

He pulled up to the curb and opened the door. "I've an errand to do, deliver some papers in Buda, but if you aren't in a hurry, I could take you home afterwards."

She looked around. Still no tram was in sight and the rain was getting stronger. She had no umbrella with her either.

"Thanks. What a surprise—you in a car," she said as she occupied the front seat.

"Needless to say, it's not mine."

"Oh?"

"I'm glad we met. I wanted to invite you to a Party meeting, next Wednesday evening."

"Well, thanks. Are you— are you an official?"

"I've become quite involved in the last couple of weeks. At last, I've mobilized myself."

"I see."

"And I feel much better now, less depressed."

"It's a cliche, but still true: Time heals wounds, even such deep wounds as yours."

"Oh, it's not just that. It was the passivity that was unbearable. Rage with no outlet."

"And now you found your outlet?"

He shrugged. "A lot must be done to change things around; to teach them a lesson. And I'll do anything just to do that," he said with determination.

"Are they teachable?" In spite of her different experiences, Kata herself wondered at times how much the average Hungarian was amenable to basic change.

"Teachable?" he asked with some irony. "My dear, power drives lessons home in a very direct way. The best vehicle!" David appeared to note Kata's reserve: "You don't seem to agree. Of course, I know you are on the fence, at best. That's why I'd like you to come to the meeting. You may see things differently then."

The touch of a smile crept into her features. David must have noted it.

"Is it possible that you still have foolish notions about democratic elections?"

His comments seemed benign, though patronizing, but she was, at the moment, a captive audience. She considered his remark. "I don't want to think that the only solution is to swing to the other extreme."

"Oh, you don't? Well, there are things, and people, that must be eradicated. But let's get back to the first question, will you come to the meeting? And, would you work for the Party? We need people like you!"

"Like me? What makes you say that?"

"Well, you've had your loss—I heard your husband was in Auschwitz; you're young, intelligent and, I suspect, energetic." He glanced at her for a moment. "You haven't been much involved, though, have you?"

She was not sure how much she wanted to say. She supposed it was ridiculous to be worried. After all, he had only just now become a Party worker.

So she continued the dialogue.

"You're right, I've not been involved with the Party. We just got through with one totalitarianism. In any case, Communism goes against many things I believe in. And then, to think of it as the 'only' way?"

"Is there any other way for us?" David asked without hesitation. "The last decade made it obvious: Those who have the power have the key to life. We must get into power; how can you question that?"

"And when you're in power?"

"When we have the power?" David laughed a little embarrassed but more with satisfaction: "We'll call the tune by which they'll dance.

"But, let's go back to you," he insisted. "I know little about you. Tell me about your work."

"Um— I'm a secretary, in welfare."

"Really? Not in the Ministry?"

She shook her head. "I'd better tell you," she said after thinking a moment, "I work for Americans."

"Oh! I got the impression from your cousin that you had continued in the same job you had before the war."

"I did for a while. My employment with the church welfare organization hasn't been long."

David turned his head with a jerk to comprehend the last statement, but then, returned his visual attention to the road ahead.

"Church! Are you one of those recent converts?" he asked. "Budapest is full of them. Of course, it was different in Tolna. I was astounded to hear how many Jews tried to hide under the cloak of the church. If it had helped, fine!" The motion of his hand reflected futility.

"But it didn't. Well, that's not the point. But to think that you're continuing the ties, even if it's for a job."

"What makes you think it's for a job?" she asked with feeling. She was becoming annoyed, at Engel, at herself. It had been foolish of her to have gotten trapped in this car, to have allowed herself to be interrogated.

"Look, I see you're getting upset," he seemed to note her mood. "Believe me," he said with civility, "it wasn't my intention to challenge you, when I recognized you at the streetcar stop. I'd been thinking of getting in touch with you, and all of a sudden, there you were. Still, how can I not react to preposterous situations?"

"And you think of my job as preposterous."

"Oh, it's not your job. I'm sorry you work for Americans. There's no future in that in Hungary. But, it's your association with a church and any religion.

"Let's face it! Either you do it for a job, for hoped-for assimilation, or you believe in that nonsense. I must say, the last possibility is the most disturbing."

They had arrived at his destination. He got out of the car to deliver the envelope. When he returned, his mood for discussion was gone. He seemed too upset to hear her any more.

At this hour there was practically no traffic. They zoomed through the Bridge, then towards her address. Engel's thoughts seemed to be in tune with his car's speed.

"I was thinking of this religious dope: Old women's tales about a God who never existed. And even if He did, He must have committed suicide if He could see what Hitler accomplished and not be able to prevent it!

"God! Christianity! The same self-righteous indignation for centuries—the Jews have killed the Savior! So then they had to use their Crusades, pogroms, prejudice.

"Well, they did teach me a lesson. 'An eye for an eye, a tooth for a tooth' is too good for them. The spear will be in our hands! We must learn to use it with precision!

"This is why I am just as impatient with the Jewish tradition. 'Be good! Be merciful! Study the writings!' They groom us for passive abnegation. That time's over! They're fighting in Palestine—good. But that's a lost cause, too. What did that girl say the other day? She doesn't want to be identified as a Jew again. Neither do I. Not as a Jew, certainly not as a Christian!"

The verbal torrent slowed down at last.

Kata edged in: "And what, what do you want to be? You're skeptical, of being 'just' Hungarian."

"If Communism takes over, as I have no doubt it will, then, there will be a society with no caste, no races: all for the common goal. But to accomplish this, there's hard work ahead. And at last I've begun in that direction.

"And that's the only answer?"

"What else? Should we just forget? In a couple of years they'd start it all over again. They'd do the same tomorrow. Can't you see that?"

Kata was silent. David was probably right. What can one expect after mass murders, exterminations, having been treated as vermin and worse than that! And yet—

"Tell me," she said humbly. "I understand, but tell me, can hate solve the issue?"

"They hated first; it started with them. Never forget that!" David snapped back with feeling. "Never forget that!" He repeated. The speed of the car accelerated.

It took time for his anger to abate. The poorly lit streets raced by. But then, he composed himself and returned to the first question.

"And how about you? I don't suppose you'll be interested in the Party then—surely not while working for the Americans. Unless— Are you planning to stay with them?

"I don't know yet. But that's not the real issue."

"What is the real issue?" he asked with willed self- control. "You stubbornly seem to feel that Hungarian Jewry has choices."

Kata thought for a while. "I don't know if they do. And I know what you think: what choices did we have in the last seven or eight years or even twenty-seven? But still, it's hard for me to give up on having choices. Look," she said with hesitation. "I don't know how I can tell you this, you went through so much more than I, but it really shakes me to think that we learned nothing from the past but to use their instruments. It will be milder, of course. Nothing can compare with the mass murder of, what do they say, six million? But still, as ridiculous as it may seem to you, I think 'love your enemies' is a better weapon in the long run."

"You're out of your mind!" David was beyond choosing a 'proper' reply. "To love them? You remember what Misi Voros said: 'They need bullets.' I agree. Don't you see they would start it all over again if they had a chance?" he asked in desperate frustration.

"I know. Maybe I'm just groping for an answer. Surely, justice has to be done! Retaliation? How far shall we go?"

"How far? I can't worry about that. One thing I know: whatever we do, it must produce steel fists. There is no place for love where millions were murdered. I'm sorry for you," he concluded. He seemed to shudder at her childish solutions. "Don't worry. I'll not cause you trouble. I'll go my way, and you? Well, I hope you'll think about this. Working for Americans will not help you here. Yes, think! There's still time to join. If you wait? I don't know how long the decision will be left open. But if you do join, there is no place for this love nonsense in the Party, no place at all here in Hungary, in 1946, after what has happened."

Kata sighed. "I heard the warning. Look, this is my street and there's the house—next corner. Thank you for the ride. Be well!"

She felt as if she were crumbling under the weight of the past, present and future. She must get rid of the terrible burden! She must forget. She could not go on constantly reliving those dreadful years, poisoning her life with hatred.

CHAPTER 16

ARPAD

N O V E M B E R   1 9 4 6-
A U G U S T   1 9 4 7

More than ever, Kata looked forward to going to work Mondays.

Her employment with the Americans represented a different world. In it she hoped to find a confirmation of the decency of human beings among representatives of a less turbulent culture than her own.

She found a haven in that church welfare organization with ideals that she could share. Furthermore, the surroundings, while not luxurious, reflected the comforts of a well-settled ambience, long missed.

Mr. Campbell was on sabbatical leave from a professorship in an American denominational college. He was thrilled to have obtained the services of Kata whose experiences during the war helped him to understand what had gone on in Europe. He encouraged her to tell of her mother's escape to Western visitors who made special tours of inspection in the war-torn country and were eager to return to the States with stories of human endurance. Yet, Kata's enthusiasm in relating the miracle was not quite without ambivalence. Would her faith-filled story soften the authenticity of the horrors which her mother had survived in so unique a way? The horrors were real and miracles did not happen to everyone.

She was surrounded by people—her employer, another American employee and the foreign visitors—who were giving, represented freedom and normalcy, and were people of faith.

She was tempted—more than tempted, in fact—to know that big fascinating America better and perhaps make it her home. Quota registration for entry into the United States opened late in 1946. She registered, wanting to assure a place for herself and Jancsi on it. But the plan for actually going was tentative; she was still exploring what life in Hungary would likely hold for her and the child. And working with the Americans was Arpad Kurucz, who represented Hungary's rocky past.

* * *

Arpad had begun to work for the agency a little after Kata. A good word from a distant relative living in America and married to a colleague of Mr. Campbell's got him the job. He was lucky, as his position in the Ministry of Interior had just ended.

"He is one of the scions of Hungarian gentry," Alice Smith, the American secretary, let Kata know. "He has had his troubles, too—lands confiscated, father killed, his mother toiling to support him with some family assistance. And, oh yes, his wife was killed by the Russians. I understand, though, it was not a happy marriage."

"Sad story," Kata acknowledged, silently noting Alice's detailed knowledge of the facts. She herself was quickly able to round out the picture in her imagination. And indeed, when she began to know Arpad—their desks were pushed opposite one to the other—his travails were confirmed in their conversations. His father had been a victim of Bela Kun's three-month Commune in 1918. That event always had unsavory recollections for the general population and to some extent even more so for Jews, who were forever reminded of the fact that Bela Kun was Jewish. Of course, the issue did not come up between Arpad and Kata, but as they talked, they were both well aware of the facts.

Neither did it need elaboration to surmise the struggle of a gentry family to maintain a certain style of living in the post-World War I period in Budapest, when Greater Hungary was divided by the Treaty of Trianon, and the surrounding countries received the lands belonging to Hungarian owners, in Arpad's case Romania. Allusion to the struggle invariably popped up in their conversations. Nevertheless, Arpad's life had had its glories as well and he readily spoke with Kata about the good times that a gentry youth, even with meager resources, could enjoy "before those damned Russians took over."

* * *

It was a different world, that of the Americans, Arpad realized. At times he felt as if on a foreign island amidst the sea of his fellow Hungarians. The key word was service. This in itself was appealing. It was impressive to know that there were people who were concerned with giving and caring. Yet, the giving had a different flavor from any charity Arpad was used to—the organized collection of contributions given at some glittering social event and distributed to an equally organized list of recipients.

The kind of service his employers offered was really not selective. It was assumed that any applicant would have some reason to ask. For some, a donation meant surplus rather than the satisfaction of basic need; others tried to foster relations with the West in the hope that their contacts might eventually open the way to an American visa. And the clientele was diverse. A good share of the applicants were from the old membership of the established Protestant churches. But there were also some whose newly forged church membership kept them from the traditional Jewish relief organizations.

Arpad had difficulty when he first interviewed some of these families.

"There are so many Jewish resources," he said. "The Jews have a vast network of collaboration and mutual help. Why don't these people use those channels?"

"Well, they seem to feel they belong here," Mr. Campbell noted. "What difference does it make who the recipient is?"

"It's hard for you to change gears, Arpad." Kata commented. She was a little annoyed, but after all, this was a new experience for Arpad. And Arpad was embarrassed, too. He respected Kata and viewed her differently from the recent converts whose motives he suspected. In fact, he was impressed by the experiences of the girl and her family. Still, how could he tell her of all the pain, all the humiliation that the changing order had meant to him? And how could he discuss with her the exasperating fact that his job in the Ministry was really lost because of the suspicion—quite unjustified—of a vengeful person who had risen from anonymity to cabinet rank in the Hungarian Communist Party?

Well, at least Kata and he could agree on their position about the Party. Neither of them was for the new order, though the vehemence of their opposition and the shades of their critical judgment were not the same. Nevertheless, because they found this convergent point of view in their outlooks, Arpad chose to dwell on the corresponding, rather than the controversial, aspects of their ideas.

As a matter of fact, he became quite interested in her. She, too, represented a different world. Not quite as different as the American secretary. Alice Smith frightened him away. Too much freedom, too little sophistication, and a considerable language barrier, too! His English was rather rudimentary. He could at least converse with Kata Fogaras and did not have to feel inferior because of his search for words and expressions, or because of anything in fact. His background still provided him with fringe benefits in the status-conscious appraisal of his countrymen.

In any case, Kata was a good-looking woman who was able to express herself with clarity and conviction, and Arpad was now a lonely man. He did not look for ideological discussions. They were painful and confusing to him, and were hardly amenable subjects for agreement between him and the girl. In all truth, he had never been accustomed to much real conversation with persons of the opposite sex. In his immediate surroundings women were viewed as desirable jewels, or tired providers. But now, he was ready to become better acquainted with another kind, and their discussions would often end with an invitation from Arpad for a simple lunch or after-office cup of coffee together.

* * *

These informal little events became quite pleasant stops in the interim period between the tragedy of the past and the enigmatic future. Kata, too, had to face the fact that part of her life was over. Yet, the real acceptance of her loss required time and she was now in a state of limbo. And if for Kata the coming years loomed heavily laden with questions, Arpad found the search for an answer to his life much more frightening. While she had questions of how she would fare in the current political arena of growing Communism, at least there was nothing in her past that could be held against her. Arpad's whole world represented the antithesis of the present political order.

Arpad did everything to avoid looking into the future. Kata tried to close her eyes to the ghosts of the past. In spite of its rocky journey, Arpad's pre-war years could be remembered with some enjoyment and glow and, strangely enough, they often found themselves "reminiscing" about the days when a gentry youth, even with limited means, was able to have fun, could participate in merrymaking, could weave brilliant hopes for the future and be on the fringe of a society where the rich and the titled held the key to success.

"The good old times," as Arpad tended to consider them, had never been really open to Kata in her adolescence. Yet, they were not directly tied to the saga of final persecution and destruction and could, therefore, be vicariously enjoyed at least for the duration of their conversations.

Arpad even took her to the opera once. He had received free tickets from a neighbor, a member of the chorus, in appreciation for monitoring packages from American relatives of the musician. It was a pleasant evening and their seats in the orchestra, though free, somehow fitted in with the picture of the carefree social background that Arpad's stories had revealed.

But their occasional times together, and now the date to the opera, were not only vehicles for return to the lighter part of pre-war gentry life. Arpad was a handsome man. Ten years older than Kata he fitted the Hungarian image for the need of a more mature, more experienced male to be the suitable partner to the "weaker" sex. His suave and polished manners bespoke his background in more definite terms than any revelation of financial difficulties would suggest. He was exotic and intriguing. And surely he could speak the language of women—complimenting, attentive, gallant and protective.

They had worked together now for almost a year and had had many opportunities to talk to each other outside of the office. The nature of the relationship provided an atmosphere of lightness and anticipation, of unformulated hopes and unsuppressed pleasure while Kata was slowly beginning to pull herself together in preparation for tackling life ahead.

* * *

"Let's go out tomorrow," Arpad suggested. "I'll take you to my favorite restaurant in Obuda."

"Are there still some left?" Kata asked. The old part of the city had suffered more destruction during the war than Pest. But traces of the pre-war past still survived. This was what Arpad had found on a day he combed a well-known sector of Obuda and spotted a family-owned restaurant he had frequented in better times.

It took them almost two hours, by the time the tramway connections were made, to reach the place, strolling on the upward slope leading to its entrance. In the garden, several small cubicles were screened from the neighbors' direct surveillance by the spreading leaves of morning glory vines. All guests had a free view, though, of the three-member gypsy band settled in one side of the garden square so as to offer equal access to its music to the visitors and an accompaniment to would-be dancers in the middle of the garden dance floor. There were not many people that day and they got excellent service and enjoyed the house's specialty, *fatanyeros*, which Arpad ordered as a treat for the evening. It was the anniversary of his employment at the agency and the day he had first met Kata.

"Anniversaries do need celebration," he said and cheerfully raised his glass to continued happy associations, "not only in the world of welfare business," he added.

Kata felt good. The drops of Badacsonyi wine slowly took away the edge of the evening coolness and helped to transform the garden in a city still not out of ruins into one of enchantment and hope.

Arpad beckoned to the gypsy who gave life to those longing, sobbing and thrilling pizzicati of the violin. And Arpad's warm baritone glowed, pleaded, wooed as he sang along with the tune: "Orgonak, tavaszi orgonak . . . " — "Lilacs, spring lilacs . . . '

One song came after the other. Even Kata ventured to join in, though she was never noted for her singing.

"You're beautiful tonight, Kata," Arpad said as the gypsy returned to his stand. "You're more beautiful now than I ever knew you before," he said slowly drawing Kata's hand to his lips.

The words, the touch, the music elicited a dreamy smile.

"Thank you," she replied and her hand returned the sentiment by its gentle squeeze of her partner's fingers. She reciprocated the look and saw that Arpad was tender and demanding.

"Kata, we have known each other for a while now." Arpad spoke again after a few minutes of silent admiration. "Where are we going?"

A little shrug, a lifted eyelid, a quizzical smile left the question open.

The band started a csardas. It shifted the mood from nostalgic day-dreaming and gave impetus to impatient feet.

"Come on, let's dance."

Arpad led her to the dance floor. She was somewhat self-conscious in this scantily populated restaurant to go along, to reveal her joy. She was also self-conscious because this was the first time she had felt like rejoicing in this way, the first time since the war was over. The first time since she had become a widow.

And yet, she could, she did enjoy herself. The dormant feelings, the numb movements of the body victoriously escaped from their prison. There was a sense of liberation as their steps moved from right to left, from left to right, his hand on her waist directing her movements, his eyes commanding her feelings.

As they returned to the table and were sipping their coffee, Arpad went back to his earlier question. "Kata, I really meant it when I asked, where are the two of us going?"

This was a different direction from the conversations of the past months, Kata thought. Her fingers absent-mindedly gathered the crumbs on the table. She formed geometrical patterns as she plowed across the checkered tablecloth. It reminded her of the fortune-seeking of Greek soothsayers, who expected an answer from the grains of sand. She was aware of her detachment—not from the situation but from the need of giving a reply to a question which somehow seemed rhetorical.

"Look at me," Arpad reached to her chin. "Let me look into those lovely eyes. Let me tell you I love you, Kata," he said with deliberation.

His glance was penetrating her. A sweet, intoxicating sensation came over her.

"I've wanted to tell this to you for some time," he continued. "I guess I was a little scared. At times you seem too serious, Kata, so beyond such frivolity. Frivolity? What am I saying? I'm not trying to be frivolous at all." Arpad corrected himself, and again clasped her hand with genuine warmth. "Kata, let's leave, it's too public here."

The wine and the surroundings enwrapped Kata in a comfortable cocoon from which she knew she would have to break out, but it was good to delay any action. She said and did nothing. Arpad took the initiative. He rose, left money on the table, helped Kata to her feet, and ushered her toward the exit.

On the winding street leading to the streetcar he held her arm firmly. Then he turned to a side street noting there a bench with a partial view of the Danube.

"Let's enjoy this a while," he said and pulled out a handkerchief to dust off the seat.

The earlier magic of the music still lingered. The air carried the intoxicating smell of lilacs, mingled with budding acacia. And the stars sparkled above.

Arpad put his arm around her, first cautiously. Then he pulled her towards him and kissed her eyes, her cheek, her lips. She could feel the surge of passion in his now impatient movements and she found herself responding to its intensity. His proclamation of love echoed in her whispered reply.

Then there were no words and indeed no thoughts but her response to his caressing touch, his increasing desire to hold and possess her.

They heard footsteps. The two straightened up. Another couple was approaching, possibly in search of a quiet nook.

"Kata, let's go home," he urged as he ushered her back to the main street. "Our feelings need privacy."

They walked in silence.

They crossed the Danube by tramway and at the corner of Karoly Boulevard Arpad helped her off. "This way," he said, guiding her by the elbow. Then, looking around in the empty Boulevard, he brushed her hair with his lips whispering: "Two more blocks, dear."

For a while Kata just walked along relishing the enchantment of the evening.

God, how good it is to feel like a woman again, she thought.

Yet, as the distance to Arpad's apartment shortened,—and she knew the address—a scare, a warning, a sobering mood intruded into the happy daze. As they crossed Baross Street the lights of a coffeehouse extended an invitation. Kata stopped.

"Let's have a cup of coffe," she suggested.

A faint shadow crossed Arpad's features, but he led her through the revolving door of the coffeehouse, which offered refuge to late patrons of the neighborhood.

For a while Kata seemed to be searching for words. There was a long silence.

"Do you feel rushed?" Arpad finally asked, with some anxiety.

No reply. The dreamy eyes again were cast on the tablecloth.

"I hope you know I don't mean this to be a cheap little affair," Arpad anxiously explained. "Maybe you want to know what my plans are? I'm not quite ready, Kata, to propose, but I haven't put the thought of marriage aside. I want you to know that. We are grown-up people. I thought we may not need a marriage certificate."

She was touched by the tone of his voice and felt the emotional pull toward him.

Finally, head down and voice very low, she said: "I really don't know. It's not just the marriage certificate. You said you were not quite ready to propose. I don't know what I am ready for, either. I've had a lovely evening, Arpad. I think you know that. But this is about all the certainty I have about us."

* * *

Soon after the evening at Obuda, Kata left for a two-week vacation, settling Jancsi and her mother in a summer cottage for the months to come.

* * *

"Kata, let's have a real date again," Arpad suggested at the end of August. "With your going and coming to Veroce and my vacation, we've had little time together, have we?" The question was laden with feeling as well as reproach. "We almost need to be reacquainted!"

The summer had raced past. Those times in the company of her son and parents, the long sunbathing on the Danube's beach and the intermittent swimming in the river's crisp-cold waters, even her walks alone in the woods with a book in her hand, had not produced an answer about Arpad and herself. And her questions were not formulated enough for much discussion with her parents.

What was she looking for in a man now? A romantic troubadour; a scion of that Hungarian society which had eluded her up to now? Could it be that this was all she wanted?

Arpad was not the intellectual Istvan was, not the philosopher like her father. And, what about spirituality? But there were plenty of things to like him for, she told herself. And she needed the personal contacts to know him better.

So Kata happily went along to Demenyi's that evening.

The coolness of the late evening made them waver for a moment before taking their seats outside. But the gypsy band was not cold, it seemed, and most of the garden cubicles were occupied.

"And how was your summer?" she asked.

"You know, I spent two weeks in Eger. Not with family, but with good friends. It was fun. Don't misunderstand me," he assured her with a chuckle. "This time flirting was not my goal. But I did go out and the gypsy played, as well as in the past. The fortnight did remind me of the happy times of my youth. Now that I'm nearing forty, the past seems to become more and more important."

Again, those good old times, Kata thought. This is what keeps him alive.

But almost as if in rebuttal to her inarticulated thoughts Arpad said: "Let's come back to the present, Kata. The important thing is that I missed you, I missed you very much!"

"You did?"

"Indeed! Come, now that we're through with the main course, let's dance!"

"You can bring the *palacsinta*, we'll be back soon," he nodded to the waiter who arrived for the order.

As they moved to join the dancers, someone from the cubicle they passed called out in happy recognition,

"Look who's here! Hey, Arpad! What a surprise!"

They stopped and two men at the table stood up immediately, heartily inviting Arpad and his companion over.

Arpad hesitated. He introduced them to Kata, but was eager to proceed to the dance floor. "We may be back later," he said perfunctorily as he led Kata away.

"You didn't seem too friendly," Kata teased. "Tell me about them."

"Oh, old friends," he shrugged his shoulder. And he held her tight and seemed to silently admire her. They moved slowly, the tango was enchanting and for a moment they felt alone in the big garden, intertwined, in anticipation.

"Oh, Kata," he whispered, "let's escape!"

"Escape?" she chuckled. "Arpad, I think your friends are watching us," she added with some sobriety and stepped back a little, conscious of their curious eyes. "Don't you want to join them?"

"Not really. Why don't we just leave?"

"Oh, I don't know. I'd feel funny just to disappear. Besides, I wouldn't mind knowing your friends, Arpad. Tell me about them."

"As you wish," he shrugged. "I know them both from *gimnazium*. Csaba was actually a distant relative of my wife Anna. I met her through him," he added pensively. "He's a district notary—I think he has recently been forced into early retirement—a reputed drinker and quite a Don Juan. I haven't seen him for some time. The other man, Lehel, has an apartment in the city and we do run into each other occasionally. He isn't doing so well now that his four thousand-acre estate had been nationalized and he's left only with the hunting lodge and the surrounding vineyard. Lehel is bitter, of course, about many things. All of us are," he added with a sigh.

"Well, here we are," Arpad announced their arrival as they moved up to the table. The announcement was hardly necessary. The party at the table was already eagerly greeting Arpad and his girl. A perfunctory introduction took away the momentary tension of meeting the "unknown."

"Enchanted," the men complimented, clicking their heels as if in riding boots and kissing her hand.

As they were settling down at the table, Kata took a better look at the two. Lehel seemed to be the more sophisticated. The benefits of four thousand acres were still exerting their influence. Csaba had the conventional curly moustache of his class and caste, the country public officer. His ringed finger boasted a family crest and he expertly held the wine glass toasting the lady in their midst, accompanying his good wishes with effusive compliments.

After the preliminary niceties, however, he seemed to be more interested in renewing contacts with Arpad.

"So you got stuck in the Americans' office, my friend," Csaba chided Arpad as they were sipping their wine. "It must surely be better than allying with the Reds and the like."

He looked sideways at Kata in an effort to assess what was "the like" that she came from. Arpad quickly explained that they knew each other from work and that Kata was the right hand of the American church officer. This called for a compliment to such a smart young woman who obviously had other assets, too, beside the command of English. It also placed Kata in the right religious setting.

As they talked, another man and his companion entered and greeted them. He was monocled and presented a somewhat supercilious savoire faire. The woman in his company showed no remarkable feature but the jewelry she wore bespoke better days, or wealthy connections perhaps, Kata thought.

"Hey, Arpad Kurucz," he reached out his hand. "I haven't seen you for years! How are things with you, my boy? I heard of the tragedy from Csaba. And now?" He looked at Kata.

"This is Colonel Pongraczy, Kata; Colonel, that is, of the past."

A stiff bow and another introduction: "Maria Kutassy. Would you mind if we joined you?" the Colonel asked, and was already pulling a chair to seat Maria.

He was obviously accustomed to being in command, Kata thought.

"Of course, of course," came the well-mannered reply. "This is indeed an unexpected old-time reunion, I must say." Arpad began to look quite happy.

"Maria and I just came from the movies and I thought we might have a bite before I took her home. Home is near here, you know," he added meaningfully.

Arpad seemed to feel the conversation should be expanded. "How are things in Fejerfalu?" he inquired from Csaba.

"Well, times are bad, the pension is nothing and my brother is under investigation."

"I'm sorry to hear that," Arpad sympathized. "What happened?"

"Nothing, absolutely nothing. These damned Jews think they own the world. He's accused of commanding a labor division. What could he have done? Wasn't it his duty to obey orders?" Arpad frowned uneasily. He took time to formulate the most appeasing response.

"These are confusing times for everybody, I'm sure," he tried somehow to give an explanation without pushing Csaba further in his oration.

"They are, to be sure. You know, my brother was never very tactful nor soft-hearted. Still, he's my brother and I'll stand up for him in face of ridiculous accusations. It's bad enough that we lost the war and our lands, and now it looks like even our future!"

Kata felt strained. Arpad glanced at her and was preparing to say something, some benign neutral comment that would divert the conversation from the delicate topic. He seemed to be seeking the right word that would make Kata feel more at ease without giving Csaba a new occasion for argument and for further easy words. Fortunately, Lehel picked up the hopelessness theme.

"It's all these Reds that make life unbearable," he said. "I would not care what their religion is: What matters is that our good life is disappearing, that our wealth has been robbed and our dreams crushed. I want to be fair—a gentleman must. Not all the accusations are for nothing. Even then, the people in the Government today turn me the other way. If it continues this way, there is no hope at all for the likes of us."

"Look, I don't like this talk," Arpad finally said. "Couldn't we turn to some more cheerful things?"

"There is little cause for cheer, you know that damned well," Csaba retorted. He could not care about the girl's sensitivity. By now he had probably guessed her background.

"You don't need to be so belligerent, Csaba," Lehel sought a less militant trend for the conversation. "Arpad is right. Let's talk of happier things—about the past, it's worth remembering!"

Arpad's face lit up a little at the mention of the past. Even Kata felt more hopeful.

"Arpad often puzzled us," Lehel addressed Kata in a confidential tone. "At times he was quiet, as if nothing else mattered than school. Then, when the girls came—yes, Arpad became a different person in the last year of *gimnazium*. Then came the university, the social events, the balls and serenades—he surpassed us all!"

"Yes, girls he was running after," Csaba picked up the conversation. "Do you remember how he spent a monthly allowance on that dark-eyed little Julcsa?"

"Drinks, hangovers, angry relatives—and the vacation was over," now Pongraczy added his past recollection. "Your uncle was proud of your successes with women," he commended his friend.

Arpad smiled. "Proud? Maybe. Stingy, too!"

"Arpad was always in trouble on account of girls. He had to account for his doings and spendings to the family," Pongraczy offered the explanation. "Your Uncle Balazs, yes, he pushed you to conquer, then he was mad as hell when the girl was in trouble."

This was what Arpad was like? God, what am I doing here? Kata's

insides churned. Was this Arpad's world? But she sat there as if paralyzed to speak, move or even think.

Pongraczy was ready to go. "I just want to say," he concluded,
"money does not make that much difference now. It went into cards,
drinks, women. Of course, now it's in the hands of the damned—" He
pursed his lip but did not finish the sentence.

"What pains me most, boys," he turned to them in an attempt at
self-justification, "is not so much the land and the lost wealth. I can still
manage, somehow. But we were someone, and now—now there is no
future at all. There's nothing to hope for!"

"Unless another war?" Csaba tried to inject the provocative thought.

"Another war?" Lehel looked at him with slightly concealed con-
tempt.

"It wouldn't do anyone any damned good. Not even us."

"Arpad is the smart one, he works for the Americans," Pongraczy
said. "Do you want to emigrate, maybe?"

Arpad took time to answer. "No, I really don't think so. What would
I do there? It's a different world. They're simple and naive, and everything is work. Work, work, work . . . '

"Well, you're doing all right with them now, aren't you?" came
Csaba's challenge.

"Ah, it's all right for a while. It's all right to sit at a desk and do what
they tell me. I can still be myself. Here I am still someone. You know
me, he knows me, my name is worth something. In America, I guess I'd
be nobody. Anyhow, one can't get a visa and perhaps not even a
passport."

"Wait, Arpad, if my brother Dini is acquitted, he will have you
occupy the Jew Gross's job as circuit judge. What about it, hey?" and
he poked at Arpad's shoulder.

"Stop, Csaba, for God's sake, stop!" Arpad finally spoke up sharply.
But he immediately continued in a conciliatory tone: "You all make me
really depressed. It might be good to think back if there were something
to look forward to, also. But is there?" And he seemed sad and the joy
was gone.

"Let's have another drink and be merry!" Csaba offered the least
controversial solution.

They drank some more. They began to sing.

"Do you remember the time Arpad consumed a case of wine glasses, throwing them one by one to the wall, and the gypsy continued playing, playing?" Csaba recalled. "We'd just finished law school. Those were the times! Those were the times, indeed!"

"*Kislany, kekszemu kislany . . .* " Arpad slid into the mood of the thirties. "*Szepszemu zsidolany . . .* " — "Little girl with blue eyes . . . Jewish girl, with beautiful eyes . . . " He sang, he drank, he was now happy and gradually he became unaware of the company.

Kata was watching impassively now as if looking at a stage; listening to actors speaking an alien language. It was just noise, intermingled with the gypsy's romantic chords, evaporating, becoming nothing in the cool of evening dusk. A surge of heat filled her. The taste of the savory supper now turned disgustingly acid in her throat. Was she going to vomit?

"I want to go home," she said, turning to Arpad with a decisive tone.

Arpad looked at her as if not quite comprehending. "Go home, so soon?" and he reached for another glass, but the bottle was empty.

"You're not used to this any more, my friend," Lehel looked at him with some concern. "We'll have to get you home—you'll need some help!"

"Did you forget I have a car for this jaunt?" Csaba turned to Lehel. "Come on Arpi, we'll drive to Pest."

Kata slid into the rear seat, Arpad after her. In a minute his head dropped on her shoulder. He fell asleep.

Lehel looked back from the front seat a few times to check if everything was all right. Then he returned to his conversation with Csaba at the wheel.

They crossed Margit Bridge and as they were sliding along Lipot Boulevard, Arpad suddenly sat up.

"Was I sleeping?" he asked with some embarrassment.

"You were knocked out, Arpi," Csaba gloated. "You could never really drink. You haven't changed, my friend; you haven't changed at all!"

"I don't know," Arpad muttered. He was still not ready for real conversation. "Csaba, I guess we'd better get out. I really need some fresh air." He turned to the driver. He was eager now to be on his own.

"Can you manage?" Csaba asked.

"Sure, of course. You don't mind, do you?" he asked Kata, finally recognizing her presence.

"I don't mind it at all. We can walk from here."

"It was good to see you Csaba, and you, Lehel, and even Pongraczy. It was good to see you all!" he repeated as he said good-bye. But Csaba insisted on the last word:

"Remember, Arpi, if my brother is acquitted, he may get you the Jew Gross's job, remember!"

"Sure—shut up—fine." Arpad mumbled.

* * *

Arpad and Kata walked for a while without talking. The fresh air helped him to come to his senses. He suggested they have a cup of coffee. He really needed to wake up.

They had their espresso but it had to be quick. The place was about to close.

They were on the way to Kata's home, turning to Andrassy Avenue. Arpad felt better. But with the return of sobriety the awareness came that the evening had been a fiasco. He tried to apologize.

"I should never have agreed to join them," he told Kata. "Csaba was always uncouth. I should have known better. Of course, Pongraczy wanted to show off in front of his girl. I'd sort of hoped, though, Lehel would save the situation."

"What about you, Arpad?" she asked sharply. "Couldn't you have taken a stand? Eh," she said, "it doesn't matter. The situation was unsalvageable, hopeless!"

She walked on briskly in silence, then erupted: "Tell me, have you ever really tried to comprehend what happened to others? Did you ever believe people were murdered for nothing?—you and your friends!"

Arpad looked at her startled.

"Kata, please. Look, I'm really sorry. But let's be quiet. There is Andrassy ut 60," he nodded to the other side. "Communist Headquarters. The guards are there!"

"Communist, yes!" Kata said in a lowered voice, "and Nyilas Headquarters three years ago. That's where my mother had her ordeal, I'm sure I have told you that!"

"I know."

They said no more. The busy clicking of her heels against the pavement accentuated the night's silence. She was practically running along the Avenue, Arpad trying to keep up with her. In no time, they were in front of her home. She pushed the bell.

"I'm sorry, Kata," Arpad repeated with a mixture of annoyance and guilt. "We should have left right after dinner. An evening for nothing!"

"Nothing?" She swallowed. "A most important evening!"

The concierge was already opening the portal. As she quickly retreated into the hallway she called back:

"See you in the office!"

And she continued her running, now up the stairs.

CHAPTER 17
SEARCH

S E P T E M B E R   1 9 4 7-
S E P T E M B E R   1 9 4 8

A pu, don't you see? I don't belong. Nowhere!"

Vaghelyi looked at her with a frown. "You feel that now?"

"More than ever! When I'm with Jews, I don't quite fit. I don't even have a number tattooed on my arm. Yet, the bonds are strong—blood, family ties, common mourning."

"Of course you do!"

"Then, there was this Arpad from work. I met his friends," she shook her head. "And to think of it that I had wanted to be one of them!"

"What about the dedicated Christians?" her father asked.

"Oh Apu, you know I don't have their kind of faith! I'm depressed! So I survived, and now? I feel lost. Maybe it would be different in America!" she sighed.

"America!" Her father threw up his hands. "You must first look for other kinds of answers. By the way, there'll be an American speaker in our church this Sunday. Why don't you come to hear him?"

"An American? I'd like to hear what he has to say. I'll come."

And on Sunday she was in church with her parents heading to the familiar nook where they always sat.

She saw the American, with Bible in hand, waiting. The congregation shuffled feet; there was a low hum of comments; it was well past time to start.

Pastor Pfeffel was walking toward Kata. "I'm so glad you're here. The translator must have been delayed. Do you think you could help out?"

"I'll be glad to." Kata went forward, was introduced to the Reverend Tydings and was given the passage to read: " . . . one time you Gentiles . . . separated from Christ, alienated from the commonwealth of Israel . . . "

The preliminaries over, Tydings was called to the pulpit. Kata was quite excited as she followed him. And after the first minutes of stage fright, she found herself fully responding to the challenge.

"Christ . . . He is our peace who . . . has broken down the dividing wall of hostility." Tydings repeatedly came back to the words. And as Kata translated them into Hungarian, the message assumed special significance for her.

* * *

They were sitting in her father's study a week later. "Pastor Pfeffel told me that he felt your presentation was more than the repetition of another person's thought," her father said. "He never thought you were taking spiritual matters so seriously."

"You know, Apu, in a way it's true; I think this was the first time that I totally identified with what I heard from that pulpit. Let's face it, I've never been the kind of Christian Pastor Pfeffel would want."

Her father tilted his head quizzically. "The Pastor likes you a great deal, and I've just told you how warmly he spoke of you."

"I know, Dad. He's a friendly man. Still, as far as he's concerned I never walked down the aisle."

"You walked up to the pulpit!"

"To translate."

"And what you said before?"

"You mean that I had no question about the message?" She stopped to digest her own words, then added: "I'm convinced of it!"

* * *

"Kata, my family just got their visas to Chile," Zsuzsa told her by phone. "I haven't made up my mind yet, but since Gyuri is dead and my mother and all her sisters are leaving, probably I'll go too. Hurry up with your plans; at least we'd be in the same hemisphere."

And Baumgarten wrote in a Christmas card: "A cousin of mine who had the good luck to be born in San Francisco, though he was brought back here by his parents as an infant, decided to validate his U.S. citizenship. He's leaving soon. How are Kata's plans coming along?"

So far, if one had a visa, it was not difficult to get the passport. But the American visa for Kata and Jancsi was not forthcoming. Unexpected applications by people who had priority status inflated the waiting list and took precedence over earlier registrations.

In the meantime the Communists had emerged in the elections with a plurality over the Smallholders Party. They were still only a segment, though the largest segment, of the political coalition. But as the months proceeded, all the other partners with their political diversity slowly disappeared. And the political shifts, resignations, realignments, willing and engineered departure of leaders from the country, and the arrest of others, culminated in the "Year of the Turning Point:" 1948. The hate campaign that followed was now diverted from the culprits of the war to the industrial rich, then on to the shopkeeper middle class, the small traders and finally the agricultural Kulaks, wealthy peasants. It engulfed hitherto powerful party officials, veteran Communists now falling in the shadow of presumed Titoist insubordination. It mounted its attacks on the church, incarcerating Mindszenty and later some Protestant leaders as well. In another year or two it would turn against a segment of the Jewish community conveniently labelled Zionist, to drain the high number of Jews from political leadership.

When the American visa was once again postponed, Kata wrote to the Stewarts in Scotland. The Reverend Stewart replied with warmth. Yes, he and his wife would procure a visa to Great Britain for Kata and the child. The visa was for work as a domestic, but who cared? It would cover just a transitory period until she and Jancsi could move to America.

And the solution had some compensations. Great Britain was so much closer than America.

Not that the family would really try to block her plan to leave. The trend of unofficial public opinion was in favor of emigration. The Kalmars, too, remembered the lucky ones who had left before the Nazis took over. Still, Scotland was nearer!

With the British work permit in hand, Kata applied for a passport. It looked as though she would soon be on her way. Others of her friends had obtained permission to leave without difficulty—Zsuzsa and family indeed were off to South America by July 1948, even with a good-sized moving van containing a major household's needs.

But the Ministry of the Interior kept delaying the issuing of Kata's passport. Travel dates were reset over and over again. Finally in August her application was rejected.

It was a total shock. It was incomprehensible. Others had been allowed to leave. Why was she an exception? Could it be her working for Americans?

She could not be trapped again! She must try to appeal the decision and do whatever else was necessary to achieve her goal.

* * *

It was a mild autumn morning when she visited Dr. Garay in the hope that the judge would intervene in her passport problem. He was one of the few survivors of the past political order who was not branded guilty by the current regime and who was able to maintain his national appointment in spite of the many far-reaching changes that had taken place since the war. Dr. Garay's empathic attitude toward Jews was well known and he was allowed to continue as a judge in the Supreme Court.

Garay was a devout Christian. His faith spurred him to take rescue actions at the risk of his life, but it was more. It also included literal and unquestioning belief in the teachings of the Bible and the need to abide by its rules, and to put unwavering faith in God's providence and guidance for one's life. When in 1944 he had recognized the immediate threat to Kata's life, he had been willing to invite her into his home. But now?

"Why are you so eager to leave?" he asked as she sat in front of him in his chambers. "Do you think you're in danger?"

"My life? Probably not. Prison? Maybe. And very likely I would have difficulty in finding another job if the Americans can't stay. But—" she leaned forward. "Dr. Garay, how shall I tell you, those ghosts of the past! Can you imagine, are you aware of the animosity, the hatred that still exists here between Jew and Gentile? Wherever I go, one side or the other tears open the wound that craves to be healed."

The judge looked at her pensively, then said: "Kata, I don't have the

power that you seem to imagine—nothing over and beyond the authority of my position. I really don't think I could help. But look, have you
thought what God's will may be in all this? At times God tells us
'Accept!' And if He wants to, He will provide a way. Think of the
miracle that happened to your mother."

Kata swallowed hard. She'd had such hopes that Dr. Garay would
help! She walked out of his office hardly able to withhold her tears.
Once on the street, she sobbed uncontrollably.

She was dimly aware of being curiously looked at by passers-by as
she walked through the crowds toward the Avenue. She needed to be
alone.

She took a Number 4 streetcar, crossed Margit Bridge and decided
to get off at the foot of Rozsadomb, Hill of Roses. There she turned
toward a quiet street.

She walked instinctively upward defying the rising road. At the top
she saw a bench in a tiny circle around a flagpole, a bench offering a
panoramic view of the city, and she decided to make use of it. She had
to think through the implications of the conversation she had just had
with Dr. Garay.

In the last few months Kata had been somewhat apprehensive about
finding herself in lonely places. She'd had the feeling that there was a
shadow following her on many occasions. And the rumors about people
disappearing were not without foundation. But nobody was in view
now and there seemed no threat.

The surrounding big villas disclosed some signs of life—a distant
window being opened, a child's voice echoing from the other street. Far
below she could see the passing of streetcars, and while life there was
at a distance, she had a sense of being part of the city with its desperate
efforts to revive, to withstand, to resist—or, perhaps, it would just
succumb.

She tried to divine what her role would be in all this and whether her
own end finally would be to succumb.

She desperately wanted to leave the country. Now not only did the
official routes seem closed but Garay had challenged the whole plan. She
was shattered, even beyond the matter of the passport.

There was something in Garay, a core of steel, a seed of unshakable
faith that demanded response.

It was true she looked at things differently from Garay. Really, how could she subscribe to everything he said? It was impossible! All those theological fine points, those dogmatic rules of law, the word-by-word adherence. And yet, there was something in the man that filled her with awe, an unequivocal stand before which she was humbled, defenseless, spiritually naked. Sitting quietly on the hill now, alone, her thoughts traveled back in time.

* * *

She and her father were walking to church one Sunday morning when she was seven years old. It was late spring and the ground floor windows of apartment houses were open, with their inhabitants leaning on the sills. A child's voice called out her name:

"Hey, Kata!" Rozsi Polgar, a little schoolmate of hers beamed. "Where are you going?"

She had felt panic, but answered with bravado: "I'm going with my father to visit friends."

For a while they marched on in silence. Then, her father lifted her chin and with tenderness she could still recall said: "It's difficult for you to speak of our church, isn't it?"

She had only nodded.

Father patted her shoulder and kept his arm around it for quite a while.

* * *

In many ways she had liked the services. The hymns were fun to sing; the enthusiasm of the preacher in a small congregation was contagious and their friendly coaxing of her as a little girl to recite poems on all kinds of occasions, had made her feel good. They wanted her and she liked to recite.

"Katoka," her mother used to say with a wide smile, "you seem to live the words as you stand there under the Christmas tree!"

* * *

"Anyu, did you become a Christian because of Father?" she had asked her mother recently.

Mother never had been quite at peace with her decision to be baptized until the miracle on the Danube shore. Ever after that she knew it had been the right step.

* * *

In Scotland Kata could forget the social implications of faith. They were there, of course, but it was easier to ignore them, and in the established milieu of a state church, the call for salvation sounded different from the demand for vigorous decision of conscience required from the devout group of her father's fellow worshipers. At that time she longed not to be singled out but to be part of the wider church offering her a more defined identity and status.

*   * * *

She thought back to a Sunday morning, back in Pest after the War— *the big Reformed Church was filled with worshipers. In spite of the encroachment of an atheistic political creed, there were still men and women searching for the spiritual. Or was it just a habit, a lingering symbol of good citizenship to declare oneself a Christian? Well, the speaker at least was not one of the traditional preachers in Calvinist robes. He came from Britain. Kata had heard about him; her father knew him personally. But today she was present just as an outsider, hoping to discover some unexpected spark that would illuminate directions.*

Paul Neumann faced the crowd in the traditional bastion of the Hungarian Reformation. He stood up, sat down and sang with the choir: "Eros Varunk az Ur Isten" — "A Mighty Fortress is our God." Had she not known that he came from abroad she would have expected the usual Bible verses, a carefully selected passage from the New Testament and a scholarly exposition on the virtues of Protestant Christianity. As a matter of fact, that is what she did expect—perhaps with a touch of Western flexibility.

Neumann rose. "I want to introduce myself. You know my name but I want to tell you who I am.

"I was born in Germany but I am not a German.

"I am a British citizen but I am not an Englishman.

"I am a deacon in the Church of Scotland, but I am not a Scotsman.

"I am a Christian but I am a Jew!"

Kata sat there—awed and wanting. And the message possessed her.

Here was a man who carried his past proudly, it was the starting principle, the foundation of his being and his faith. Courage like this was the kernel of faith. Or was it the other way around?

*   * * *

She had had so little contact with her father's family. They lived in another country. But she had visited them at the age of fourteen. They were wonderful, God-fearing people. Their archaic religious practices—dietary law, not even the turning of the electric switch on the Sabbath, the ritual bath—had been* *utterly strange to her, the city girl being groomed to be a member of a sophisticated educated middle class.*

But weren't some of the practices of devout Christians just as alien, an affront to her intellect and a denial of the world of abundant gifts from the Creator? She never could respond to the pounding of the "Are you saved?" approach and was repelled by the constant "do not's" of zealous Christians. And yet . . . both her forebears and the brothers and sisters in father's church shared in singlemindedness and dedication to their particular faiths. In fact, in that devout Christian group she felt less compelled to give up her past than in the more formal, often nationalistic atmosphere of the Hungarian Reformed Church.

* * *

Jesus Christ had not broken with his past! He had extended the limited circle of God's chosen people to all who wanted to be part of such "elect." He had stretched the concept of local patriotism to an allegiance of all people seeking to know the Heavenly Father.

But this had nothing to do with the horrors of concentration camps.

Nothing? No, God himself could not possibly punish His people. But He did! God you did! You are a God of destruction!

She sobbed in pain and terror. It was not only Istvan, the beloved whom she had learned to mourn for years now and whose loss she had gradually accepted through much weeping. But, as if for the first time, the memory of her aunts, uncles and an array of cousins came to her, family who had vanished, and she had never once shed a tear for them. Now, she had to face that her loss was not only one beloved person whose life had become a part of hers and would continue not only in memory but through their child, but the loss of ties to the people to whom she belonged, whose blood she shared.

* * *

"Didn't you have any losses?" Misi Voros had asked.

"Yes, yes, yes!"

"What kind of Father are you, God, who sends His people to the gas chambers?" she challenged again. "Who sent even His only begotten Son to the cross."

She stopped, pain in her chest, her throat constricted.

She felt alone, perverse, uttery hopeless—now not only as to her plans; but more profoundly, regarding her relationship to the Source of

Life which pulsated around her and was and would ever be in this globe and the millions of stars and planets, billions of years before her and in the unfathomable Eternity after she was gone.

* * *

"God, forgive me, forgive my unbelief," she moaned. "Let me understand that terrible, incomprehensible will of yours!"

The will of God! Now that the rage for what God had allowed—(no, never His will! He may have allowed it perhaps)—was consumed, she went back to the events of rescue here and there, her mother's escape, the step-by-step guidance by the hand she had experienced.

But still, what about Istvan, the family, the hundreds and thousands in Hungary and the countless millions in Europe who had died? Could it possibly have been His will?

* * *

"What is man that you are mindful of him?" asks the Psalmist.

"I am . . . dust and ashes," Abraham says.

"I came that they may have life," proclaims Jesus, the Son who was sent to the Cross.

Despair-hope. Destruction-revival. Even on the Cross.

EVEN on the Cross!

"My God, my God, why hast Thou forsaken me?"

"Father, into thy hands I commit my spirit!"

* * *

How can one bring God to task? Job had tried.

"No purpose of thine can be thwarted," he understood at last.

* * *

And the tomb is empty! But to conquer death He had to die!

* * *

She had not had to die. She had survived.

But the graves of Auschwitz were filled with nameless rotted masses. Their odor spread all over the Continent filling survived lungs with imagined lethal gas. And the heirs of the victims and those of the killers still desperately clashed.

What was survival worth in poisoned air?

Was there no answer to the new hopelessness?

She took a deep breath. She sat motionless. She was numb, empty, spent.

Suddenly, in the void she heard the words with clarity and force:

"Christ Jesus . . . He is our peace . . . who has broken down the dividing wall of hostility . . . Christ Jesus . . . who has made us one."

Her heart jumped.

The message she had translated a year ago! The message that had gripped her! In it the sought-for hope for the world and specifically for her! Here the potential for breaking down hostilities, for finding the common core of mankind so that the bonds that unite, rather than the strife and passion that separate, prevail.

A moment of quiet, a sense of that peace, then a stirring within! It was a breeze, ready to gain momentum and grow into a sweeping wind, to leave the confined spot on this very Hill, the wild sensation of Kata Vaghelyi Fogaras—to expand, accelerate, envelop those unknown figures far below and fill the unknown millions of places never imagined.

And she searched her memory further into the text:

"He might create in himself a new man in place of the two," Jew and Gentile, "and might reconcile us both to God . . . bringing the hostility to an end."

A new man. Not a Jew, not a Gentile, but a new man, a new woman, reconciled to God.

She finally belonged! Her place was firmly set among God's people reconciled to each other and their God.

True survival.

* * *

In one way, the search was over and yet it had just begun. What her faith meant and where she belonged was answered for now. The split, was she Jewish or Christian, had been repaired.

But the will of God?—for her who had survived?

As she was sitting there on the bench, threads of music reached her through a window just opened. A strange and powerful melody came to her, at first in a rather undecipherable way and then assuming some pattern. What was this dramatic, dissonant and yet faintly known theme?

Whether her recognition was correct or not, her thoughts linked the tune to *Parsifal*, the opera Istvan and she had heard together on their first date.

She sat back, not so much listening to the music—it came from some distance and she was not really able to follow its sequence—rather, she thought back to the beautiful evening when their young love began to blossom.

They had tried to understand the meaning of Parsifal's search and what the Grail contained.

The Grail? Maybe it contained different things for everyone. Maybe it was the search itself that was important, the commitment to reach the top, to reach the holy vessel.

Her search for God's will would go on, her directions were set. The path? She did not know. She would learn, step by step.

She felt the autumn breeze on her cheek. She once again turned to the calm in the midst of which she sat and the devastated struggling beauty of her Pest yonder across the Danube below. What was God's will for the city? What was God's will for her?

There must be some way of going into the world and through one's own life bringing the spirit of love and compassion there, not as an anointed prophet or priest but as an ordinary human being in touch with life.

She might never be a sword-rattling or scripture-waving warrior of the faith, but she was ready to live the theme of reconciliation wherever she could—there were so many high walls to be breached, so many deep chasms to be bridged.

Where?

The answer would have to be God's.

She rose, stretched her arms and felt her muscles loosen after the long, intense period of sitting. She turned her palms upward. Then, she let them drop, turned and began, walking down the hill toward the tramway.

CHAPTER 18

FATHER AND DAUGHTER

AUGUST 1948

It was the middle of August, eleven months later, when Kata absent-mindedly rang the bell of the apartment. It had been a frightening and exhilarating afternoon.

Her father opened the door, surprised.

"Left your key home?" he asked as he bent down to kiss her.

Kata shook her head.

"I was absorbed in a lot of thinking. Will you have time for me later?"

His glance seemed to assess the urgency of her question. "Will it be all right after eight? I'm expecting someone."

She did not move, so he added: "Come on in til then, we have a few minutes."

He led the way to his office.

The apartment was quiet. Her mother was in the country with Jancsi. As in the past, when she had spent the summers in some modest vacation village where her husband could easily commute for weekends, Sarolta was renting rooms in a cottage at Zebegeny. Istvan's mother was spending some time there, too, sharing costs and pleasure. And on weekends the working members of the clan would take the two-hour train ride to enjoy the family as well as the fresh air of the surrounding woods and the cool flow of the Danube.

"I've been getting my things together," Dr. Vaghelyi said, pointing to the stack of books on the desk, "reading for vacation. You know, I'm planning to stay away from the city for the rest of the summer. And you? Were you able to make arrangements?"

She made a grimace. "We'll see."

Her father was well aware that there were problems with her job. Mr. Campbell had been called back to Cleveland several months before and Alice Smith had left at about the same time. Arpad had decided to wait out happenings in his friend's place at Eger. The office was in the temporary care of a Hungarian staff member, until it would be clear whether there was any point in maintaining a program in Budapest. The Hungarian government was less and less interested in ties with Americans, or with any church group for that matter. This, of course, added to Kata's worries. By now, not only Party membership but earlier affiliations with it were often essential for employment. It was scary to think of the future in every way.

It was scary—until today.

"Apuka, there's a lot to talk about," she said, anxious to start.

Her father raised his eyebrows in patient expectation. He usually let Kata proceed at her own pace.

Oh, sweet, wonderful, understanding Apu, Kata silently acknowledged her father's patience in sitting there and quietly waiting. What would her news do to him?

She looked at her watch "It's—it's really difficult to begin, particularly as we'll be interrupted." She hesitated for a moment, then burst out: "I am leaving with Jancsi on Tuesday."

"What did you say? Leaving?" There was a pause. "Where to?"

The question seemed artificial.

"I think you know, Apuka, I've hinted at the possibility." She herself was bargaining for time.

"But how? What happened all of a sudden? No, this is impossible. I don't understand."

The doorbell rang.

"I'll open it for you," Kata offered.

"Never mind." He got up and walked heavily toward the entrance to let the visitor in.

It was cruel to tell him now, Kata thought. They didn't really have time to talk about it.

She went wearily to her quarters.

She herself did not want to think about the whole matter now. She busied herself with tidying up the room, did some quick laundry in the bathroom, washed her face and put on fresh powder and lipstick. The weekends spent with the family in the summer cottage had given her a healthy tan and she needed no other make-up.

She went to the kitchen and set the table for a snack. The icebox contained some leftovers, but she had no desire to eat and she waited for her father to express some wish for a meal.

The visitor left in half an hour. Kata tried to pretend this was like any other evening. She asked about supper. Dr. Vaghelyi had had a big midday meal—so he said.

"Let's go for a walk, Kata," he suggested.

She nodded. It was her father's end-of-the-day routine. They descended the stairs and moved on in silence toward Andrassy Avenue. It was at the intersection of their street that Andrassy turned residential and they moved in the direction of the private homes.

Kata often accompanied her father on his after-work strolls. At times they would proceed without many words, reflecting on the day's events. At other times they could hardly wait to tell something to each other. And today—today they walked on as if it were the most usual, most uneventful evening.

"Summer will soon be over," Kata remarked casually. "Jancsi loved it there in Zebegeny."

Her father nodded. "I know. And he learned to swim—a little, anyhow. That Csukas boy taught him. Of course, your mother was nervous about it—she worries too much about currents." Slight smiles crept to the cheeks of both at the thought of Jancsi and grandmother's fussing.

"This is a beautiful avenue," Kata said, almost in reverence, as she held her father's arm while they walked on. They passed the handsome residential homes and stopped mechanically before one or the other to admire their shape anew, or to note the still present effects of the war. Of course, some of the houses looked more empty, more lifeless than before. Yet, many still carried their baroque lines with dignity. And the

horse chestnut trees hung their ripening fruit over the grassy path just
for strollers paralleling the sidewalk.

It was hard for her to think that all this would soon be behind her.
Not only Visegrad and Domos and Zebegeny—what about this beautiful boulevard, this Andrassy Avenue, which had been a part of her for
twenty-eight years? Yet, she decided she and Jancsi would leave it
all—if they could.

"Do you want to sit?" her father asked and he occupied one of the
benches under the row of trees.

An elderly couple sat down beside them. Their common-place chatter
was distracting as well as intrusive—not that father and daughter would
discuss anything important in public. But still, sitting so close to stran-
gers made even an allusion impossible.

"Shall we go?" Kata asked when it was obvious the other couple was
well settled.

They rose and continued a little further toward Hosok Tere—Square
of the Heroes.

After a few minutes her father stopped. Leaning on his walking stick,
he looked up and down the avenue to take in its full length, to prolong
the moment.

"It's a warm night," he said.

Then, he pulled her head toward him, gave her a gentle kiss and led
her back on the boulevard toward the little sidewalk confectionary shop
on the Korond corner.

"Let's have a piece of cake and a cup of coffee," he said.

Kata accepted the suggestion gratefully. The coffee and cake served
as a substitute for the supper at home for which neither of them was
ready. Also, the presence of other people would distract their thoughts
from the looming issue. It was safe to feel for a little while longer that
life was continuing as ever. The garden tables were set up as they
always had been since the days she had had her first date in that place.
It had survived the war, though its patrons undoubtedly had changed.
There were fewer young couples and more elderly fathers.

Where were the young? On the snowfields of Russia and in the gas
chambers of Auschwitz. She shivered.

* * *

They arrived home just before ten.

After changing into more comfortable clothes, Kata was as ready as she'd ever be. Father sat down first, motioned Kata to the other armchair and with imposed calmness in his voice said: "Now, tell me."

It was not easy to start. She was apprehensive and tense. Then she remembered the many occasions when she had gone to Apuka with her questions and doubts. She recalled that at times it had been with trepidation, wondering what Father would think, whether he would permit, whether he would approve. Yet, most of the time the anticipated ordeal had become yet another occasion for her growing love and admiration for him—the man who had taught her self-respect and confidence in people and in the world around her.

Often his convictions seemed unrealistic, of course, but without them she could never have survived. One needed faith in the possibility of the impossible in order to fight extinction. And one needed the faith in God, too.

That faith of Father's! "Everything will work out." But of course not everything did. Istvan had never returned.

Istvan! She had had to fight for her father's acceptance of her marital choice at first. But, wasn't this understandable? After all, she and Apu were suddenly no longer as close as before.

Poor Apu! After all, she'd found her prince then. He could not expect— No, he could not expect me not to, but he was affected by that new alliance. And now, he can't expect again— But what would it do to him? Kata was beginning to be too enmeshed in her internal monologue.

The repeated "Well, tell me!" of her father finally brought her out of the world of reminiscence and fantasies. It must be done. She must tell him and see what he thinks. She wanted freedom for herself and her son, and that desire was strong.

"You know, Apu," she started, with her head resting on the back of the tall armchair and her eyes for the moment staring at the ceiling of the room to lessen the pain of personal contact, "you know, Apu, how much I have wanted to go to the States. I've been finding it very hard here—the memories, the hatred. You remember my despair when they turned down my passport last year."

"I know, but then you seemed to be so much more at peace," her father sighed.

"I was. I felt I was not meant to leave."

"And now?"

She was quiet for a few moments, searching for words.

"Apu, I often wonder what 'acceptance' means. I can't believe it means not to try. Of course, there are times it is not wise to move. With the Mindszenty Trial on, I took no further steps. But months have passed and things are growing only worse. Don't you agree?"

Vaghelyi made a slight move of his head. "It's a difficult situation," he admitted, "but it's not the first time."

"You want me to go through it again?" Her face twitched. The impartial, philosophical approach of her father, so often soothing in the past, now seemed inappropriate.

"I'm not saying that things are not bad, Kata," her father proceeded, apparently noting her edginess.

"But tell me, what's happened? How can you leave now, when for months it didn't seem possible?" He put into words the fact which, in spite of the deterioration of the situation around them, had given encouragement to his own aging years.

"You're right. It did seem impossible for quite a while. The doors that at first appeared to be opening didn't lead anywhere. In any case, as I said before, I'd come to terms with many things. We've talked about that. That Sunday with Tydings started a process. And then, after my defeat, I gained a sense of direction. I felt more alive. And—this may sound contradictory—I was really looking for guidance: Would God really close the doors or let me go?"

"And?"

"Well, rumor has it, the border will be sealed very soon. And I feel I must try once more."

"And you think you really have a chance?"

"It looks as though I do," she said with reserved enthusiasm. "Look, Apu, it's a complicated thing. I heard of a man who helped out some people I knew, and this man is to leave town soon. I thought I'd better have a talk with him. I hardly expected any results, but didn't want to miss a chance. He said he would see whether anything could be done and would get back to me in a couple of days. I didn't hear from him. Then two weeks later, when I was about to table the whole issue, he called. I went to see him.

"He gave me the address of a 'friend' who'd talk to me. I went to see this friend. He put me in contact with a young woman. I now understand from her that everything will be ready Tuesday night.

"That's all." Kata leaned back again, ready for her father's reactions. A long pause followed.

"Do you know these people well?" her father asked. "Can you trust them? One hears of so many deceptions."

"But Apu, everything has its risks! When I think back—" She paused, then said, "Even marrying Istvan had its risks—you told me so!" There was a slight irony, a hurting edge, in the comment. She felt ashamed.

"Apu, I had four wonderful years with him," she added in way of justification. "How foolish it would have been to be afraid."

Dr. Vaghelyi instinctively reached out and squeezed her hand. It was a belated gesture of truce for the opposition he had offered many years ago—opposition that was well founded in a way, but which was to some extent spurred by the ties they had, ties which were so hard to cut.

But now, this would be the end! The impending reality seemed to come home to him and he withdrew his hand as though not to precipitate any decision and not to approve of any action too hastily.

He now tried a different approach. "But how can you risk such a trip with the child? There are so many potential traps—*agents provocateurs*, careless arrangements, minefields, police. Oh, Kata, how can I even list them all."

The point he made was disturbing. She had been thinking about all these herself, to be sure. It was a tremendous responsibility—for herself, but even more, for her child.

"I know. I can't be sure," she admitted. "I can only count the odds. The contact seems good. I know they've helped many successfully. I won't go into details—it won't help you or me—but I know people who left with them and arrived. I'm pretty sure I can trust them. The rest? Again, all I can go on is their previous success. But I'll still have to talk over the details, how they will minimize the danger to Jancsi."

Her father kept shaking his head. "A daring undertaking. In every sense! Tell me," he pursued, "what about there? Where is 'there?' " He realized that beyond the crossing Kata had told him nothing.

"The first step is Austria. I don't know what after that," she said haltingly. "England? The United States finally? Some other place? It's impossible to have this planned to the last detail now," she said with impatience. "It's impossible to undertake it without any risk at all. Nothing can be done without risks!"

It was annoying and at the same time imperative that she should remind him. "My whole adult life was full of risks. I don't know what will await us beyond the border. All I can hope for is that we will get there. After that? I'm young, I can work, I speak languages. God has helped me through inconceivable, seemingly insoluble situations."

In spite of the pain she knew he felt, Vaghelyi managed an almost invisible smile. This was his daughter, in a way this was his creation. And the pride this thought gave him helped him to continue, to try to understand better what was on Kata's mind.

"All right, you don't know much about 'there,' but still, you must have given it some thought. What'll you do with Jancsi? What'll you live on and who'll take care of him? You aren't going in a regular way, with passage paid. If you knew it was America, at least Campbell would be there, and others, too. There's my cousin Helen. You might not want to rely on her too much, but there would at least be someone interested, who could advise you, to whom you could turn. But in Austria? It's still an occupied country, not even settled. What will you do there?"

Kata thought for a while.

"I've been wondering about this myself," she admitted. "What will I do with the child? I suppose there's always some program, or there are women who are eager to take care of children. You know there are tens of thousands of Hungarian refugees all over Europe and other continents. Many of the women aren't equipped to work outside of their homes, particularly in a strange country, but would be happy to earn some extra pennies by taking care of other people's children along with their own.

"I really don't know, though." A touch of doubt crept into her initially confident portrayal of the future. "Jancsi is six now and he should start school this fall. This is good. It's always easier to find some solution for a couple of hours in the afternoon than for a whole day. But, I don't really know. What do you think?"

Her attempt to assert her right or to gain approval of her plans was tainted with the many questions the plans posed. And though she had hoped for guidance from Father, now she went on in a defensive manner without waiting for his answer.

"Of course, there were questions about Jancsi right from the beginning. Should we have had a child at all? I guess only the future will tell whether our decision was wise. But Istvan and I very much wanted a child and Janos came. Then we had to decide whether to send him away from home. Istvan and I decided we would. What a cause for trepidation that was! You know! Now he's back.

"And now? To be honest, it's really not so much that I fear who will take care of him," she said in a humbler tone. "The real question is, what will it do to him? What will it mean to him that I take him away from loving grandparents, from the safety of a home and family—as long as that safety holds—and force him into strange surroundings? This is what's bothering me most. And what will it do to you and Anyuka?"

Her father was slow to reply this time. His face was working with feeling. It seemed he had begun to realize for the first time how imminent the danger was and how final its impact could be upon his life. He was preparing to grasp his last chance of assertion—for his and his wife's happiness: assertion to hold tight, and keep his daughter and grandchild before it was too late.

"Well, you said it. I don't see how you can contemplate the trip. There's danger, real danger, in those border crossings and I know your mother will be deathly frightened. And she will worry beyond words for the future of the child. After all, who'll look after him, tell him stories, guide him as he grows—you, a lone woman?"

Kata's face sank under the foreboding questions which only echoed her own. Noting this, Dr. Vaghelyi softened somewhat and his anger turned to pleading.

"Kata, when I was on the hospital bed, the night your mother had her ordeal on the Danube shore, I prayed mainly for her. She needed my supplications. When I heard of her being rescued and rejoined with you, a tremendous weight dissolved. Then the two of you came home and you brought back Jancsi. It became a new kind of life for me." His voice softened. "The dying hulk of an old man became alive once more. He had all whom he loved dearly, all under his roof. He had a grandson who listened, who could be taught, who could develop and be shaped. There was a future."

He got up and began pacing the room. "There was a future," he muttered as if to himself. "This is what you want to take away from us—from your mother and me—the future. How can you?"

It was extremely unusual for Dr. Vaghelyi to express himself in such a claiming way. He usually left the decision to Kata, gave her time. But there was no time now. He seemed ready to muster all his persuasive powers: psychological, intellectual, moral, and, at the end when all else failed, the power of love to keep them with him at all costs.

He continued to walk from one door of the room to the other. He seemed somewhat confused. There was too great a mixture of feelings—love and resentment, pleading and anger.

"Kata, this is too much all at once," he soberly commented. "Let's go to bed. Let's sleep on it. Can we continue tomorrow?" Again there was pleading in his voice, a plea for a reversal of the contemplated verdict. A plea, at least, for time.

Kata stood up, gave him a decisive but short kiss which contained just as many mixed emotions as her father's words.

"Yes, Apu, let's try to sleep. We'll continue."

* * *

Sleep didn't come. Kata tossed back and forth, turning the thoughts, trying to recapture the fervent desire of only two days ago that her wish would come true, and master the creeping fear that invaded her now when she thought of the venture. It had seemed all so reasonable, so perfect—to be able to leave at last. And now that the vague possibility was becoming a probability and perhaps a fact in a few more days, now she was hesitating, fretting, feeling at a loss as to what she really should do.

What's the matter with me? She posed the question to herself with annoyance. And I thought a talk with father would help.

She sighed, thinking again of the border crossing and its dangers. And still this aspect of the plan she could visualize. She could anticipate the odds, plan for the details, talk over every little item if not with her parents then with the people who were arranging the flight. It did seem reasonably certain that at least Jancsi would be safe. It was the aftermath that lurked like a frightening puzzle in the background. She was fearful. It would be a different life, alone with her child.

As she contemplated what all this would mean, her thoughts reverted more and more to her ties with her father. It was hard to explain. Hadn't she left once, married, and had her own happy life? And even when things went badly, hadn't she done things on her own? And yet, she knew that in a way it was Father who still directed her life.

She knew the news would be a blow to her Mother, but somehow this was not what was foremost in her mind. Mother would survive, she had Father to take care of. But Apu, poor, poor old Apu. And there in the darkness of her room, her tears flowed freely as she sobbed her mental farewell to the father she so very much loved.

She must have dozed a little but heard the church bell at the corner chime one. She also heard some movement at the other end of the apartment. She put on a robe and entered the living room. She sat there for a while in the chair. And her thoughts continued, a mixture of past and present with some occasionally hopeful, at times fearful glimpses into the future. But, above all, what loomed over her was not the danger, the practical steps she and the child were to take in three more days now, nor the places they would be in a week or within two or three months. The most painful thoughts revolved about the separation between her and her parents, her and her father.

She again heard movements in his bedroom, an adjusting of the window sash, some quiet steps, then relative silence. Yet, amidst the silence, the tossing back and forth, the squeaking of the bed was discernible. She tiptoed to the door, and gently knocked.

"Come in," she was told.

"I can't sleep, Apu."

"I know. Come and sit here," her Father said.

Dr. Vaghelyi was sitting up in bed, dressed in his summer robe. Apparently he had been up several times since he first began preparations for the night and was attired for more ups and downs, walks to the bathroom, back and forth in the room, and, if needed, a short sojourn to the desk to be distracted by some favorite poet. But now here she was, sitting at the edge of the sofa bed, leaning against the wall at her father's feet.

How appropriate, she thought to herself. At the foot of her master.

They sat this way for a while. She waited. She knew her father would speak to her when he was ready.

The two o'clock gong of the church clock chimed. "It's really not so late yet," she made the inconsequential comment, as if to start an exchange of words.

"No, not so late yet," her father responded. "For some things, though, quite late." Another silence followed.

A passing car's lights found their way into the otherwise darkened room, drawing enigmatic sketches on the ceiling and then quickly disappearing with the noise of the engine.

"I was thinking of the day you were born," her father finally started. "What a great morning it was! I stayed at the hospital and you were born at around two. I waited for a while to see my offspring and express my gratitude to her mother. You know, I married late in life. The studies, lack of money, the first war made it a long pull for me. Also, my conversion, my falling in love with Christianity, was a wonderful thing but in many ways I had to wait to meet the girl who would share my unconventional road of faith. Your mother was willing, though she did not always find it so easy. Then, we were expecting you and it seemed life had finally fulfilled its every promise. There you were on your mother's arm, early morning. I was allowed just a few seconds—she had to rest and they had to minister to you. But to see the two of you was one of the most exalting experiences of my life. I think I even had some tears in my eyes—not quite becoming to a middle-aged man, I know— but the joy and hopes spurred within me were overwhelming. I kissed your mother and barely touched your hair, then left. As I was walking out of the hospital, dawn broke and it symbolized the birth of a new day, a new epoch. I walked whistling to the house, a good half hour. The fresh morning air, the increasing light, the solitude the city offered at that hour were the lovely accompaniment of a secular worship service.

"You were a very sweet child, Kata. And smart, too. You may know your mother was unable to have any more children; she was not so young either, and it may have been all right the way it was. It was hard to contemplate having anybody replace you or even having another toddler demanding attention reserved for you.

"I said you were a lovely child. But really the joy came more as you grew. In the early years, your mother spent most of her time with her baby, as it is normal to do. She was very good to you, Kata. She is a very dedicated person, you know."

"I know, Apukam."

Her father continued: "You were about eight when you wrote your first poem, do you recall?"

"Yes, Apuka, it was about two pigeons hearing the church bell and praying. Apu," she turned to him with a start, "what was your relationship with your own parents like? I never met them, did I?"

"No," Dr. Vaghelyi quietly said. "My mother was long dead by the time you were born. My father still saw you as an infant. The relationship? They loved me. Since my student days we were separated by distance, it's true."

"And by ideas, beliefs?"

"In a way, to be sure. But their faith—though I took the big next step—it was their faith that sparked mine."

The old man reached out toward his daughter. "Come, sit nearer."

Kata rose and sat up in the bed alongside her father. "You are right, we can hear each other better this way." She got another pillow, and sitting with her arms crossed, looked at the patterns of light and dark reflected on the ceiling which offered some focus for her gaze.

"Then came high school," her father continued the reverie. "You were good then, Kata, you learned well. But it was not really the grades that impressed me, you know that. It was the eager interest with which you would listen, the inquisitive questions you could put, the emotion-filled responses that you would provide when I spoke to you about the riches of the world. Riches? You know I'm not talking of money. I know you would not have minded a little more of it. But when we started with Aesop's fables and then slowly moved to some Hungarian poetry— how beautifully you used to recite 'Janos Vitez,' do you remember?— then as you grew I would tell you about the travels of Aeneas and the Golden City, long before you had to tackle it yourself in the classes. Then came your literary endeavors, the writing, and I had much hope in you. Somehow you never quite fulfilled that hope. This is something I was a little sorry for. I hope someday you will."

It was Kata's turn now to reminisce.

"Apu, do you remember the evenings, when after some meeting you would finally come home and it was time for me to go to bed, but then we stood leaning against the warm logwood stove and began to talk and continued to talk and talk? Poor Mother, how many times she would call us, tell me to go to bed, it was late. We knew she was right but it was just too exciting not to continue. You had to tell me about the book you were planning then, you outlined chapters, discussed ideas. I'm not sure I always really followed you in everything, Apu," the belated confession was out, "but it was just wonderful to have you share all that with me."

"It meant everything to share it with you, Kata," his needy and humble words touched her soul. "Then you grew up into a lovely girl, Kata." The tone of the reminiscences took on a different and more sober tone. "After you returned from your studies in England you were changed. A mature, accomplished young lady, yes. But you were on your own."

"Yes, and I know, Apu, you felt badly about that, didn't you? It was hard for you when I started to see Istvan. I was a little bit annoyed at you then, I must say. You did not seem to understand as you had understood me in the past." Kata's voice now had just a touch of edginess in it. Her father waited a while.

"You can't comprehend that, Kata, not now. But wait until Jancsi grows up and goes his way. You want your child to be on his own and happy, but it's hard to relinquish your treasure." His voice became husky and Kata knew his hands were trembling. He clutched them in the usual way, as he always did, when the ever-increasing tremors took over, particularly in moments of emotional upset.

"Come, Apu, come." She reached out toward his hand and put it to her lips. She kept it there for a moment.

Dr. Vaghelyi was shaking. Was he crying? Kata wondered. There was an uncertain silence. Then he blurted out: "I love you, Kata, I love you; I love you—so very much. It is heartbreaking to let you go," her father continued. "I can't think of it," he added in a very quiet and painful voice.

There they sat together with hands clasped. By now Kata had put her head on her father's shoulder looking for comfort and the promise of solutions that she had always gotten from him as a child. It seemed somehow very wrong that she should break the magic tie that existed between them, that she should torture her parents like this—her mother, too. Of course, Mother was much younger than he; there were many other hopes for her yet. And she was practical, too. For Father, these were really the years of dusk. Could she do this to him? It was not just the guilt, the remorse. She herself felt the pain of parting. She knew that once she left she would be quite alone in the world—yes, in the world literally. She didn't even know where she was going. Jancsi, yes, he would be with her, but he was a child. Comfort comes from the wise and the old. And Father loved her and she loved him, too. She began to rationalize the temptation to stay in order to temper the pain of parting for all, including herself.

Perhaps she should be content to have married, had a son and such a wonderful father. Maybe this was all she should want from life. She had to find some reason to help her say the next sentence:

"Apu, maybe I shouldn't go," she offered. "I can't see you suffer this way. I wonder if I can go through with it myself. It is an act of abandonment—for you as well as for me," she admitted with an enormous sigh. She was glad she could say it. The whole plan now seemed just too much to carry out.

No words came from him now. But she could feel her father gently stroking her hair as if she were small and in need of caressing. He kept doing this for a while and she knew he was thinking.

Then, all of a sudden, he slipped his arm under her shoulder, gave her a strong, almost passionate embrace and kiss, and leaning forward, abruptly broke the spell:

"All right, my dear, we'd better try to sleep. It will be all right."

"But Apukam," Kata asked somewhat baffled. "I said I would stay." And she got up.

"I know, Kata," her father answered, rising and pacing the room once more. "I know you said you would be willing, but I cannot accept the sacrifice."

"Apu, I suffer too, this is very hard for me, too. Maybe it would be better even for me to stay."

"No, dear. I know this is what you have wanted for years. It is time for me to let you go. I did it once, you know, when you married. It was hard then. Fathers take it hard; I may have taken it harder than most. You were more to me than most daughters. But even then it had to be done. Your happiness depended on it then—it does now. You must carry out your plans. You will be all right; God be with you!"

By now, the first streetcar was passing on the street, morning was there with its sobering beginning lights. Relief and natural concern came to her as she asked: "But how about you, Apu, what will be with you?"

Dr. Vaghelyi, in his usual way of finding answers in quotations said:

"Do you recall in Ecclesiastes: 'There is a time to plant and a time to pluck up what is planted . . . there is a time to seek and a time to lose'?"

CHAPTER 19

AUGUST 1949

The train pulled slowly out of Nyugati Station. As it left the protection of the concave roof—many of the glass panes were still broken—the noises of the platform bustle merged into the sound of rolling and accelerating wheels. Their jaunty melody provided background music to the scene of nearby sunny streets and the scurrying figures of men and women on their way to work.

Bomb-shattered apartment buildings along the city tracks still displayed wooden or cardboard substitutes for window panes. Four years after the siege and still not repaired!

Soon the train was passing by streets with less human traffic, and the buildings flanking the rails yielded to puffing factories. The stale smell of the city's uncollected garbage was replaced by the sporadic stench of industrial waste, sporadic since only a small number of the plants had resumed their pre-war activities.

It was warm in the compartment where Kata and the child sat. She stood, let the upper sash down as far as it would go and remained standing in front of it for a while. She wanted to take with her a lasting glimpse of the receding city. It was farewell.

There were not many passengers and Kata was relieved that the two men who were in the compartment, after a few casual comments about the weather and the preparations for next day's holiday, St. Stephen's Day, turned to their newspapers.

The train now passed smaller buildings, houses plastered with grey and yellow with sunny goldenrods within their small fenced gardens and morning glory hugging the walls.

Jancsi kneeled on the seat beside his mother, holding tightly to her waist as he shared the view with her even as the suburban gardens stretched into wider fields. Ox-drawn wagons moved slowly over country roads and the scent of haystacks from the fields reached them through the open window.

The view, the child's occasional "why's," the uncertainties of the next few hours mingled in a peculiar conglomerate of awareness and dreaming. And into it intruded the scene two days ago—her farewell from Father.

"How is it, how is it, that you're leaving now?" he had asked.

Her mother, when she was finally told, had been more acquiescent though obviously distressed. She had expressed her emotions cautiously in front of Jancsi—the child must not suspect the true purpose of the planned journey. Then, when the boy was in bed she had wailed: "Oh, Kata, how will we do without you and Jancsi?" she cried, sealing her words with an emotional embrace.

But her mother had her feet on the ground and she had no question that being able to leave the country was a boon. Only, Mrs. Vaghelyi prayed, only, that they get to their destination safely. And Kata's mother-in-law and the Banats, the only others who were told, concurred.

"Would the little boy want an apple?" one of the passengers offered, changing the trend of Kata's thoughts.

"Thank you, we'll keep it till after lunch," she said, giving Jancsi permission to accept it.

Some time was spent with eating, with very general comments about the vacation to be taken by mother and child. There was a short round of checkers and reading those favorite tales of Hansel and Gretel and Little Red Riding Hood.

One of the passengers got off at Komarom, the other joined an acquaintance in the next compartment. Boarding passengers glanced in but seemed to shy away from a child, leaving Kata and Jancsi alone.

"Sleep a little, sweetheart," Kata said, noting her son's drowsiness. Jancsi put his head in Mother's lap, providing Kata the warmth and reassurance that she so desperately needed now as they were leaving country, friends, family behind.

Her father had really been shaken!

And as she re-lived those precious hours of farewell, she prayed that her father's trust in God's words might be her own lasting inheritance.

"Szombathely!" She heard the conductor's voice as the train was slowing down. Gathering Jancsi and her overnight bag, she ushered the child toward the door.

* * *

A young woman and man in casual clothing were looking at the exiting passengers intently. When they saw Kata and the boy they moved up to them with some hesitation.

"Aunt Katalin?" they addressed her questioningly and introduced themselves as Dini and Boske. They referred to the letter of Zoltan Huncut who had informed them of their coming. Kata felt relieved hearing this name.

"This is Jancsi," she turned to her son and prodded him to kiss Aunt Boske and Uncle Dini, college students!

Dini took the small suitcase as they walked toward the Dobos home. Jancsi was the one who kept the conversation going as he could not quite figure out his relationship to their companions and wanted to know how his mother knew Mrs. Dobos and how it was that he had never seen Boske and Dini before. These inquiries served to fill the time during the ten-minute walk to the house and by the time Kata had given a somewhat unconvincing recognition to her "cousin" Juliska, and Jancsi had introduced himself with due description of his rank in the Kindergarten, birthdate and some details about the summer he had spent with grandparents, it was appropriate to suggest that the two of them have a little rest before the family took off to the summer home.

They lay down behind the shuttered windows. Kata at first found it hard to fall asleep. Thoughts of the night to come were not easy to dispel as her mind tried to grasp what the next twenty-four hours might bring. She clutched Jancsi lying beside her in order to assure him of

Mother's presence and to encourage him to sleep. When she heard the boy's heavier breathing, she herself firmly decided to leave foolish daydreaming and have some rest.

Her sleep was not smooth. Pictures of forest paths, silently spreading cleared land, a challenging entry to new territories made her open her eyes from time to time so as to assure herself that at the moment, at least, she was in the safety of these four walls near the Szombathely station.

We still could take the evening train back, she tempted herself as she lay half-awake.

Nonsense! If she turned back now, there'd be no other chance.

Her eyelids closed again and a few minutes' sleep followed.

After two hours, her body at least felt rested from the train travel. She dressed Jancsi energetically.

"Yes, you can go with the boys, Dini will take you on his bike," she answered Jancsi's queries. "Oh me? Of course I'm coming. Boske and her friends prefer to walk and we'll all meet when we get to Remenyhegy."

After they had had some coffee, milk and cake, the little group— mother, son, Boske and Dini—kissed Mrs. Dobos and talked of seeing her at the summer home next morning.

Two more young fellows and three girls joined them as they descended the stairs. Jancsi was fascinated by the young men and, after a few glances at Mother to make sure she was near, and that she approved, was quite willing to accept first Dini's hand, then the back of his bicycle seat as the three boys mounted the two-wheelers and slowly moved ahead toward the edge of the town.

The girls and Kata followed.

It did not take them more than half an hour to reach the next village. At the edge of Remenyhegy they met two older country men who greeted the youngsters with easy familiarity. The students suggested that they would have to return soon but first they all strolled through the central marketplace before they left on their bikes.

Jancsi was confused. It was difficult for him to take leave of Dini, who had allowed him to ride with him and be part of the big boys' company. Nevertheless, the exhilarating experiences of the last hour made it possible for him to look ahead cheerfully to the days when the vacation, which had started with so much fun, would continue and he would find his friends the next morning when they would return with Mrs. Dobos.

By now it was dark. The faint lights of the village street witnessed Kata's handshake with one of the men before he, too, left and Kata, Jancsi and the other man turned towards a side street in order to find the cottage.

* * *

To Jancsi, the street seemed long. He asked about this house and the other, whether it was the one they would occupy. He could not quite understand his mother's somewhat impatient bid for less talk and brisker walking. Soon they turned again, and the row of houses gave way to longer stretches of gardens between smaller and smaller buildings. Shortly the gardens seemed to run into empty fields. Jancsi was puzzled by this walk in the darkness.

Mother pointed to a distant black patch which, so she said, would be their destination.

In a way Jancsi did not mind the walk. He felt like a grown-up. When on vacation with grandmother, he had had to be in early, eat his supper, say his prayers and go to bed while the older members of the family would continue their intriguing talk around the table on the screened verandah. Today, Mommy must want him to feel that he could keep her company even after the stars were out and the half-moon threw its shaft on the dirt road under their feet. Yet, he was beginning to be tired and only his pride in his recently won status as Mother's escort stirred him on to continue with relatively little fussing. But the house they were aiming for still seemed far away and the road became more and more deserted.

"When are we getting there?" he asked, a little suspiciously.

"Another ten minutes, dear," Kata reassured the boy and suggested that once in the hut, which was more visible now, they would rest.

The cabin was a disappointment to Jancsi though it had an exciting aura of mystery. It was just a one-room place with all sorts of implements inside. There was no window that he could notice, neither was there any lamp to light. Mother and the man kept the squeaky wooden door ajar so that they could enjoy the evening air and have a glimpse of the lights of the village left behind.

Kata spread a blanket that her companion had taken from the corner and suggested that they rest.

"Mr. Acel has to go back to the village to meet a friend, but the other man whom you saw, Jancsi, will be with us soon and will help us to find the cottage that we're heading for."

Jancsi had some questions as to why Mr. Acel had to leave them there and why the other man could not come with them right away, but it was late, well past his usual bedtime and the long walk from the village stopped his talking and made him want to lie on the blanket quietly while Mother watched the countryside for the arrival of Mr. Tornac.

"Here he is, honey, and a friend of his, Mr. Cserkesz," he heard his mother's voice as she awoke him from sleep. As they stumbled out through the low door and silently took the road leading away from the village lights, Mother promised a story for Jancsi as soon as they were on the straight road and would not need to pay so close attention to which way to turn.

* * *

Kata walked steadily toward the destination that only Tornac knew for sure, as the moonlight gave an enchanted quality to the flanking fields. It was a lovely August night with twinkling stars connecting her with the Maker of the universe. The occasional distant sound of a dog's barking, the nearer croak of frog in the roadside ditch, the passing of a lightning bug here and there illuminating its path in the air, reinforced Kata's love and trust in nature and her dedication to the joys of the Hungarian countryside. It was a walk she could have taken years ago with Istvan at her side as hand in hand they had exchanged dreams of a happy future together. Kata still had dreams, but of a different sort. What would become of these dreams?

Jancsi finally became rather insistent that she tell him the story and let him know how long they would have to walk in the night. He was getting tired.

Kata gently squeezed her son's hand. "You know how much I love you, dear," she whispered as she bent down to the boy. Janos responded with a big hug and the reassurance that he loved Mommy, too.

"But tell me about the trip, Mommy, where are we going?"

"Do you remember, Jancsi, we always wanted to go to America to visit Aunt Helen there?" Kata started. "Well," she swallowed, "we're on the way to America now!"

The words sounded preposterous and incredible even to Kata.

Jancsi turned to his mother and repeated the sentence in the form of a question: "We are on the way to America now? When are we going to get there? Are Grandma and Grandpa coming, too?"

"Listen, dear, we're in the very beginning of our trip. In order to make it true, in order to make sure we can get there, you must be very quiet as we walk with Mr. Tornac now. Nobody must hear us make any noise. You know, it was difficult to start on this trip. If all goes well, we're really on the way to America. But nobody must find us here. It must be our secret. If we make noise, policemen may come and take me away. Nothing would happen to you, dear, they would take you back to Grandmother," Kata eagerly assured the child. "But I might be in a bit of trouble and you wouldn't see me for a while. If we manage to walk quietly and not draw the attention of anybody from the village to us, you and I'll stay together and in a while we can see Aunt Helen in New York. Maybe at some other time Grandma and Grandpa can join us, too. This is our private adventure now."

Silence.

Walk, walk, walk on the dirt road. Little steps moving quietly alongside the grown-ups' strides. A little hand desperately snuggling within Mother's palm and the trembling of a frightened body expressed in the shaking little fingers. Kata put her arms around the child. His shoulders were moving, his teeth chattering. Nonetheless, Jancsi walked on bravely.

"Sweetheart, I know you're scared, but I'm sure nothing will happen to us. You're such a smart little boy, and I know you and I'll get to America safely," Kata added. "First we have to get through this forest— you see the end of the road? Mr. Tornac will help you if you're tired. Then, you'll still have to stay very quiet until we get to another country called Austria. I'll tell you when. After that, we can have fun and celebration. We'll let Grandmother know that we arrived and I'm sure one of these days we'll get a letter from them saying how happy they are for us. And then, later, maybe a letter will come that they will join us there."

"Grandmother and Grandfather will also walk this long road to America?" Jancsi queried in whisper.

"We'll see."

Now the tall forest trees towered over them, offering their canopy of protection. As they slid into the rustling foliage with less light than they'd had on the open road, Tornac took Jancsi on his back and placed his feet around his own waist and Jancsi himself carefully fastened his arms around Mr. Tornac's neck so as to remain safely in the saddle. From time to time he would turn his head toward his mother but after a while he accepted the fact that the four of them had no other way to go but where Mr. Tornac led them and he was even able to rest his head on the man's shoulder, enjoying the adventure of man-riding in the middle of the night.

Only a few hushed words were spoken in brief questions and answers concerning how long a time and how much distance remained. From time to time Kata would smooth the boy's sweater as it was lifted by an unexpected movement or an interfering branch from the trees. She did this not only to reassure Jancsi of her presence but perhaps even more to reassure herself that whatever else life might bring, she was with her child.

Walk and walk, and more walk. "How near are we?" she again asked Cserkesz.

"Another fifteen minutes, Madam, and we will be out of the forest."

Kata felt a flutter in her stomach as the anxiety of the last leg of their adventure mounted.

"In fifteen minutes we come to a clearing and in another fifteen minutes all should be over," Cserkesz added.

The next half an hour would be the crucial one! As frightening as it was, she began to feel relieved by the knowledge that the outcome was within a certain time limit.

Jancsi became alert. He suddenly turned and called for his mommy.

"Here I am, dear, we'll arrive there soon."

Cserkesz stopped. Kata and Tornac moved up to his side. He put Janos down and placed the boy's hand in his mother's. The four of them stood silently.

Nothing stirred.

"I'm going to move ahead to that fence," Cserkesz pointed toward the double row of barbed wire which cut into the moonlit vista. "I'll stand there for a while to be sure no guard is around. There shouldn't be any. We've calculated the hours of change. A guard is responsible for

ten kilometers alongside the fence and the one on duty started out at
ten. At this point he should be at the other end of his itinerary.
Nevertheless, to avoid mischance, I'll move up to the fence and stand
there for a few minutes. If anybody hails me, I'll meet him. I live in the
village and it's conceivable that I just came out for an evening walk. If
nobody appears, I'll signal and you can all move forward."

Cserkesz walked deliberately toward the wire. When close to it, he
took a few steps, no longer trying to be particularly silent. Should there
by anyone near, it would be better if he were caught alone.

There was no sound.

Kata, Jancsi and Tornac left their hiding place in the foliage and Kata
could feel her heart pounding in her chest. After a few steps they
stopped for a moment to assure themselves that nobody had seen them.
There was no sound besides their own breathing.

"All right. Let's go!"

As they reached the fence, Cserkesz, who had Kata's small overnight
case in hand, threw it to the ground between the two lines of barbed
wire. This served as another safety measure in case there was an
undetected mine there. But the bag plopped safely on the grass and the
clearing contained only the rays of the moon and the stars engulfing the
four silhouettes standing close together.

Cserkesz took a step. He forced himself through the enlarged space
between two wires forming a barrier on the Hungarian side of the
border. He stopped near where the overnight bag landed. Tornac did
the same, but he moved on through another enlarged circle in the
second row of wires and stood, legs apart, on Austrian soil.

"Give me the boy," Cserkesz urged Kata.

Jancsi was handed through the hole to Mr. Cserkesz, who placed him
in Tornac's hand, without touching the ground. They had carefully
planned this maneuver, so that should there be a mine between the two
fences which they had not discovered after all, Jancsi would not become
its victim.

Jancsi was safe!—at least from the mines.

Do help us on, dear Lord, help us!

With this, Kata carefully pushed herself between the wires. Cserkesz,
still in the middle, helped her to regain her balance; then through the
second row where Tornac's hand assisted her. Finally, Cserkesz also
reached their side.

"Here we are," he said, "this is Austria," and with that, he headed toward a narrow patch of trees.

In a few minutes, the rolling Austrian countryside was before them. Through the cloudless night they could view in muted light the gate to freedom.

They moved on. As they were on the road leading them to a nearby farm, Kata embraced her son and her voice vibrated with relief and joy as she told him: "Darling, we're safe! We just left Hungary!" Faint echoes of her restrained laughter lingered and followed them as they continued their walk.

It took a few more minutes for Janos fully to grasp the meaning of the statement and hear again and again that the danger was over and they were in safe territory. Actually this was not quite true. Their point of crossing was into the Russian-occupied part of Austria. True, the Hungarian police were powerless here. However, Jancsi caught his mother's joy. The hours of restrained silence that he had miraculously accepted and was able to observe now evoked a reaction. He suddenly tore his hand from that of his mother, started to somersault on the path and accompanied the physical release with an audible series of exultant shrill cries.

"Quiet, quiet!" Kata anxiously tried to stop him and even Cserkesz curtly ordered Jancsi to silence. They had hardly uttered these warnings when the strong beam of a searchlight swept the horizon and fell dangerously near them. Kata quickly caught up to her son, pulled him into the roadside ditch some steps away and put her hand over his mouth.

"Sweetheart," she whispered urgently. "You must be quiet. That's a searchlight. We can't let them see us!"

Jancsi grasped the anxiety in his mother's voice and crouched quietly with her, hiding behind the roadside bushes. The two men were also kneeling, flattening themselves to the least visible profile.

The searchlights continued for a while. Then, all was quiet again.

"Let's walk in the ditch," Tornac suggested, "just in case they might be watching."

They carefully pushed their way through to another patch of young woods. After about half an hour under the shelter of the trees, they emerged. A working farm's activities reached their ears and they could see light from the farmhouse windows. They followed a path to the back. As they neared the night-threshing crew, Tornac went ahead and called aside one of the owners who had anticipated their arrival. The four of them were led into a guest room where Kata and Janos would spend the night before starting off for Vienna next morning.

After a few minutes of arrangements about that trip and a swift thank you as well as good-bye to the guides, the weary travelers found themselves in a small farm room, in a new country, where they would sleep and dream—now with more certainty—about the future. Jancsi was able to fall asleep shortly alongside his mother. It took Kata longer. At first, she tried to relive the exhausting and trying hours of the previous day and forecast what might be awaiting them tomorrow. Some muffled German words were audible as a group of Austrian peasants stopped to rest, near the window of the room. She had the strangest association. She thought again of Wagner and of that opera night ages ago when her romance with Istvan had really begun. Yes, it was Parsifal, he was on his way in search of the Grail. She was trying to remember where the Grail was or why it was important to find it, but her sleepiness interfered. She even tried to say a short prayer, but somewhere in the middle of her supplication, she found that she could continue no longer.

The familiar noise of threshing machines, familiar from bygone vacation days on her uncle's farm, offered a long-forgotten lullaby and linked the present with her childhood past when life was full of wonders and exciting opportunities to come.

After her sleep, what would there be? There was no dream to answer the question.

FORTY YEARS LATER IN BUDA

S U M M E R   1 9 8 9

Kata walked on Uri ucca, an old segment of Buda with Philip, her American husband, at her side. It was a time of powerful changes, first in Poland and now—was freedom coming to Hungary, perhaps?

The street in the Castle District led to the Coronation Church, the old Ramparts and the former Royal Palace. They strolled by beautiful little houses from a bygone era. Most of them carried a plaque: "This building was erected from remnants of medieval structures"—here in 1795, there in 1813.

The small one-room "Oldest Jewish Synagogue" on the street, now a museum, carried a similar sign.

"Look, Philip," and she translated the words into English for him, "new edifices built from the remnants of old. The ruins were not discarded, they were used to build. Just like life, my life!" she said with excitement.

In a flash the highlights of the last forty years appeared: the lengthy trail to America, a second widowhood, Janos grown—a noted scientist now; her marriage to Philip, even her parents' joining her in New York to witness some of the happenings. And now, back again in the land, the place of joys but many more tragedies, humiliations, losses. She was wondering about the sum of these experiences—not only the tumults in Hungary, but later her life as a refugee, having to make it, struggling to make it, needing new skills and renewed strength. There were the responsibilities, illnesses to face, children to bring up, decisions to make. How did she do it?

Only occasionally did she consciously look for her Grail. Yet, the resolution forty years ago to build her life on the premise of reconciliation—not to destroy but build, not to reciprocate evil but to bring out the best in her adversaries—this determination pulled her through, strengthened her and gave meaning to her life. She was not ignoring the actual events, the little and bigger accomplishments of hers and her family. But in times of discouragement, frustration and fear she remembered the past. Strangely, she recalled now Baumgarten's words in the midst of terror: "If God wants to save your mother, He will." And her mother had lived.

The sun was above their heads. She heard the noontime bells of Coronation Church. Had they been ringing all these years? Surely, people were allowed to claim religion now.

She had had a rich heritage. God-fearing parents—her father with his unwavering faith and Christ-centered life, her mother demonstrating undaunted faith, whether subject to mass murder on the Danube shore or dealing with step families in America. Philip, too, was a man of faith.

Was her Grail in the search? In a way, yes. But the search itself provided the spiritual sustenance that she could rely on in times of need and bounty.

And the future? What will it bring—here and for her, even in America?

"If God wants to—," she will continue on her journey of building.

"I'm glad we came this way," she said to Philip as they turned towards the Fisherbastion. "Things came together for me about the past and the future."

And as they mounted the steps of the Rampart through the opening she could see her native Pest across the shimmering waters of the Danube, beautiful as ever. She felt peace.

POSTSCRIPT

There were some real life people who inspired me to write this novel. Among those who acted out their faith and made survival possible some particularly stand out. Janos Pechtol, Dr. Elemer Graf, Dr. Sandor Csia (not the one convicted of war crimes) and Maria Nagy will always be remembered with the deepest gratitude and love.

And now a word should be said about the question that haunted me when writing this novel. "I have mercy on whom I have mercy" was my lifeline in despair during the horrors I myself experienced. Those words give some answer even now to the question: How come? But it still leaves me to wonder: Why me?

Veronica Foldes Frame

271